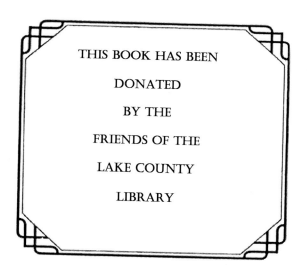

THIS BOOK HAS BEEN

DONATED

BY THE

FRIENDS OF THE

LAKE COUNTY

LIBRARY

Advance Praise for
More Mortgage Meltdown

"Whitney's presentation makes complex financial concepts easy to understand, and I appreciate that. Despite the gloomy economic forecast, I actually found his calm and rational demeanor very comforting."

—Debbie Ermiger, Hewlett-Packard Company

"Not only is this topic daunting, but it is also somewhat difficult to understand; however, Whitney does a fabulous job of making it both interesting and comprehensible. His careful consideration of the details really provides an accurate, truly expert view of the economy."

—Heba Macksoud

"Whitney Tilson's insights and comments are invaluable."

—Marilyn Tahl

"Whitney Tilson's sobering review of the debt bubble, and what we might expect to see in the next 1 to (gulp . . . 25 years is an excellent reminder that we need to constantly plan and be prepared for potentially ugly scenarios in both our personal and our business lives. Tilson also provides an excellent perspective on the current situation.

"I've found that people tend to accept a situation and find a way to move through it when they have a fuller understanding of what happened and why. Tilson's presentation of what happened offers that 'what' and 'why.'"

—Jesse M. Keyser, *The Motley Fool*

"I found Whitney Tilson's presentation on the mortgage mess riveting as well as frightening. I don't know whether to stuff my mattress or help the economy and buy a mattress! I really appreciated learning what he had to say."

—Elaine C. Sherwood, Customer Experience, Manager, Sun Microsystems, Inc.

More Mortgage Meltdown

6 Ways to Profit in These Bad Times

Whitney Tilson
Glenn Tongue

WILEY

John Wiley & Sons, Inc.

Published by John Wiley & Sons, Inc., Hoboken, New Jersey.
Published simultaneously in Canada.

For general information on our other products and services or for technical support, please contact our Customer Care Department within the United States at (800) 762-2974, outside the United States at (317) 572-3993 or fax (317) 572-4002.

Wiley also publishes its books in a variety of electronic formats. Some content that appears in print may not be available in electronic books. For more information about Wiley products, visit our web site at www.wiley.com.

Library of Congress Cataloging-in-Publication Data:

Tilson, Whitney, 1966-
    More mortgage meltdown : 6 ways to profit in these bad times / Whitney Tilson, Glenn Tongue.
       p. cm.
    Includes bibliographical references and index.
    ISBN 978-0-470-50340-9 (cloth)
      1. Mortgages—United States. 2. Housing—Prices—United States.
  3. Investments—United States. I. Tongue, Glenn, 1959- II. Title.
HG4655.T55 2009

332.63'2440973—dc22

                                         2009010821

Printed in the United States of America
10 9 8 7 6 5 4 3 2 1

Contents

Acknowledgments

T his book would not have been possible without Chris Woolford, who chased down endless amounts of data, created nearly every chart, and wrote the chapter on American Express. We'd also like to thank Tim Melvin, who drafted parts of the book; Jeannie Reed, who did invaluable editing; and our office manager, Kelli Alires, who keeps things running smoothly.

Special thanks also go to John Heins and John Schwartz, our partners, respectively, on Value Investor Insight and the Value Investing Congress. Much of the book's content comes from work originally done for the conference or the newsletter, which John and John have helped make into invaluable resources for value investors.

Kudos to Pamela van Giessen, Emilie Herman, Kevin Holm, and the rest of the team at John Wiley & Sons for their guidance and astonishingly fast turnaround of this book.

Sean Dobson of Amherst Securities was the original inspiration for this book, and his team, including Laurie Goodman and Emir Boydag, provided us with reams of data.

Finally, we'd like to thank our families and friends, whose love, patience, and support make everything we do possible.

Introduction

I t was a cold day in early February 2008 as we biked to the Peninsula Hotel in midtown Manhattan to meet Sean Dobson, the CEO of Amherst Securities. We were there because we were intrigued by this e-mail a friend had sent us a few days earlier:

> Sean is the best mortgage technician I know and has developed a unique database that includes virtually all mortgages originated since 1998, sliced by month of origination, product type, and further stratified by a proprietary coding system that picks up loan-level characteristics with unusual predictive capability. He has monthly delinquency and default statistics, new defaults as a percentage of current outstanding and CPR [conditional prepayment rate] stats. Loans can be assigned to securitizations and you can see where you can go from there for RMBS [residential mortgage-backed security] tranches and CDOs [collateralized debt obligations].
>
> He runs a mortgage broker-dealer and advises many hedge funds and institutional accounts on their mortgage-related investments, including CDSs [credit default swaps] and the various indexes. He is definitely someone you should get to know.

Sean presented slide after slide filled with wild, multicolor charts and squiggly lines, explaining them in a strange language we didn't understand (which we now call "mortgagese").

From what little we could understand, the message was clear: The U.S. housing market had experienced a bubble of enormous proportions, and countless mortgages were defaulting at unprecedented, catastrophic rates. More importantly, there was no sign of a letup and, in fact, Sean argued that things were likely to get much, much worse.

We started to ask him a lot of questions, trying to figure out what all the squiggly lines meant and understand terms like DTI, CDX, sTr, cTr, SMM, and vPr. Fortunately, Sean was patient and, as we began to understand mortgagese, our eyes got big and our jaws hit the floor as we realized: Holy cow, he's right! This bubble is much bigger and more far-reaching than almost anyone realizes, and is only in the early stages of bursting.

This conclusion was in sharp contrast to the consensus view among investors, government regulators, and policy makers, who thought that the worst was behind us. It wasn't an unreasonable view, given that almost a year had passed since subprime mortgages had started to default at high rates, defaults in other areas weren't yet at alarming levels, and the fallout seemed to be contained to a handful of firms and funds that had blown up, like Novastar, New Century Financial, and the Bear Stearns hedge funds. But Sean's data told a very different story: that we were in the second inning, not the seventh inning, of the mortgage meltdown.

As we write this book a year later, we're now in roughly the fifth inning, which has important implications for investors (not to mention policy makers, bankers, and CEOs).

■ ■ ■

Before we met Sean, we'd been following the housing and mortgage markets for years and had long believed that a significant bubble had occurred and was in the process of bursting. Thus, we were skeptical of the calm assurances throughout 2007 and well into 2008 that the worst was behind us that were offered by President Bush, Fed Chairman Ben Bernanke, Treasury Secretary Henry Paulson, the CEOs of financial and real estate firms, and Wall Street analysts who, with very few exceptions, simply parrot what CEOs tell them. Given our skepticism, by the time we met Sean we'd already sold a number of stocks with exposure to the housing market that had previously been among our favorites, such as USG Corporation and Mueller Water Products, and had shorted a number of financial stocks, including Allied Capital, Ambac, Farmer Mac, Lehman Brothers, and MBIA Inc.

Nevertheless, in February 2008 we were much too sanguine about the economy and the markets and thus had left ourselves dangerously exposed, with a long portfolio nearly four times the size of our short portfolio. Our meeting with Sean was the catalyst for us to do a lot more work.

We went back to the office that day and started digging . . . and digging . . . and digging, seeking to understand the U.S. housing market and what the future might hold. Every data point we uncovered confirmed Sean's thesis, so as we developed greater conviction we began to take action. Within two months, we'd trimmed our long exposure by a quarter and increased our short exposure by nearly a third, such that our longs were only twice as much as our shorts; and we maintained a more defensive position throughout the rest of the year than we otherwise would have.

These steps enabled us to survive the carnage of 2008. A number of the smartest value investors we know lost 40 percent, 50 percent, 60 percent, or more during the year as markets around the world crashed—and we would have likely been in the same boat had we not developed tremendous conviction about how bad the mortgage meltdown would be and acted on it.

With the benefit of hindsight, which is always 20/20, we should have been even more aggressive. In particular, we failed to anticipate how widespread the damage would be. We believed the mortgage meltdown would create a significant economic headwind, to be sure, but thought that the government would throw enough money at the problem to contain it. We certainly didn't foresee the near-Armageddon fallout that instead occurred, so we left our portfolio exposed to many retail and consumer-related stocks, which were crushed. Fortunately, however, we had big gains on the short side such that our main hedge fund was down less than half of what the S&P 500 declined. We survived the Great Bear Market of 2008—a year I suspect we will tell our grandchildren about someday.

■ ■ ■

Most investors, having discovered a valuable treasure trove of data like Sean's and coming to firm conclusions with powerful implications for the markets, would have kept this information to themselves. But we didn't. We started shouting from the rooftops—writing articles, speaking at conferences, appearing on television (most notably on *60 Minutes* in December 2008), putting together and widely disseminating a slide presentation with the data we'd collected from Sean and others, and finally writing this book.

Why have we spent so much time and energy being the bearers of bad tidings? In part because, by talking about our ideas, we've gotten a lot of valuable feedback and information. But the main reason is that we feel a duty to teach and share.

Neither of us has a traditional money management background, in which one learns at the feet of a master for many years and only then launches a fund, in the Tiger Cub model (the name given to the many successful hedge fund managers who started their careers by working for famed investor Julian Robertson of Tiger Management). Instead, we are largely self-taught. But that doesn't mean we started from scratch. We owe a huge debt of gratitude to the legendary investors who taught us through their writings and/or public speaking, starting with Benjamin Graham, Warren Buffett and Charlie Munger, but also including Phil Fisher, Peter Lynch, Seth Klarman, Joel Greenblatt, Bill Miller, Marty Whitman, Bill Nygren, Mason Hawkins, and the managers of Tweedy Browne and Ruane Cuniff.

There's a great tradition in the value investing community of teaching and sharing. Having benefited so enormously from it, we wish to continue this tradition.

■ ■ ■

In writing this book, we're not claiming that we know more about the housing market than anyone else—Sean Dobson has probably forgotten more than we'll ever know—nor that we were the savviest or earliest investors to figure out what was happening—John Paulson, Seth Klarman, and Bill Ackman, among others, figured it out before we did. That's one reason why they're a lot richer than we are!

But having presented our work dozens of times to thousands of people across the country and all over the world (including Italy, Mexico, and Peru), we think we've figured out a way to present what we've learned so that anyone can understand what happened and why, where we are today, and what the future holds.

The focus of this book is the U.S. mortgage market, the single largest debt market in the world and the one that is the locomotive of the credit crisis. Until the carnage here is dealt with—or simply begins to ease due to the passage of time—it's hard to imagine that the U.S. (and world) economy is going to turn around.

It's important to understand, however, that this bubble was not limited to mortgages but infected nearly every type of debt, and it wasn't just a U.S. phenomenon but a global one.

In the first half of the book, we explain what happened and why, where we are now, and what the future holds. In the second half of the book, after some general thoughts aimed at all investors, we share six in-depth case studies of stocks that we were long or short in the hedge funds we manage as of March 2009. In doing so, we are not trying to give you hot stock tips, but rather hoping to teach you to be a better investor—to share with you how we think about certain companies and investment situations so that you can learn and apply these tools in your own investing career going forward.

Part One

What Happened and Why, Where Are We Now, and What Does the Future Hold?

Chapter 1

What Happened during the Housing Bubble?

T alk to your parents or grandparents about buying their first home and they'll tell you it was the fulfillment of the American dream, a long process that involved years of saving and sacrificing to gather enough cash for the 20 percent down payment. They'll tell you that the day they bought their first home was one of the greatest days of their lives, that it represented more than just a place to live. In fact, that home was the single biggest purchase most would ever make, and it represented stability, safety, and security for themselves and their families.

In those days a mortgage was regarded as a sacred obligation, to be paid off steadily over time. And when it was paid off, there was often a mortgage-burning party to celebrate owning the house free and clear.

Home Prices over Time

Historically, there was good reason to believe that homes represented stability, safety, and security. For more than half a century, home prices had marched steadily upward at a rate exceeding inflation by about one-half of 1 percent annually, with very little volatility, as shown in Figure 1.1.

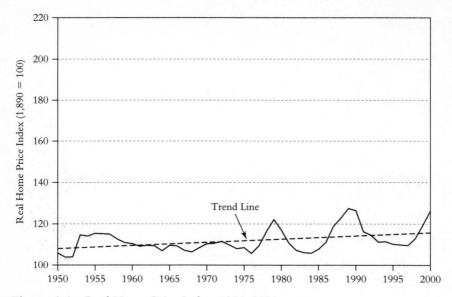

Figure 1.1   Real Home Price Index, 1950–2000
Source: Robert J. Shiller, Professor of Economics, Yale University, *Irrational Exuberance: Second Edition,* Princeton University Press, 2005.

Beginning around 2000, however, home prices started to rise at a rapid rate and became completely disconnected from their historical trend line (shown in Figure 1.2).

There were many reasons for the upward movement, as we'll explain in detail in Chapter 2, but the biggest driver of the housing bubble was the simple fact that the amount an average homeowner was able to borrow to buy a house tripled in a relatively short period of time, as shown in Figure 1.3.

Prior to 2000, the typical borrower could borrow roughly three times his income to buy a house. Figure 1.3 shows that in January 2000, a person with pretax income of nearly $34,000 (the national average) could take out a mortgage of 3.3 times this amount, or $110,000. Of course, the borrower had to have a 20 percent down payment and a decent credit history, and banks were rigorous about evaluating the ability to repay. But all this began to unravel as the years passed.

By January 2004, average pretax income had risen 9 percent to $37,000, but the amount that could be borrowed rose 60 percent

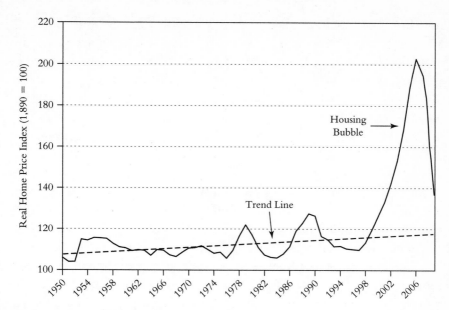

Figure 1.2 Real Home Price Index, 1950–2008
SOURCE: Robert J. Shiller, Professor of Economics, Yale University, *Irrational Exuberance: Second Edition*, Princeton University Press, 2005, as updated by the author.

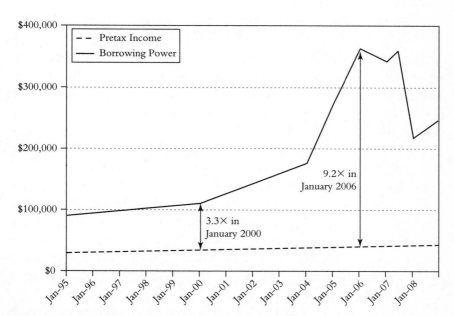

Figure 1.3 Average Income and Borrowing Power
SOURCE: Amherst Securities.

to $176,000, a 4.8× ratio. A year later, the figures were $38,000, $274,000, and 7.2×, and by January 2006, with income of only $39,600, the amount that could be borrowed to buy a house was an astonishing $363,000, a 9.2× ratio. This enormous borrowing power persisted for another year-and-a-half until the housing bubble began to burst in mid-2007.

There were a number of factors, including falling interest rates, driving this threefold increase in borrowing power in only six years, but by far the biggest was that lenders grew willing to lend up to the point that debt payments consumed 60 percent of a borrower's pretax income, whereas historically the permitted ratio didn't exceed 33 percent. Worse, little or no down payment or documentation was necessary, and interest-only loans proliferated.

Suddenly throwing such a massive amount of capital at a relatively stable asset base caused prices to skyrocket, which led to a self-reinforcing cycle: In order to afford a home, prospective homeowners had to borrow more and take on risky, exotic mortgages instead of conservative 30-year, fixed-rate, fully amortizing mortgages. In turn, exotic mortgages and loose lending terms allowed homeowners to borrow much more money, thereby driving prices ever higher.

The bubble manifested itself in different ways in different parts of the country. As discussed later, in inner cities like Detroit, equity-stripping schemes were common; in Florida, Arizona, and Nevada, there was widespread speculation and overbuilding; and in California, which has 10 percent of the nation's homes but is where 34 percent of the foreclosures are happening (44 percent by dollar value), the bubble was primarily an affordability problem. That's not to say there wasn't equity stripping in California's inner cities nor an affordability problem in Florida, but these are the general characterizations.

Figure 1.4 shows what happened to housing affordability in three cities in southern California: Los Angeles, Riverside, and San Diego. One can see that the percentage of households that could afford the average home in these three cities, as measured by the National Association of Home Builders (NAHB)/Wells Fargo Housing Opportunity Index, plunged as this decade progressed, to the point that fewer than 10 percent of households could afford the average home using a standard mortgage.

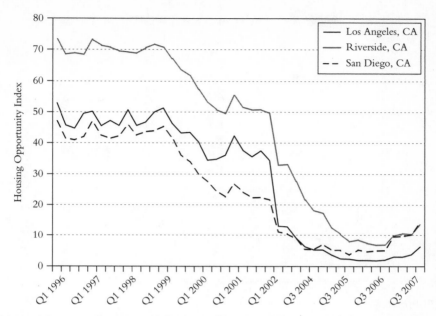

Figure 1.4 Home Affordability in Three Cities
SOURCE: Copyright © National Association of Home Builders 2009. All Rights Reserved. Used by permission. "NAHB" is a registered trademark of National Association of Home Builders. "Wells Fargo" is a registered trademark of Wells Fargo & Company.

Homes as ATMs

Another factor was at work as well: As home prices rose and interest rates dropped, millions of Americans were able to refinance their mortgages at lower rates but also—this is critical—take out *bigger mortgages*, thereby converting the rising value of their homes into cash. Called a cash-out refinancing or refi, this practice soared during the bubble. In total, as shown in Figure 1.5, Americans pulled more than $2.5 trillion out of their homes from 2004 to 2007, fueling consumer spending and accounting for approximately 8 percent of total disposable income during that period.

The combination of these factors meant that Americans were taking on more and more mortgage debt and had less and less equity in their homes, as shown in Figure 1.6. In fact, in 2007, for the first time ever, American homeowners had more debt than equity in their homes.

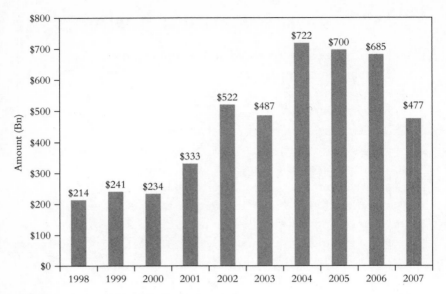

Figure 1.5   Net Home Equity Extraction

Source: Updated estimates provided by James Kennedy in "Estimates of Home Mortgage Originations, Repayments, and Debt on One-to-Four-Family Residences," by Alan Greenspan and James Kennedy, Federal Reserve Board Finance & Economics Discussion Series (FEDS) working paper no. 2005-41. Home equity extraction is defined in the paper as the discretionary initiatives of homeowners to convert equity in their homes into cash by borrowing in the home mortgage market. Components of home equity extraction include cash-out refinancings, home equity borrowings, and "home turnover extraction" (originations to finance purchases of existing homes minus sellers' debt cancellation).

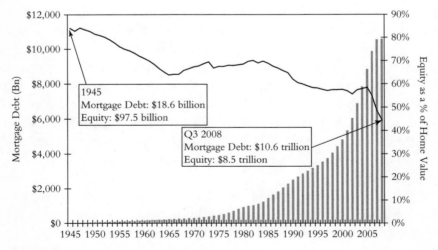

Figure 1.6   Mortgage Debt and Home Equity

Source: Federal Reserve Flow of Fund Accounts of the United States.

The Collapse of Lending Standards

Lending standards collapsed to an almost unimaginable degree during the great bubble, to the point that in some areas if you had a pulse, you could get a mortgage. The collapse manifested itself in many ways.

In 2001, the combined loan-to-value ratio for the average mortgage was 74 percent, meaning the buyer had put down 26 percent of the cost of the home (see Figure 1.7). When doing any kind of lending, it's critical that the borrower has meaningful skin in the game, so there is a strong incentive to repay the loan, even if the value of the asset falls.

Over the next five years, the average loan-to-value ratio rose to 84 percent, meaning that the average borrower was putting down only 16 percent, affording lenders much less protection in the event home prices tumbled. The situation was even more extreme for first-time home buyers, who were putting down only 2 percent on average by early 2007.

Not surprisingly, the percentage of mortgages for which the borrower put no money down—and was effectively getting a free call

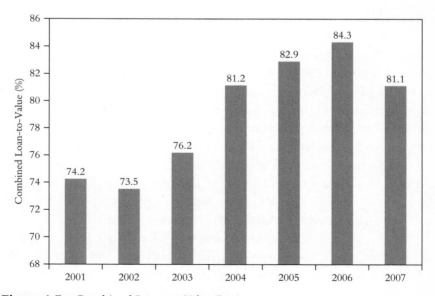

Figure 1.7   Combined Loan-to-Value Ratio
SOURCE: Amherst Securities, LoanPerformance.

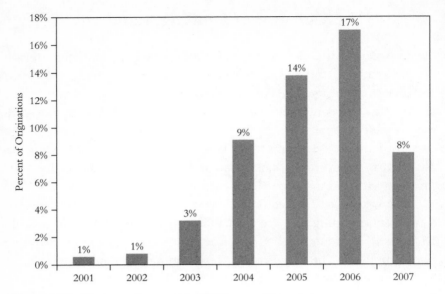

Figure 1.8   Mortgage Loans with 100 Percent Financing
SOURCE: Amherst Securities, LoanPerformance.

option on home price appreciation—soared from virtually nil to one-sixth of all mortgages in 2006, as shown in Figure 1.8.

Another change in lending practices compounded the problem. Historically, a lender was careful to verify a borrower's income and assets by asking to see pay stubs and tax returns—an obvious precaution to ensure that the borrower could afford the payments on the mortgage. There were exceptions made for certain self-employed borrowers like doctors, but this was not common. During the bubble, however, such requirements went out the window as low- and no-documentation mortgages rose to account for nearly two-thirds of all mortgages at the peak, as shown in Figure 1.9. More and more often, a lender simply looked at a borrower's credit score and the appraisal on the house and made the loan based on whatever the borrower stated as income.

Limited-documentation loans were an invitation for fraud, either by the borrower or by the mortgage broker (often both), and fraud is indeed what happened: One study shows that 90 percent of stated-income borrowers overstated their incomes, half of them by more than 50 percent. Another study found that "the average income for stated-income applicants

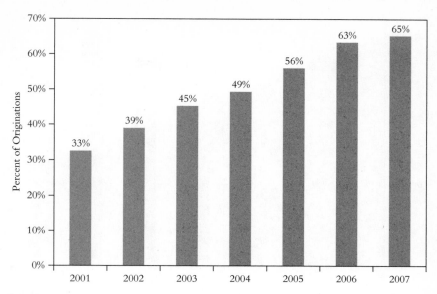

Figure 1.9 Mortgage Loans with Low and No Documentation (aka "Liar's Loans")
Source: Amherst Securities, LoanPerformance.

was 49% higher than the average for fully documented loans and the average income on loans with limited documentation was 92% higher."[1] It's little wonder that these loans are now known as liar's loans.

The most dangerous loans of all are those for which the borrower puts no money down and the lender doesn't bother to check income or assets. Such loans were unheard-of prior to the bubble, but they accounted for 11 percent of all mortgages in 2006, as shown in Figure 1.10.

Historically, one of the most important factors to consider when making a loan was the credit history of the borrower. People who had previously defaulted on many of their loans or bills were rightly considered poor risks and were charged high rates for a mortgage—or, more likely, couldn't get one at any rate.

The most common measurement of a person's credit history is called a FICO score, which ranges from 350 to 850. The median score is 723, and 45 percent of people fall between 700 and 799.[2] Roughly speaking (lenders and analysts use different cutoffs), a score under somewhere between 620 and 660 is called subprime, above 720 is

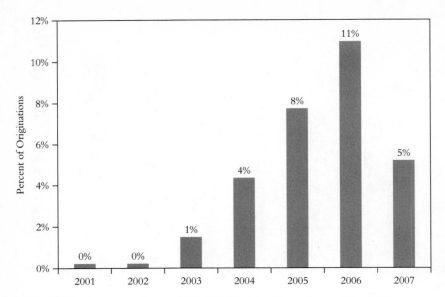

Figure 1.10   Mortgage Loans with 100 Percent Financing and Low/No Documentation
SOURCE: Amherst Securities, LoanPerformance.

considered prime, and in between is called Alt-A, though this category is also defined by limited-documentation loans.[3]

As shown in Figure 1.11, prior to 2002 subprime mortgages were rare, never far exceeding $100 billion worth per year, but then the volume rose rapidly, peaking at roughly $600 billion per year in 2005 and 2006. Subprime had been a small industry generally characterized by reasonable lending standards, but it ballooned to the point that nearly anyone, no matter how poor or uncreditworthy, could get a mortgage, often with no money down and no requirement to document income or assets. Such mortgages were called NINJA loans: no income, no job or assets. True madness.

As much attention as subprime mortgages have garnered in the media lately, it is important to understand that they were just a small part of the marketplace—only 20 percent of the market at the peak of the bubble. Unfortunately, the bubble extended far beyond the sub-prime arena and, as we discuss later, losses among the other 80 percent of loans that were written during the peak years of the bubble will cause many problems going forward.

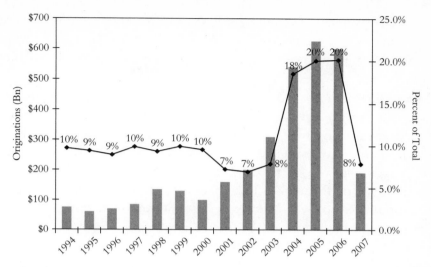

Figure 1.11 Subprime Mortgage Volume and Percentage of Total Originations, 1994–2007
SOURCE: *Inside Mortgage Finance*, Inside Mortgage Finance Publications, Inc. Copyright 2009. Reprinted with permission.

To understand how far lending standards had fallen by the peak of the bubble, let's hear from Mike Garner, who worked at the largest private mortgage bank in Nevada, Silver State Mortgage, who was interviewed by *This American Life* in early 2008:[4]

Alex Blumberg, *This American Life*: Mike noticed that every month, the guidelines were getting a little looser. Something called a stated income, verified asset loan came out, which meant you didn't have to provide paycheck stubs and W-2 forms, as they had [required] in the past. You could simply state your income, as long as you showed that you had money in the bank.

Mike Garner: The next guideline lower is just stated income, stated assets. Then you state what you make and state what's in your bank account. They call and make sure you work where you say you work. Then an accountant has to say for your field it is possible to make what you said you make. But they don't say what you make, just say it's possible that they could make that.

Alex Blumberg: It's just so funny that instead of just asking people to prove what they make there's this theater in place of you having to find an accountant sitting right in front of me who could very easily provide a W-2, but we're not asking for a W-2 form, but we do want this accountant to say, "Yeah, what they're saying is plausible in some universe."

Mike Garner: Yeah, and loan officers would have an accountant they could call up and say, "Can you write a statement saying a truck driver can make this much money?" Then the next one came along and it was no income, verified assets. So you don't have to tell the people what you do for a living. You don't have to tell the people what you do for work. All you have to do is state you have a certain amount of money in your bank account. And then the next one is just no income, no assets. You don't have to state anything. Just have to have a credit score and a pulse.

Rising Home Ownership

One apparent benefit of what was going on was that home ownership rates were going up substantially, as shown in Figure 1.12. Initially, this

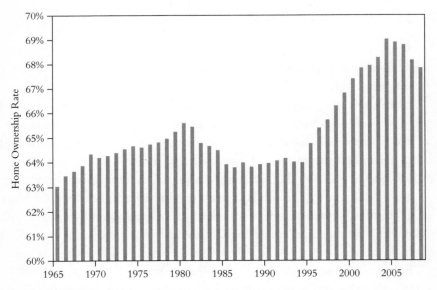

Figure 1.12 Percentage of Households Owning Homes
Source: U.S. Census Bureau.

was a good thing, as lenders stopped red-lining low-income, typically minority areas, which helped many people achieve the American dream of home ownership.

But this dream turned into a nightmare during the bubble, as people were given mortgages they couldn't afford, which has already led to over a million subprime borrowers suffering the financial and emotional trauma of losing their homes. The reality is that only a small fraction of people with poor credit histories are ready to become homeowners; the remainder of people with low incomes, uneven employment histories, and/or an inability to control their spending should simply continue renting until their financial situation is stable enough to support a mortgage. As Warren Buffett noted in his 2008 annual letter to Berkshire Hathaway shareholders, "Putting people into homes, though a desirable goal, shouldn't be our country's primary objective. Keeping them in their homes should be the ambition."

The Human Face of the Housing Bubble

So far, we've told the story of the mortgage meltdown with statistics, charts, and graphs, which makes it easy to forget that nearly every mortgage involves real people and families and their homes. Millions of Americans are struggling to pay their mortgages, and a meaningful percentage will lose their homes, which is often an economic and emotional catastrophe.

Yes, some people were greedy and reckless or engaged in outright fraud and should lose their houses, but many others are vulnerable people who were exploited in equity-stripping schemes, and many more were misled by the housing and mortgage industry, which aggressively marketed the message that housing was a totally safe investment because home prices never go down and one can always refinance. And for decades this had proved to be true, so it's little wonder that a lot of people got caught up in the bubble and took on mortgages they couldn't afford.

To put a human face on this bubble, we'd like to share some stories we've come across that capture a wide range of the people who got caught up in the frenzy.

Florida's Speculative Frenzy

A truth of markets, whether they be stocks or tulip bulbs, is that rising prices attract speculation. Real estate is no different. Beginning in the late 1990s, housing prices started rising at phenomenal rates. With people able to buy houses with little or no money out of pocket, the returns were staggering and speculators moved in with a vengeance. Property flipping became common, especially in new developments and among condominiums, whereby homes were purchased at preconstruction prices and then resold at higher prices a short time later. It is estimated that at the height of the bubble 85 percent of the condos in the overheated Miami market were bought by investors who had no intention of living in the properties. The speculation served to create false demand and push prices even higher.

As the mortgage market changed, so did the way home ownership was viewed, which had a striking impact on the structure of the mortgage and housing markets. Many homeowners no longer sought to pay down their mortgages but instead saw their homes as investments and sources of cash. They became accustomed to refinancing on a regular basis, effectively using their homes as ATMs to fuel consumer purchases or, in some cases, to buy additional property to speculate on the fast-rising real estate markets.

The *New Yorker* published a lengthy report, "The Ponzi State," that captures the speculative frenzy that took place in Florida.

> By 2005, the housing market in Florida was hotter than it had ever been, and the frenzy spread across all levels of society. Migrant farmworkers took jobs as roofers and drywall hangers in the construction industry. Nearly everyone you met around Tampa had a Realtor's license or a broker's license or was a title agent. Alex Sink, the state's chief financial officer and a Democrat, said, "When the yardman comes and says he's not going to mow your yard anymore because he's going to become a mortgage broker, that is a sure sign that something is wrong." Flipping houses and condominiums turned into an amateur middle-class pursuit. People who drew modest salaries at their jobs not only owned a house but bought other houses as speculators, the way average Americans

elsewhere dabble in day trading. Ross Bauer, a manager at a Toyota dealership in Tampa, told me that between 2000 and 2007 he bought and sold half a dozen properties, in a couple of instances doubling his money within two years. "Looking back, it was right in our face," he said. "That's a heart attack. It's not normal."

Jim Thorner, a real-estate reporter in the Tampa office of the St. Petersburg *Times*, said, "There were secretaries with five to ten investment homes—a thirty-five-thousand-dollar salary and a million dollars in investments. There's no industry here, only houses." When Thorner went to buy a new house, in 2005, the customer ahead of him in line at the sales center said that he intended to turn his property around in six months and make fifty thousand dollars. It was not an outlandish plan. Home values around Tampa rose twenty-eight per cent that year. "I'm telling you, it was the Wild West," Alex Sink said. "And Florida has always been susceptible to the Wild West mentality. If it's too good to be true, we're going to be involved in it."

In Fort Myers and the neighboring city of Cape Coral, two hours south of Tampa, things got wilder than anywhere else. A Fort Myers real-estate agent named Marc Joseph, who entered the business right out of college, in 1990, and had the jaundiced eye of a veteran, told me, "Money was flowing, easy money. Anybody could qualify—I mean anybody." He knew a bank teller with an annual salary of twenty-three thousand dollars who had received a two-hundred-and-sixteen-thousand-dollar mortgage, with no money down and no income verification—not even a phone call from the lender. "I wish I could say the market here was driven by end users and retirees, but it wasn't. Two-thirds were speculators. You could flip 'em before you had to close on 'em." Karen Johnson-Crowther, another real-estate agent in Fort Myers, showed me the sales history of a property in an upscale gated community which she had recently bought at a foreclosure auction. Building had begun in 2005. On December 29, 2005, the house sold for $399,600. On December 30, 2005, it sold for $589,900. On June 25, 2008, it was foreclosed on. Johnson-Crowther bought it in December for $325,000. I said that the one-day increase in value must have been some kind of record, and she looked at me pityingly: "No."

When I told Alex Sink about the house that had appreciated by almost 50 percent overnight, she said, "That's a fraudulent transaction." According to an investigative series in the Miami *Herald*, oversight by the state's Office of Financial Regulation and its commissioner, Don Saxon, was so negligent that more than ten thousand convicted criminals got jobs in the mortgage business, including four thousand as licensed brokers, some of whom engaged in fraudulent deals. Until the rules were recently changed, felons in Florida lost the right to vote but could still sell mortgages.[5]

Subprime Borrowers Fleeing Bad Neighborhoods

Most reports about the mortgage bubble, like the previous one, focus on people speculating or buying more house than they could afford, typically using exotic mortgages. But less often told are the stories in which mortgage companies exploited low-income, poorly educated, disproportionately minority borrowers. These schemes typically included many (if not all) of the following techniques:

- Paying higher fees or rebates to mortgage brokers for inflating interest rates or using exotic mortgages.
- Charging above-market interest rates, excessive points, and exorbitant fees.
- Putting people into adjustable-rate mortgages (ARMs) without regard for whether they could make the monthly payments after the teaser rate expired.
- Establishing prepayment penalties that prevented borrowers from refinancing.
- Promising one thing verbally, but having the documents say something else.
- Generating fees and stripping borrowers' equity through unnecessary refinancings.

60 Minutes has done a number of excellent reports on the mortgage crisis. In one that aired in January 2008,[6] Steve Kroft interviewed an African-American couple who purchased a house for $436,000 in Stockton, California, from which they ran a small day care center. Kroft gave the background:

> They say they wanted to move to a better neighborhood. A mortgage broker approached the Fontenots and offered to get them a loan. They told her the most they could afford . . . was $2,500 a month. But the monthly payment on the adjustable rate mortgage she gave them quickly jumped to $4,200.

Here's the conversation:

> "Did you understand any of this?" Kroft asks.
>
> "No, not really. Not much of it," says Phil Fontenot, who also says he didn't have a lawyer look over the paperwork.
>
> "But you knew this was a big decision, right? You were borrowing hundreds of thousands of dollars," Kroft remarks.
>
> "I didn't really look at it like that," Fontenot says.
>
> "How did you look at it?" Kroft asks.
>
> "I looked at it as far as my family. I can get my family off of this block," he replies.
>
> "And that we could pay the payments that she said that we could pay," Fontenot's wife Kim adds. "But after it was all said and done, and the paperwork was drawn up, it was something different."

Here's a similar example from a CNBC report:[7]

> Cynthia Simons craved a better life for her family and wanted to leave the crime-ridden area of Compton, California. She thought her prayers were answered by a mortgage broker from her church who found the family a house in a safe neighborhood. Was Simons' dream house too good to be true?
>
> Simons says her broker grossly exaggerated her income and without her knowledge arranged TWO mortgages . . . one a

loan for her down payment, the other an adjustable rate mortgage on the home.

Now Simons still has the house but can no longer keep up with her mortgage payments.

These are your typical peak-of-the-bubble subprime loans, so it's easy to understand why these loans have been defaulting at catastrophic rates.

Equity Stripping in Inner Cities

You might think the previous stories represent the worst of what mortgage companies did in inner cities, but equity strippings were even worse. In these cases, lenders trolled inner-city areas of Detroit, Cleveland, Newark, Akron, and the outer boroughs of New York, looking for homeowners who had built up equity in their homes so as to convince them to borrow against it. These loans generally had high interest rates and the payments weren't affordable for many of the homeowners, often elderly, on fixed incomes and financially unsophisticated.

Niall Ferguson, in his excellent book, *The Ascent of Money*, describes what happened in one city:

> In the space of ten years, house prices in Detroit—which probably possesses the worst housing stock of any American city other than New Orleans—had risen by nearly 50 per cent; not much compared with the nationwide bubble (which saw average house prices rise 180 percent), but still hard to explain given the city's chronically depressed economic state. As I discovered, the explanation lay in fundamental changes in the rules of the housing game, changes exemplified by the experience of Detroit's West Outer Drive, a busy but respectable middle-class thoroughfare of substantial detached houses with large lawns and garages....
>   . . . Subprime lending hit Detroit like an avalanche of Monopoly money. The city was bombarded with radio, television, direct-mail advertisements and armies of agents and brokers, all offering what sounded like attractive deals. In 2006 alone, subprime lending injected more than a billion dollars into twenty-two

Detroit ZIP codes. In the 48235 ZIP code, which includes the 5100 block of West Outer Drive, subprime mortgages accounted for more than half of all loans made between 2002 and 2006. Note that only a minority of these loans were going to first-time buyers. They were nearly all refinancing deals, which allowed borrowers to treat their homes as cash machines, converting their existing equity into cash. Most used the proceeds to pay off credit card debts, carry out renovations or buy new consumer durables.[8]

Addie Polk of Akron, Ohio, is a typical victim of this type of predatory lending. She and her husband moved into a working-class neighborhood in Akron in 1970 and purchased a home for $10,000. Her husband worked at the nearby Goodrich plant and eventually retired from there in 1995, when they finished paying off the mortgage.

After her husband died, Mrs. Polk's only income was Social Security and her husband's small pension, so she began to borrow against the house to pay day-to-day expenses. She refinanced the home four times over the next decade, the last time at the age of 86 in 2005 when Countrywide gave her a 30-year fixed-rate mortgage of $45,620 at 6.375 percent, plus a credit line of $11,380.

This loan should never have been made, as there was no way the elderly widow could afford the monthly payments. Sure enough, she began to miss payments and eventually Fannie Mae, which by then owned the loan, foreclosed on the home. After leaving 30 eviction notices on her door, the sheriff came to evict Mrs. Polk in September 2008. When he knocked on the door, he heard a loud noise. A neighbor crawled through a second-story window and found her lying in bed, a gun beside her. She had shot herself twice.

Fortunately, Mrs. Polk survived and, thanks to the publicity surrounding her case, Fannie Mae quickly forgave her loan. But there are hundreds of thousands of Addie Polks out there in working-class and poor neighborhoods whose loans will not be forgiven and who will lose their homes. They were sold on the idea of using their homes as ATMs and in most cases didn't realize the likely consequence of their actions: the dreaded sheriff's knock on the door and eviction from their homes.

Betty Townes is another elderly African-American widow who is about to lose her home thanks to being sold a series of option ARM mortgages she can't afford. World Savings, now part of Wells Fargo, refinanced her home four times in four years. When Scott Pelley of *60 Minutes* asked her what she was thinking, she replied, "All I know is that they told me this loan was best for me." It turns out that a staff person at World Savings, without her knowledge, declared on the loan application that her income was more than $4,000 per month, based on her husband's income. The only problem? Her husband had passed away! Her true monthly income was only about $1,875.

A final story of equity stripping is that of Clarence Nathan. He worked three part-time jobs and earned about $45,000 annually. He got himself into financial trouble and was able to borrow $540,000 against his house without any income verification. He later learned (after he'd defaulted on the loan) that the broker, who earned a commission of $18,500, had declared his income at $195,000 per year. He commented:

> It's almost like you pass a guy in the street and say, "Lend me $540,000." He says, "What do you do." "Hey, I got a job." "OK."
>
> I wouldn't have loaned me the money. And nobody that I know would have loaned me the money. I know guys who are criminals who wouldn't loan me that, and they break your knee-caps. I don't know why the bank did it . . . $540,000 to a person with bad credit.[9]

One could argue that the Fontenots, Mrs. Polk, Mrs. Townes, and Mr. Nathan should have known better—but who really should have known better: these financially illiterate borrowers or the large, sophisticated mortgage lenders who preyed on them.

WaMu's Depravity

The class action lawsuit against Washington Mutual (WaMu), which can easily be found on the Internet, provides rich fodder for how one of the biggest mortgage lenders in the country went completely off the rails and sank to extreme levels of depravity. JPMorgan Chase is going to have its hands full trying to clean up this mess.

The 470-page complaint is filled with examples from dozens of former employees about how the bank threw its loan standards out the window to underwrite as many mortgages as possible. Obviously fraudulent loans were jammed through. Appraisers were pressured to inflate prices to make loans work. Loans were not properly documented. Loan terms, especially for option ARMs, were not fully explained to buyers. Marketing materials emphasized low initial teaser rates and did not fully explain the loan reset features. Borrowers were encouraged to take fast-track or no-documentation loans, even when a lower interest rate and a more favorable loan structure were available with a fully documented loan. In short, if you had a pulse, you could get a loan from WaMu—after all, with Wall Street willing to buy virtually any loan, what did WaMu care?

Soledad Aviles is one of many examples from the lawsuit. He is an immigrant from Mexico who cannot speak or read English. He was working as a glass cutter and earning a whopping $9 an hour. The combined family pretax income was about $5,000 per month. Despite this, WaMu gave him a home loan of $615,000 and told him payments would be slightly more than $3,600 a month. All of the loan documents were in English and, excited about owning a home, Mr. Aviles signed them.

At 72 percent of the family's income, even $3,600 per month would have been unaffordable, but it turns out that monthly payments were actually $4,800—96 percent of income! So how did WaMu justify this loan? The loan documents showed his income was $13,000 per month. Someone falsified his income, which was what usually happened when a lender was foolish enough to do a low- or no-doc loan.

In situations like this, the borrower quickly defaults and loses the home—but by then WaMu had probably already sold the loan. Unfortunately for WaMu and its equity and debt holders, though, it wasn't able to sell enough of its loans, and the losses on the loans it held caused it to file for bankruptcy in September 2008. But the losses haven't disappeared—they will be borne by JPMorgan Chase and taxpayers for years to come.

Job Loss and Health Emergency Lead to Foreclosure

Job losses now spiraling upward to the highest levels in at least 16 years will surely exacerbate the collapse of the mortgage bubble. In addition, medical bills are contributing to many household financial crises, hardly surprising given that 46 million Americans don't have health insurance.

The *St. Louis (MO) Beacon* told the story of Stacy Haynes,[10] who fell victim to both and lost her home, which she'd purchased in 1999 with a conventional mortgage and a $20,000 down payment. She refinanced it with a GMAC mortgage of $216,000 in the form of an interest-only ARM with an initial interest rate above 8 percent. She was paying over $18,000 a year in interest without a penny of principal being repaid.

Then, in early 2008, disaster struck. Haynes was hospitalized with a critical case of pancreatitis and because she was employed as an independent consultant, she had no health insurance. Then, a few weeks later, she was laid off due to the economic downturn. Unemployed and deeply in debt, she struggled to keep her home, going so far as to sell possessions on eBay and Craigslist to make a few payments.

Haynes also tried to sell the home, but got no offers above the amount of the mortgage (it ended up being sold at foreclosure for $153,000, and the new owner later offered it for $129,900). Haynes had to move in with her daughter and file for bankruptcy.

This isn't a case of greed or exploitation on anyone's part—just another sad story of a life gone awry due to a bad economy and bad luck. Incidentally, contrary to popular perceptions that distressed homeowners behave like speculators and mail in their keys once they're underwater (or upside-down) on their mortgage, note how hard Haynes tried to keep her home, making a few last payments even when it was clear she was going to lose it.

Zombie Homeowers

The media have coined the term *zombie banks* to refer to banks that are crippled by severe losses—but not so severe that they actually go under, so instead they limp along, unable to lend and function properly. Less well understood are the millions of zombie homeowners who are trapped in homes in which they are underwater on their mortgages, unable to sell, move, or save.

Zachary and Tracy Campbell are good examples of zombie homeowners. In 2005 they moved from San Diego to Phoenix and bought a home in Maricopa, a suburb of Phoenix. They scraped together

$50,000 for a down payment on a new four-bedroom home that cost $250,000. The *Wall Street Journal* captures their dilemma:

> Today, Ms. Campbell figures, the home is worth perhaps half what they paid in 2005.
>
> Even that might be optimistic. Along a nearby highway, young men hired by a local real estate brokerage wave red signs touting "Homes From $69.9 K."
>
> The Campbells planned to sell their house for a profit after a few years and move back to San Diego before their daughter starts kindergarten. Today, they couldn't hope to sell the house for enough to pay off the mortgage. They fear the down payment they made on the house is money they won't see again. . . .
>
> "We're trapped," says Tracy Campbell, as she watches her 2-year-old daughter romp on a playground. . . .
>
> Some people in the neighborhood are simply walking away from their houses, leaving them for the lenders to fore-close. "We're surrounded by empty houses on three sides," Ms. Campbell says. But she and her husband have kept up on their payments, and want to keep their credit record clean.[11]

The Campbells' situation is perhaps the most common type of problem today, with an estimated 20 percent of all mortgage holders in the United States now underwater. They didn't do anything wrong, nor did the lender, but their situation, even if they don't default, isn't good for them—or for the country, as it reduces mobility, which is especially important during tough economic times when people need to move to areas in which jobs are being created.

The $132,000 Shack

The *Wall Street Journal* had another interesting story from Arizona,[12] this time about a shack that was appraised for $132,000, thereby justifying a loan of $103,000 against it. It was a 30-year ARM with an initial interest rate of 9.25 percent that was capped at over 15 percent. The mortgage broker collected $6,000 in fees at closing and pocketed another $3,000 selling the loan to Wells Fargo.

The borrower was Marvene Halterman, a 61-year-old former alcoholic who had not worked in over 13 years. The shack—you really have to see pictures of it to believe it—was in such poor condition that she eventually moved out and rented a place that was safer. Her son moved in but could not make the payments, so it was foreclosed on and a neighbor purchased it for $18,000 simply to tear the eyesore down.

Fraud

During the bubble, outright fraud was widespread, in part due to the laxness of lenders. The *New Yorker* article quoted earlier had another lengthy story about one con artist in Florida.

> Last fall, Michael Van Sickler, of the St. Petersburg *Times*, tracked the real-estate deals of a local tattoo parlor owner named Sang-Min Kim, also known as Sonny. Starting in 2004, Sonny Kim made ninety sales around Tampa, mostly in poor neighborhoods, on which he cleared four million dollars. Van Sickler found that many of Kim's buyers, who put little or no money down, were untraceable; some had been convicted of drug dealing and other crimes. Kim, who has not been charged with any crimes and could not be reached for this article, closed a third of his deals with a title agent named Howard Gaines, who now faces up to forty-five years in prison on a fraud conviction elsewhere in Florida. According to law-enforcement experts, drug dealers often become flippers, in order to launder money.

> One night in December, Van Sickler took me on a tour of some of the abandoned and foreclosed properties that had once belonged to Sonny Kim's real-estate empire. We stopped at an ill-lit corner in a mostly black slum of single-family houses called Belmont Heights, which is cut off from downtown Tampa by Interstate 4. Van Sickler—incongruous-looking in a dress shirt and dark slacks—pointed out a decaying two-story stucco house.

Its windows were boarded up, and mattresses lay in the overgrown yard, near a "For Sale" sign. Van Sickler learned that Kim acquired the house in 2006 with a deed that was witnessed by a convicted drug dealer, then flipped it for the sum of three hundred thousand dollars, with the help of a no-money-down mortgage from a subsidiary of Washington Mutual Bank, which later foreclosed on the house. (Last year, WaMu went into receivership, after becoming the largest bank failure in American history.) According to mortgage-fraud experts, the straw buyer is typically paid a small slice of the flipper's take and then disappears without moving in. When Van Sickler recently asked a real-estate agent about the house, he was told, "That's selling for fifty-two thousand, but it can be yours for thirty-five thousand in cash."

"Sonny Kim may not be the biggest, he may not be the worst, but he really epitomizes the laxness of the banks during the boom years," Van Sickler said as we stood outside the house. "It raises the question, Did anyone from the bank do a drive-by to eyeball this place?" Kim's deals had been financed by Wachovia, Wells Fargo, Bank of America, Lehman Brothers, Fannie Mae, and Freddie Mac. While Van Sickler, who was having trouble selling his own house in Tampa, was investigating the trail of Sonny Kim in September, the country plunged into the worst economic crisis since the Great Depression, and the banks that had greased Kim's deals were at the center of it. "We're not *all* to blame for this," Van Sickler said. "Decisions were made, and people looked the other way. This did go all the way up the ladder."[13]

Conclusion

Now that we've seen how lending standards completely collapsed and the mortgage market became an orgy of utter depravity, from the individual homeowners all the way to the offices of Wall Street CEOs, in Chapter 2 we explore the reasons for this insanity.

Chapter 2

What Caused
the Bubble?

I t seems almost inconceivable that two-and-a-half years of reckless
lending, the biggest part of it in the U.S. mortgage market, could
create such an enormous bubble that its bursting would bring the
world financial system to its knees and plunge nearly every economy in
the world into a severe recession (or worse). How did this happen?

The answer is that a confluence of factors created a perfect
storm—what Berkshire Hathaway's Charlie Munger calls "Lollapalooza
effects"—resulting in the greatest bubble in history.

A Mountain of Money Looking for a Home

Let's start with the big picture. By the middle of this decade, the world
was awash in cash. The International Monetary Fund (IMF) estimates
that over $70 trillion of global savings in fixed-income securities, more
than double the amount in 2000, was held by sovereign wealth funds,
endowments, pension funds, insurance companies, central banks, and

the like. That's a lot of money—roughly equal to the entire world's gross domestic product (GDP)—and it needed a home.

Typically, the largest fraction of it would have been invested in U.S. Treasuries, but for three years beginning in late 2001, Treasury yields were particularly unattractive thanks to Federal Reserve Chairman Alan Greenspan cutting short-term interest rates to extremely low levels and keeping them there in an attempt to keep the economy out of a prolonged recession after the bursting of the Internet bubble and 9/11. As shown in Figure 2.1, the federal funds rate was a mere 1 percent by June 2003, the lowest level since the 1950s.

Greenspan knew that these actions would have an impact on home prices. In fact, in testimony before Congress on November 13, 2002,[1] he said: "Besides sustaining the demand for new construction, mortgage markets have also been a powerful stabilizing force over the past two years of economic distress by facilitating the extraction of some of the equity that homeowners have built up over the years." Greenspan was counting on consumers using the equity in their homes to create demand and keep the economy out of recession. He had no way of

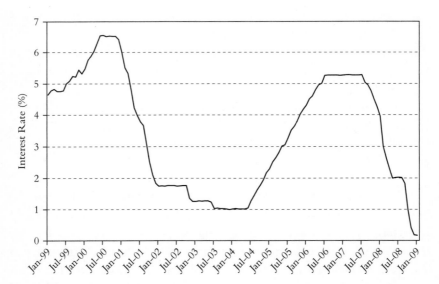

Figure 2.1   Effective Federal Funds Rate, January 1999 to January 2009
SOURCE: Federal Reserve Bank of St. Louis.

knowing then how right he was—and how disastrous the consequences would be. It is widely accepted now that Greenspan cut interest rates too much and kept them too low for too long, because this provided the liquidity and motivation to fuel the worldwide debt bubble.

Wall Street Responds

With safe investments like Treasuries paying such low rates, the investors of that $70 trillion started taking more risk in search of higher yields—and Wall Street was happy to oblige. Here's how Mike Francis, who helped build the U.S. residential mortgage trading desk at Morgan Stanley, described it when he was interviewed by *This American Life*:[2]

> It was unbelievable. We almost couldn't produce enough to keep the appetite of the investors happy. More people wanted bonds than we could actually produce. That was our difficult task . . . trying to produce enough. They would call and ask, "Do you have any more fixed rate? What have you got? What's coming?" From our standpoint it's like, there's a guy out there with a lot of money. We gotta find a way to be his sole provider of bonds to fill his appetite. And his appetite's massive.

To meet this enormous demand, Wall Street turned to the U.S. mortgage market to buy loans that it could package and sell to institutional investors around the world. It was appealing not only because it was the largest debt market in the world but also because it appeared to be very safe, as defaults had historically been extremely low.

Wall Street had a problem, though: It couldn't compete against the government-sponsored entities (GSEs), Fannie Mae and Freddie Mac, for plain-vanilla conforming mortgages, so it had to look elsewhere. In particular, Wall Street started buying subprime and Alt-A mortgages in enormous quantities. As shown in Figure 2.2, Wall Street firms' purchases of such mortgages accounted for more than one-fourth of the entire mortgage market in the peak bubble years of 2005 and 2006 and totaled $2.6 *trillion* for the four-year period from 2004 to 2007.

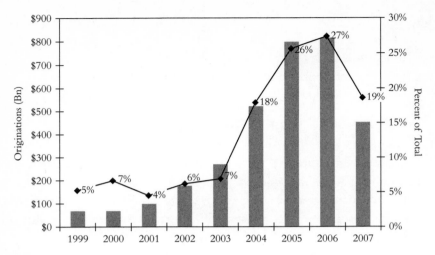

Figure 2.2   Subprime and Alt-A Mortgage–Backed Securities
SOURCE: *2008 Mortgage Market Statistical Annual,* Inside Mortgage Finance Publications, Inc.
Copyright 2008. Reprinted with permission.

The Siren Song of Securitization

The mechanism by which Wall Street (and the GSEs) took mortgages
and sold them to investors around the world is called securitization,
which is simply a process by which a group of loans are pooled and
then the pool is sliced into pieces called tranches (the French word for
"slices"). The most senior tranche gets the first cash earned by the loans
in the pool and is the last to suffer losses, so it's typically rated AAA
by the major rating agencies, whereas the most junior tranche (usually
called the "equity tranche") is the last to get cash and the first to suffer losses, so it's usually unrated and is held by the institution putting
together the securitization. A typical pool of mortgages, also called a
residential mortgage-backed security (RMBS), might have 15 to 20
tranches, including multiple AAA-rated tranches (the "super senior"
being the most senior, then some "junior AAA" tranches).

Table 2.1 is a simplified look at a $1 billion pool of mortgages,
which might consist of 5,000 loans with an average loan size of
$200,000. Figure 2.3 shows graphically what this pool looks like. Note
that 95 percent of the pool is rated investment grade.

Table 2.1 Structure and Ratings of a Typical Pool of Mortgages

Bond Tranches	Thickness of Tranche	Dollars (millions)	Loss Support
AAA	80%	$ 800	20%
AA	5%	$ 50	15%
A	6%	$ 60	9%
BBB+	2%	$ 20	7%
BBB	1%	$ 10	6%
BBB−	1%	$ 10	5%
BB (below investment grade)	1%	$ 10	4%
Overcollateralization (equity)	4%	$ 40	0%
	100%	$1,000	

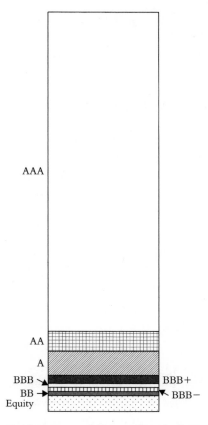

Figure 2.3 Structure and Ratings of a Typical Pool of Mortgages
SOURCE: T2 Partners.

To understand why securitizing dicey mortgages was such a lucrative business for Wall Street, consider that the average subprime mortgage in 2006 had an interest rate in the 8.5 percent range, yet through the magic of securitization, 80 percent of a pool of these mortgages (the tranches with an AAA rating), paid investors only around 3 percent, and even the lowest investment-grade tranche yielded less than 4 percent. That's an enormous spread: on a $1 billion pool, the interest received would be $85 million (assuming the homeowners all paid) and the interest paid out would be less than half that. The magic of securitization turned turds to gold, so it's little wonder that Wall Street firms wanted to buy as many high-interest-rate mortgages as possible.

To be clear, there's nothing inherently wrong with securitization. It has been around since 1970 and is used for many types of debt, including credit cards, auto loans, and debt used to back buyouts (leveraged loans). But securitization has some inherent dangers that must be considered. The biggest is that it separates the person or entity making the loan from the consequences of the loan defaulting, which is a recipe for disaster unless three parties to this process act rigorously:

1. Wall Street firms needed to make sure that the banks and mortgage brokers and wholesalers from which they bought loans had adhered to high standards when underwriting the loans.
2. The rating agencies needed to maintain high standards and refuse to rate pools filled with poorly underwritten loans.
3. The institutional buyers around the world needed to do their own due diligence on what they were buying (rather than blindly relying on the ratings) and refuse to buy securities based on pools filled with poorly underwritten loans.

Needless to say, none of the three safeguards happened.

A Race to the Bottom

There was a race to the bottom among Wall Street firms, none of which wanted to lose business (and profits) to competitors. Mike Garner, who worked at the largest private mortgage bank in Nevada, called Silver State Mortgage, described what happened:[3]

Mike Garner: Three of them [mortgage brokers] would show up at your door first thing in the morning and say, "I lost 10 deals last week to Meritius bank. They've got this loan. Look at the guidelines for this loan. Is there any way we can do this? We're losing deals left and right." I'd get on the phone and start calling all these Street firms or Countrywide and say, "Would you buy this loan?" Finally, you'd find out who was buying them.

Alex Blumberg, *This American Life*: So, Merrill Lynch would say no. And Goldman Sachs would say no. And you'd finally hit on somebody and they be like "Yeah, we'll buy that loan."

Mike Garner: Yeah, and once I got a hit, I'd call back and say, "Hey, Bear Stearns is buying this loan. I'd like to give you the opportunity to buy it, too." Once one person buys them, all the rest of them follow suit.

Alex Blumberg: So, what were you thinking when you're turning around and selling those to Wall Street? Were you ever thinking, "What are you guys doing?"

Mike Garner: Yeah. And my boss was in the business for 25 years. He hated those loans. He hated them and used to rant and say, "It makes me sick to my stomach the kind of loans that we do." He fought the owners and salesforce tooth and nail about these guidelines. He got the same answer. "Nope, other people are offering it. We're going to offer them, too. We're going to get more market share this way. House prices are booming, everything's gonna be good." And the company was just rolling in the cash. The owners and the production staff were just raking it in.

To give you an idea of how much money people on the ground were making, *This American Life* profiled Glen Pizzolorusso, an area sales manager at WMC Mortgage in upstate New York who was making over $1 million annually:

Alex Blumberg: Glen had five cars, a $1.5 million vacation house in Connecticut, and a penthouse that he rented in Manhattan. And he made all this money making very large loans to very poor people with bad credit.

Glen Pizzolorusso: We looked at loans. These people didn't have a pot to piss in. They can barely make a car payment and we're giving them a $300,000, $400,000 house.

Alex Blumberg: But Glen didn't worry about whether the loans were good. That's someone else's problem. And this way of thinking thrived at every step of this mortgage security chain. A guy like Mike Francis, from Morgan Stanley—he told me he bought loans, lots of loans, from Glen's company, and he knew in his gut they were bad loans. Like these NINA loans.

Mike Francis: No income, no asset loans. That's a liar's loan. We are telling you to lie to us. We're hoping you don't lie. Tell us what you make; tell us what you have in the bank, but we won't verify. We're setting you up to lie. Something about that feels very wrong. It felt wrong way back when, and I wish we had never done it. Unfortunately, what happened . . . we did it because everyone else was doing it.

Alex Blumberg: It's easy to ignore your gut fear when you are making a fortune in commissions.

The Money Being Made on Wall Street

Wall Street firms were making a fortune from the bubble, which fueled their reported profits and share prices. Figure 2.4 shows the stock prices from 2003 to 2006 of the major Wall Street firms, Goldman Sachs, JPMorgan Chase, Morgan Stanley, Lehman Brothers, Merrill Lynch, and

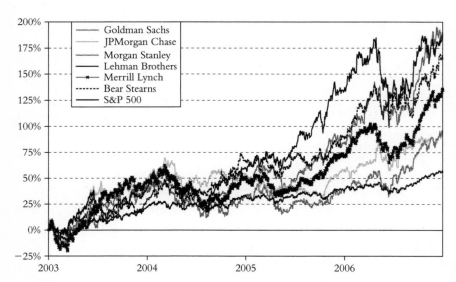

Figure 2.4   Stock Prices of Wall Street Firms vs. S&P 500, 2003–2006
SOURCE: Yahoo! Finance (http://finance.yahoo.com).

Bear Stearns, all of which roughly doubled or tripled, handily outpacing the S&P 500, which rose only 50 percent during the same period.

It wasn't just these firms, of course. All across the financial services industry, massive profits were being made from the credit bubble, such that financial services firms' profits soared to more than 45 percent of all profits made in the United States, as shown in Figure 2.5.

The employees of financial firms were also making a lot of money, nearly doubling their share of national income over 30 years, as shown in Figure 2.6.

What these charts don't capture, though, is how much money was really being made by a lucky few on Wall Street. According to a study by Equilar, a compensation research firm, executives at seven major financial institutions that have collapsed (American International Group, Bear Stearns, Citigroup, Countrywide Financial, Lehman Brothers, Merrill Lynch, and Washington Mutual) received $464 million in performance pay from 2005 through 2008, according to an analysis performed for the *New York Times*.[4]

Another *New York Times* story examined compensation at Merrill Lynch, whose adventures in toxic mortgages are threatening to bring down Bank of America.[5] Of the $5 billion to $6 billion in total bonuses paid at the firm in 2006, $1 billion to $2 billion went to the 2,000

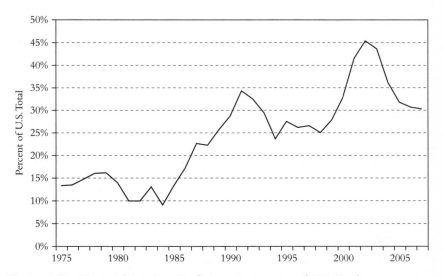

Figure 2.5 Financial Services Profits as a Percentage of U.S. Total
SOURCE: Moody's Economy.com.

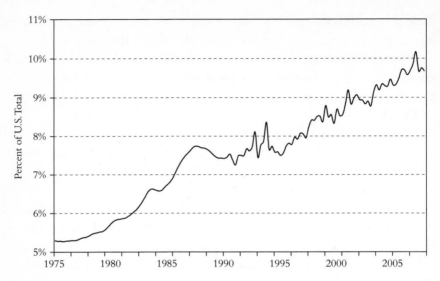

Figure 2.6   Financial Services Wages and Salaries as a Percentage of U.S. Total
SOURCE: Moody's Economy.com.

employees in the fixed-income and mortgage division; 1,900 of them received bonuses averaging $700,000 each, while the top 100 received at least $1 million each, with an *average of $5 million!* In that year, Dow Kim, co-head of investment banking and global markets and the person who oversaw the fixed-income and mortgage units, made $35 million, nearly as much at Stanley O'Neal, Merrill's CEO, bringing Kim's six-year total compensation to $117 million.

Rating Agencies

Given the amount of money being made, Wall Street certainly wasn't going to do anything but fuel the bubble, but what about the rating agencies? Sadly, rather than acting as a brake against reckless behavior, they enabled it by giving trillions of dollars of toxic assets their prized AAA rating. That they were massively wrong isn't in doubt—the only question is: why?

In part, it was total incompetence. We have looked at some of the pricing models used by the rating agencies and investment banks for packaging and pricing mortgage-backed securities, and every one of them assumed for all scenarios that home prices would continue to rise. In other words, they never even modeled a scenario of flat, much less declining, home prices! This might have appeared reasonable based on history, but rating agencies, when awarding the highest AAA rating, are supposed to understand the markets they're rating (it wasn't hard to find evidence of a housing bubble), model a range of future scenarios and stress test 100-year storms to make sure the bonds will still pay.

It wasn't just incompetence, though. Given the magnitude of the errors and the terrible conflicts of interest, it's impossible to believe that the rating agencies made an innocent mistake (or, to be more accurate, thousands of innocent mistakes). We think the rating agencies suffered from willful blindness, driven by the massive amounts of money to be made (at least as long the bubble was still inflating).

Rating structured finance products was many times more profitable than the rating agencies' bread-and-butter business of rating corporate and municipal bonds, so as securitization boomed on Wall Street, so did the profits of the rating agencies. Figure 2.7 shows Moody's stock price from 2003 through Q1 2006. In light of this, it's not hard to see why the rating agencies prostituted themselves and ruined their good names.

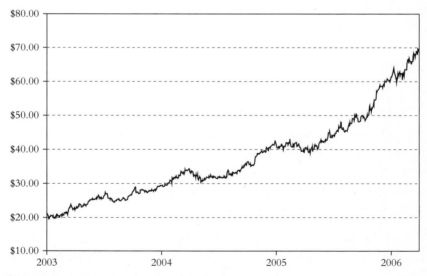

Figure 2.7 Moody's Stock Price, 2003 to Q1 2006
SOURCE: Yahoo! Finance (http://finance.yahoo.com).

Institutional Fixed-Income Managers

With Wall Street firms and rating agencies having sold their souls, what about the managers of the $70 trillion of global savings in fixed-income securities? Surely they would exercise caution when investing the savings entrusted to their care? *Ha!* They threw caution to the wind as they piled into the ever more toxic products being dreamed up by the financial wizards of Wall Street, rarely asking any questions and blindly trusting the ratings of the rating agencies. And it wasn't even for very much money: One of the most remarkable aspects of the bubble is how much risk was taken for only a few extra basis points of return.

Why would they do this? In part, institutional fixed-income managers didn't know any better. What chance does the treasurer of a small city or the manager of a small union pension fund have against a smooth-talking Merrill Lynch salesperson saying, "This CDO has an AAA rating from Moody's, so it's totally safe— and it yields 50 basis points over Treasuries!" But it also has to do with the way these managers are evaluated and compensated. If they stuck to safe investments like Treasuries, their returns would trail those of their peers quarter after quarter, which is a good way to lose one's job. As Jean-Marie Eveillard once noted, "It's much warmer inside the herd."[6]

Banks and Mortgage Lenders

While there's plenty of blame for Wall Street firms, the rating agencies, and the managers of the $70 trillion, at the end of the day the debacle occurred because banks and mortgage lenders threw their underwriting standards out the window and made millions of bad loans. What could they have been thinking? In part, they were blinded by the money they were making and, in addition, their loss experience was very low, which lulled them into complacency, as Morgan Stanley's Mike Francis explained on *This American Life*:[7]

Mike Francis: All the data that we had to review, to look at, on loans in production that were years old was positive. They performed very well. All those factors, when you look at the pieces and parts: A 90 percent NINA loan from three years ago is performing amazingly well. [It] has a little bit of risk. Instead of defaulting 1.5 percent of the time, it defaults

3.5 percent of the time. That's not so bad. If I'm an investor buying that, if I get a little bit of return, I'm fine. . . . All the data that we had to review, to look at, on loans in production that were years old was positive.

Adam Davidson, National Public Radio: As we now know, they were using the wrong data. They looked at the recent history of mortgages and saw that the foreclosure rate was generally below 2 percent. So they figured, absolute worst-case scenario, the foreclosure rate may go to 8 or 10 or 12 percent. But the problem with [that] is there were all these new kinds of mortgages, given out to people who never would have gotten them before. So the historical data was irrelevant. Some mortgage pools, today, are expected to go beyond 50 percent foreclosure rates.

Even if a loan defaulted, the lenders didn't think they'd suffer any losses, for two reasons: Either they had sold the loan to someone else or they assumed that home price appreciation would bail them out. When home prices are rising rapidly, almost no borrowers default, because anyone in trouble can simply refinance. And, even in the event of a default and foreclosure, the losses are small because the home can be resold for a good price. But when home prices start to decline, watch out below! Figure 2.8 shows that as long as home prices are rising 10 percent or

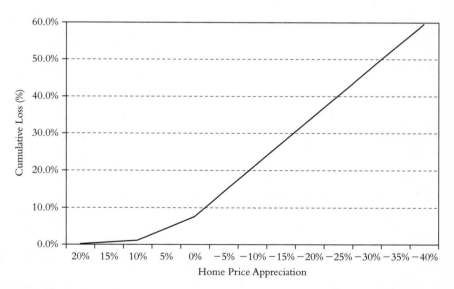

Figure 2.8 Cumulative Loss Estimate over Five Years in a Bubble-Era Pool of Subprime Mortgages for Various Home Price Scenarios
SOURCE: T2 Partners estimates.

more annually, losses in pools of even the worst subprime mortgages are minimal, but losses quickly spiral upward as home prices decline."

The Government

Even the briefest study of the history of financial markets shows that they are prone to boom-and-bust cycles unless governments carefully regulate them. Thus, it's not surprising that the housing bubble was made possible by a complete failure of government at all levels to properly monitor and regulate many different areas. Here were some of the key events:

- During the 1990s, the Clinton administration pushed Fannie and Freddie to support more lending in low-income communities and used the Community Reinvestment Act to encourage (some would say coerce) banks to do the same.
- In April 1998, the President's Working Group on Financial Markets brought together Alan Greenspan, Treasury Secretary Robert E. Rubin, and Securities and Exchange Commission (SEC) Chairman Arthur Levitt Jr., all of whom—according to a report in the *Washington Post*[8]— successfully pushed Brooksley E. Born, the head of the Commodity Futures Trading Commission, to abandon her efforts to regulate derivatives, including credit default swaps. These derivatives subsequently exploded in size and were a major contributor to the credit crisis.
- In 1999, Congress repealed the Glass-Steagall Act, thereby allowing commercial and investment banks to exist under one roof and paving the way for the creation of "too big to fail" behemoths like Citigroup.
- Congress, primarily Democrats, protected Fannie and Freddie from various efforts to rein in their growth and better regulate them. Consequently, they became massively overleveraged, which led to their downfall. In addition, their willingness to buy dodgy loans and securities based on such loans was an important contributor to the bubble.
- The Bush administration and the Federal Reserve under Chairman Alan Greenspan were strong proponents of letting the private sector monitor itself, with a minimum of government regulation.

This *New York Times* article summarizes the Bush administration's role:[9]

"From his earliest days in office, Mr. Bush paired his belief that Americans do best when they own their own home with his conviction that markets do best when let alone.

He pushed hard to expand home ownership, especially among minorities, an initiative that dovetailed with his ambition to expand the Republican tent—and with the business interests of some of his biggest donors. But his housing policies and hands-off approach to regulation encouraged lax lending standards.

Mr. Bush did foresee the danger posed by Fannie Mae and Freddie Mac, the government-sponsored mortgage finance giants. The president spent years pushing a recalcitrant Congress to toughen regulation of the companies, but was unwilling to compromise when his former Treasury secretary wanted to cut a deal. And the regulator Mr. Bush chose to oversee them—an old prep school buddy—pronounced the companies sound even as they headed toward insolvency.

As early as 2006, top advisers to Mr. Bush dismissed warnings from people inside and outside the White House that housing prices were inflated and that a foreclosure crisis was looming."

- Eliot Spitzer, who at the time was the governor of New York, blamed the Bush administration for yet another reason in a *Washington Post* column:[10]

"Even though predatory lending was becoming a national problem, the Bush administration looked the other way and did nothing to protect American homeowners. In fact, the government chose instead to align itself with the banks that were victimizing consumers.

. . . Individually, and together, state attorneys general of both parties brought litigation or entered into settlements with many subprime lenders that were engaged in predatory lending practices. Several state legislatures, including New York's, enacted laws aimed at curbing such practices.

What did the Bush administration do in response? Did it reverse course and decide to take action to halt this burgeoning scourge? As Americans are now painfully aware, with hundreds of thousands of homeowners facing foreclosure and our markets reeling, the answer is a resounding no.

Not only did the Bush administration do nothing to protect consumers, it embarked on an aggressive and unprecedented campaign to prevent states from protecting their residents from the very problems to which the federal government was turning a blind eye.

- In response to the European Union's threat in 2002 to regulate the foreign subsidiaries of the Wall Street firms, the SEC in 2004 adopted an oversight plan—but then made it voluntary! Soon afterward, the Wall Street firms took on substantially more leverage, which contributed to their downfall. As former SEC Chairman Christopher Cox admitted in September 2008, "The last six months have made it abundantly clear that voluntary regulation does not work." The program "was fundamentally flawed from the beginning, because investment banks could opt in or out of supervision voluntarily. The fact that investment bank holding companies could withdraw from this voluntary supervision at their discretion diminished the perceived mandate" of the program, and "weakened its effectiveness."[11]
- Alan Greenspan essentially said that fixed-rate mortgages were too expensive and many Americans were foolish to prefer them, which gave the mortgage industry a green light to promote the risky adjustable-rate mortgages that have now gotten millions of homeowners into so much trouble, when he praised their virtues in this speech on February 23, 2004:[12]

[R]ecent research within the Federal Reserve suggests that many homeowners might have saved tens of thousands of dollars had they held adjustable-rate mortgages rather than fixed-rate mortgages during the past decade, though this would not have been the case, of course, had interest rates trended sharply upward.

American homeowners clearly like the certainty of fixed mortgage payments. This preference is in striking contrast to the situation in some other countries, where adjustable-rate mortgages are far more common and where efforts to introduce American-type fixed-rate mortgages generally have not been successful. Fixed-rate mortgages seem unduly expensive to households in other countries. One possible reason is that these mortgages effectively charge homeowners high fees for protection against rising interest rates and for the right to refinance.

American consumers might benefit if lenders provided greater mortgage product alternatives to the traditional fixed-rate mortgage. To the degree that households are driven by fears of payment shocks but are willing to manage their own interest-rate risks, the traditional fixed-rate mortgage may be an expensive method of financing a home.

In summary, politicians from both parties as well as regulators took a number of actions that contributed to the conditions for a bubble. Then, as things started to get crazy, they failed to recognize what was happening and take steps to address the problem—and, in some cases, they even exacerbated it.

And Finally: Homeowners

A final cause of the mortgage bubble is the behavior of homeowners. Some people believe that the homeowners who are struggling to pay their mortgages and even are losing their homes are getting what they deserve. At the very least, they bought a house they couldn't afford, or did a cash-out refi to support an unsustainable lifestyle, or, worst of all, lied about their income or were speculators, flipping homes, and condos trying to make a quick buck as prices spiraled upward, seemingly without end.

Indeed some people were dishonest, greedy, and/or reckless and probably deserve to lose their homes, but in general we have a sympathetic view toward the millions of homeowners who are now in trouble, most of whom were simply trying to realize the American dream by providing a decent home for their families, fell victim to the illusion that home prices would go up forever, trusted their lenders, and/or simply didn't understand the financial implications of their mortgages.

The last-named reason is completely understandable, given that financial illiteracy is alarmingly high in the United States. Various studies have shown that two-thirds of Americans don't understand how compound interest works, 29 percent don't know the interest rate on their credit card, and an additional 30 percent think it's below 10 percent when it's likely double that; no wonder only 43 percent pay off their credit cards in full every month.

When it comes to mortgages, which became extraordinarily complex during the bubble, a Federal Reserve study in January 2006 showed that significant numbers of adjustable-rate mortgage borrowers didn't understand the reset period, the rate cap, or the terms of their mortgages. This problem is particularly acute among the most vulnerable segments of the population, who, not surprisingly, are suffering the most as the bubble bursts. A report in May 2006, at the peak of the bubble, by the Consumer Federation of America (CFA) found that:

> [L]ower-income and minority consumers were more likely than other consumers to prefer ARMs but they were less likely to understand the risks. More than three-fifths of young adults, African Americans, Latinos, those with incomes below $25,000, and those without a high school diploma did not know how to estimate what would happen to monthly mortgage payments if interest rates rose two percentage points. Those who were willing to estimate the increased monthly costs underestimated the increase by between 40 [and] 50 percent. . . .
>
> It is likely that this lack of knowledge has helped encourage borrowers to take out loans based on their initial repayment schedule without appreciating the possible risk of rising interest rates and increased monthly costs. Borrowers who are basing their mortgage decision on the initial monthly payment level could face significant payment shock as soon as the mortgage adjusts.[13]

Given this level of financial illiteracy, there is a clear and compelling need for strong government regulation to ensure that unsophisticated borrowers aren't taken advantage of. Unfortunately, as noted earlier, the government fell down on the job (thanks, in part, to massive lobbying by financial firms), so it's not surprising that there was large-scale exploitation.

We don't entirely excuse homeowners for their behavior, especially those who committed mortgage fraud—most commonly by lying about their incomes—but we even have some sympathy for the most dishonest, greedy, and/or reckless borrowers, which we can best explain with the following analogy: Imagine that someone took a huge bag of $100 bills and walked into a crowd anywhere in the world and started throwing the bills into the air. What do you think would happen? There would of course be a mad scramble, as people climbed over one another and grabbed for the money. In short, it would be an ugly scene with all sorts of bad behavior—very similar to what we saw during the mortgage bubble.

But who would you blame for this: the individuals behaving badly or the person throwing the bills into the air? While we don't completely absolve the individuals, we think the person who created the chaos is 80 percent to blame. Show us the system, and we'll show you the human behavior.

In the case of the mortgage bubble, a system developed that rewarded awful behavior on the part of everyone in the system, from homeowners all the way up to Wall Street CEOs—so, not surprisingly, that's exactly what we got. It's the system that's primarily to blame—the resulting behavior, while deplorable, is simply the inevitable consequence.

Chapter 3

What Are the Consequences of the Bubble Bursting?

I n this chapter we examine the consequences of the bursting of the
housing bubble, both in the housing sector and beyond, but first let's
take a look at the U.S. mortgage market. Approximately two-thirds
of U.S. homes have mortgages—a total of 55 million—and of these, 56
percent are owned or guaranteed by the two government-sponsored
enterprises (GSEs), Fannie Mae and Freddie Mac, as shown in Figure 3.1.

Delinquencies and Foreclosures

Delinquencies and foreclosures have skyrocketed to the point where, as
shown in Figure 3.2, nearly 8 percent of all U.S. mortgages were affected
as of year-end 2008, an all-time high since the Mortgage Bankers
Association started tracking this in 1972. This represents more than four
million homes and roughly $1 trillion of mortgages. And the problem is
rapidly getting larger, as in January 2009 alone more than $30 billion in

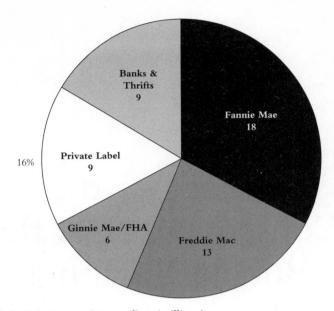

Figure 3.1 Mortgages Outstanding (millions)
SOURCE: Freddie Mac, Q3 2008, as reported by James B. Lockhart III, Director, Federal Housing Finance Agency, at the Association of Government Accountants 7th Annual National Leadership Conference (Washington, D.C., February 19, 2009).

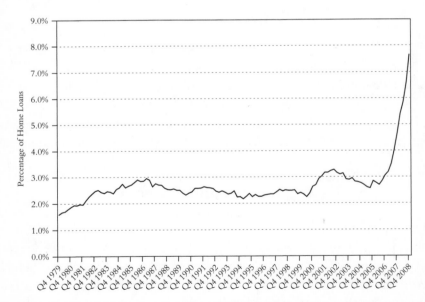

Figure 3.2 Total Delinquencies (Seasonally Adjusted) and Foreclosures
SOURCE: National Delinquency Survey, Mortgage Bankers Association.

mortgages defaulted and 274,000 homes received a foreclosure-related notice (default notice, auction sale notice, or bank repossession).

The problem mortgages are not evenly spread out, however. While only 16 percent of mortgages are "private label," meaning that they were sent to Wall Street and securitized, they accounted for 62 percent of seriously delinquent mortgages as of Q3 2008, as shown in Figure 3.3.

The rate of monthly foreclosures has more than tripled since the peak of the bubble, as shown in Figure 3.4. RealtyTrac.com estimates that over 1.5 million bank-owned properties are on the market, representing around one-third of all properties for sale in the United States.

While the number of foreclosures appeared to be stabilizing in early 2009, the main reason is that a number of states and banks (plus Fannie and Freddie) have enacted foreclosure moratoriums, in part due to anticipation of an Obama administration foreclosure mitigation plan, the outline of which was released on February 18, 2009, and the details of which were released on March 4, 2009. We discuss in Chapter 5

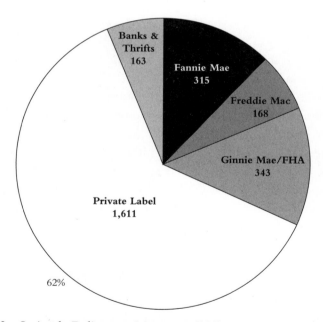

Figure 3.3   Seriously Delinquent Mortgages (000)
SOURCE: Freddie Mac, Q3 2008, as reported by James B. Lockhart III, Director, Federal Housing Finance Agency, at the Association of Government Accountants 7th Annual National Leadership Conference (Washington, D.C., February 19, 2009).

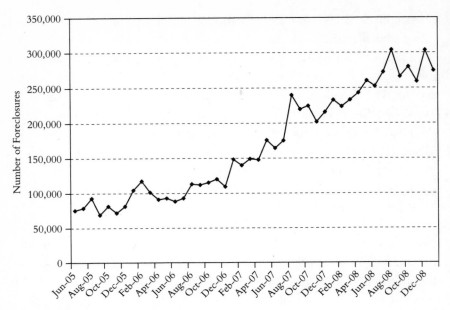

Figure 3.4   Foreclosure Activity by Month
SOURCE: RealtyTrac.com U.S. Foreclosure Market Report.

why we believe this plan is a step in the right direction but will likely have only a moderate impact in reducing the tidal wave of foreclosures, which Credit Suisse forecasts at four million to 10 million from 2009 to 2012 (depending on the economy, home prices, and the effectiveness of foreclosure mitigation plans).[1]

Further, attempts at foreclosure mitigation have so far been a bust, as most loan modifications haven't addressed the underlying problems of deep-underwater homeowners and unaffordable monthly payments, so the majority of modified mortgages have redefaulted in less than six months, as shown in Figure 3.5.

Existing Home Activity

Existing home sales declined from their bubble-era peak to an annual rate of 4.5 million units in January 2009, down 8.6 percent year over year and the lowest level since July 1997, as shown in Figure 3.6.

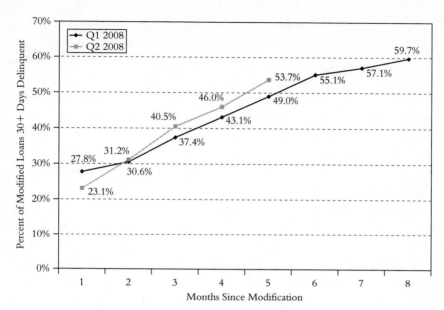

Figure 3.5 Total Percentage of Modified Loans 30+ Days Delinquent

SOURCE: Office of the Comptroller of the Currency and Office of Thrift Supervision Mortgage Metrics Report, Disclosure of National Bank and Federal Thrift Mortgage Loan Data, Third Quarter 2008.

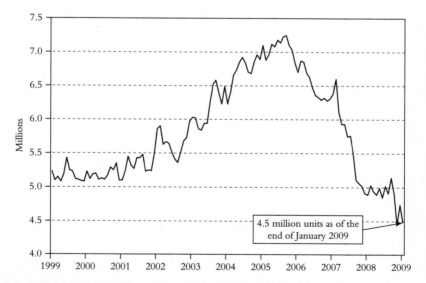

Figure 3.6 Existing Home Sales (Seasonally Adjusted Annual Rates, in Millions)

SOURCE: NATIONAL ASSOCIATION OF REALTORS® Existing Home Sales data series.

This decline is not as severe as one might expect, mostly because in California sales in January were up 54 percent (albeit from very weak levels the previous year) as banks moved to sell foreclosed homes and prices fell to more affordable levels.

As of January 2009, there was a 9.6 months supply of existing homes inventory, more than double normal levels, as shown in Figure 3.7.

Very counterintuitively, the National Association of Realtors (NAR) reported that total housing inventory actually declined 2.7 percent in January 2009, leading Lawrence Yun, NAR's chief economist, to comment: "The drop in total inventory is an encouraging sign because the number of homes on the market has declined steadily since peaking in July 2008, and inventory is at the lowest level in two years."[2]

If only it were true. The inventory backlog is almost certainly far worse than NAR is reporting for two reasons. First, many homeowners have pulled their homes off the market (or aren't even bothering to list them) because prices are so low that they either can't sell because they're underwater on their mortgages or won't sell because they're in denial and think home prices will rebound.

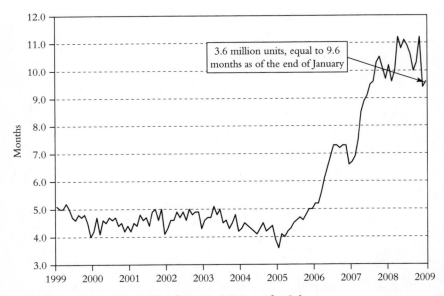

Figure 3.7   Months Supply of Existing Homes for Sale
Source: NATIONAL ASSOCIATION OF REALTORS® Existing Home Sales data series.

Second, as NAR itself points out, there is an enormous "shadow" or "ghost" inventory of homes that banks have in their inventories but aren't listing (called real estate owned or REO) because they're so back-logged, or perhaps they're deliberately holding onto houses in the hope that prices will recover—or to avoid having to recognize losses.

How big is this overhang? In a study of 500,000 distressed proper-ties in four states (California, Maryland, Florida, and Wisconsin), NAR found that the multiple listings services maintained by real estate agents, which NAR uses to measure inventory, captured only one-fourth of the foreclosed homes that banks were holding.[3]

A report from Deutsche Bank that examined 26 markets estimated that the foreclosure inventory alone was equal to an average of nearly three years of sales in bubble markets (the highest was Miami, at a mind-boggling *eight* years) and 14 months even in non-bubble markets.[4]

Finally, Mark Hanson of the Field Check Group, in a study of California, which accounts for one-third of all foreclosures, found that "half the 2008 REO is still in inventory somewhere" and concluded that the true inventory level in California is 22 months.[5]

New Home Activity

In light of all the vacant and foreclosed homes, many of which are only a few years old and are in good condition, there's little market for new homes. Builders are finally adjusting to this fact, which is reflected in the collapse of new home starts, completions, and sales, as shown in Figure 3.8.

The result is a sharp drop in the number of new homes available for sale—but not sharp enough to offset the decline in actual sales, so the supply rose to 13.3 months by January 2009, as shown in Figure 3.9.

Home Vacancies

Further exacerbating the bursting of the bubble is the fact that the number of empty homes has roughly doubled from its historical aver-age, as shown in Figure 3.10. As of the end of Q3 2008, the vacancy rate was nearly 10 percent for homes built this decade, as shown in Figure 3.11, reflecting the massive overbuilding during the bubble.

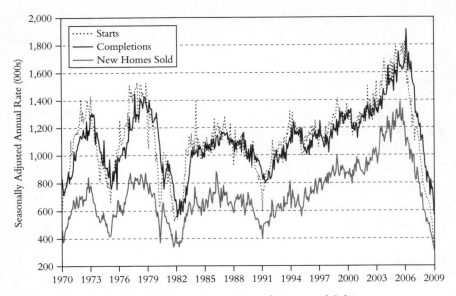

Figure 3.8   Single-Family Home Starts, Completions, and Sales
SOURCE: U.S. Census Bureau.

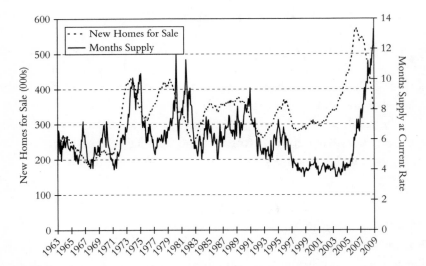

Figure 3.9   Single-Family Homes for Sale and Months Supply
SOURCE: U.S. Census Bureau.

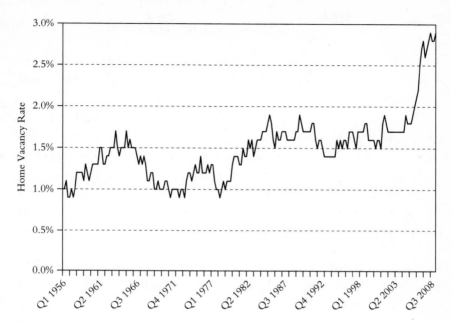

Figure 3.10 Home Vacancy Rate, 1965 to Q3 2008
Source: U.S. Census Bureau.

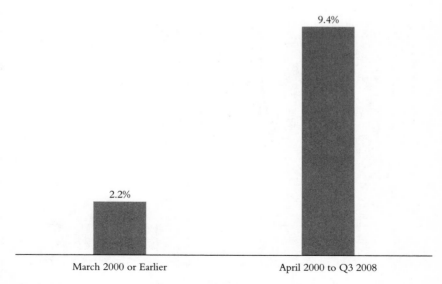

Figure 3.11 Home Vacancy Rate by Date of Construction
Source: U.S. Census Bureau.

Home Price Declines

All of these factors have led to a sharp decline in housing prices, which is measured in numerous ways. There is no right way, so we present three different measures.

The most widely followed metric is the S&P/Case-Shiller 20-city composite home price index, which includes numerous bubble cities such as Las Vegas, Phoenix, Miami, and many in California. Thus, this index shows the greatest rise in prices during the bubble as well as the greatest decline, relative to other national home price measures that include a wider swath of the housing market. For perspective, we include in Figure 3.12 the S&P/Case-Shiller national index, the Office of Federal Housing Enterprise Oversight (OFHEO)'s Purchase-Only Index, and median sales prices of existing homes from the National Association of Realtors, in addition to the S&P/Case-Shiller 20-city composite index.

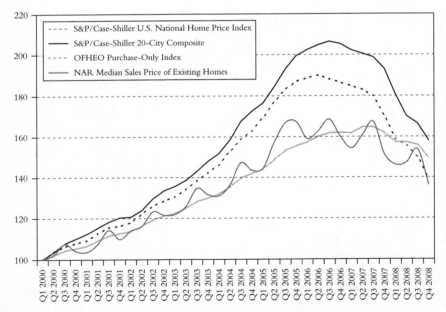

Figure 3.12   Nominal U.S. Home Prices, 2000–2008

Source: Standard & Poor's, OFHEO Purchase-Only Index, NATIONAL ASSOCIATION OF REALTORS® Existing Home Sales data series.

Underwater Homeowners

As home prices have fallen, more and more homeowners are underwater (or upside-down) on their mortgages, as shown in Figure 3.13. Once homeowners owe more on their mortgage than the home is worth, they are much more likely to default—though how much more likely is unknown. One 1995 study concluded that default is "essentially instantaneous" when negative equity exceeds 10 percent,[6] but a more recent 2008 study of 100,000 underwater homeowners in Massachusetts in the early 1990s showed that "fewer than 10 percent of these owners eventually lost their home to foreclosure."[7]

The underwater problem is particularly acute for certain types of loans, as shown in Figure 3.14, and in certain cities, as shown in Table 3.1.

Falling home prices are causing more and more homeowners to go underwater, triggering more defaults, foreclosures, and home sales by banks, which in turn puts more pressure on home

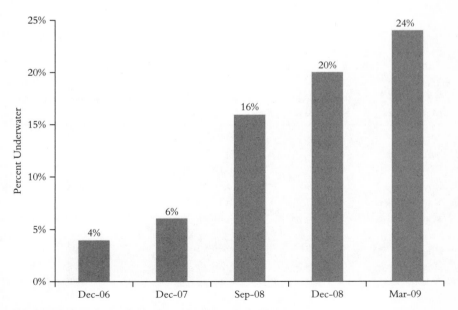

Figure 3.13   Percentage of Loans Underwater by Date
Source: Moody's Economy.com, First American CoreLogic, T2 Partners estimates.

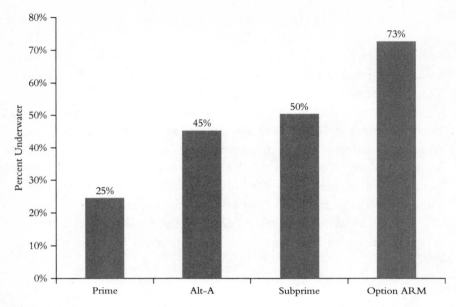

Figure 3.14   Percentage of Loans Underwater by Type (as of January 2009)
SOURCE: Amherst Securities, LoanPerformance, Standard & Poor's.

Table 3.1   Home Price Declines and Underwater Mortgages in 10 Cities

Metro Area	Price Drop Since Peak	Price Index at Lowest Level Since	Past Five Years' Purchasers with a Mortgage Who Are Underwater
Miami	−36.6%	2004-Q1	65.1%
San Diego	−34.4%	2002-Q4	63.9%
Las Vegas	−41.8%	2003-Q4	61.4%
Los Angeles	−32.0%	2003-Q4	56.4%
San Francisco	−27.8%	2003-Q3	51.2%
Washington, D.C.	−24.8%	2004-Q1	50.3%
Phoenix	−37.7%	2004-Q3	36.4%
Boston	−21.8%	2002-Q2	27.8%
Atlanta	−10.4%	2004-Q4	23.2%
New York	−15.2%	2004-Q3	23.0%

SOURCE: Zillow.com Q4 2008 Real Estate Market Report.

prices, creating a self-reinforcing decline. Figure 3.15 shows what happened in California from January 2006 through January 2009, as home prices fell more than 50 percent from their peak while homes sold out of foreclosure soared to more than 60 percent of all sales.

Figure 3.16 is a close-up look at one bubble city, San Diego, from January 2008 to January 2009. Normal home sales rose 9 percent, but overall home sales were up 62 percent due to a 170 percent increase in foreclosure sales, which led to a 35 percent year-over-year decline in home prices.

Impact on the Broader Economy

The train wreck in the U.S. housing market has triggered a credit crunch that has caused a severe economic decline worldwide. This, in turn, is exacerbating the problems in the housing market, creating a vicious circle. For example, if a business has difficulty borrowing

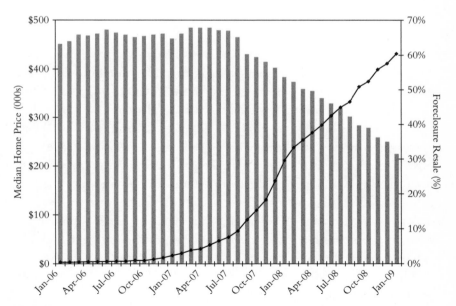

Figure 3.15 Case Study: California Home and Condo Resales
SOURCE: MDA Dataquick.
NOTE: includes new construction.

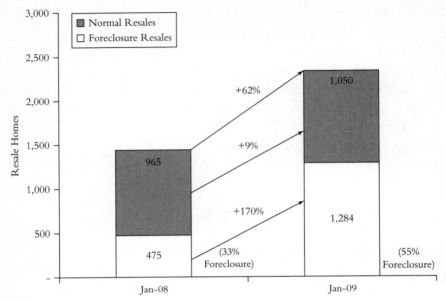

Figure 3.16   Case Study: San Diego County Resales
SOURCE: MDA Dataquick, T2 Partners estimates.
NOTE: Excludes new construction.

money or refinancing its debt, it most likely has to downsize by laying off employees. These employees, in turn, are much more likely to default on their mortgages, triggering more losses to financial institutions, which are then even less likely to lend, and so on. . . .

The U.S. economy is experiencing a recession that is already approaching the severity of the 1974–1976 and 1981–1983 recessions. Gross domestic product (GDP) growth turned negative in the third quarter of 2008 and, according to the Bureau of Economic Analysis,[8] declined at an annual rate of 6.2 percent in the fourth quarter, the largest drop since the first quarter of 1982, when it fell 6.4 percent. In addition, exports and private investment fell at 23.6 percent and 21.1 percent annual rates, respectively, in the fourth quarter.

The United States is losing jobs at an alarming rate. The economy shed 651,000 nonfarm jobs in February 2009, as shown in Figure 3.17, the 14th consecutive month of losses, totaling 4.4 million jobs. Consequently, the unemployment rate has jumped to 8.1 percent, the highest level since December 1983, as shown in Figure 3.18. If one

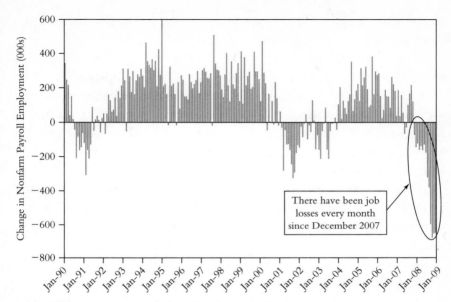

Figure 3.17 Change in Payroll Employment (Nonfarm)
Source: Bureau of Labor Statistics.

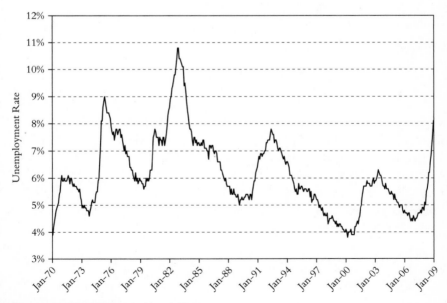

Figure 3.18 Unemployment Rate
Source: Bureau of Labor Statistics.

includes the underemployed, nearly 14 percent of Americans were not working full-time as of the end of February 2009.

The unemployment rate will continue to rise, as more than 600,000 people per week filed new claims for unemployment insurance benefits in February 2009. While the unemployment rate has not yet reached the levels of the 1974–1976 and 1981–1983 recessions, we are currently experiencing a decline from peak employment that exceeds those two downturns—and the decline appears to be accelerating, as shown in Figure 3.19.

Further, job losses and the collapse of the housing market caused consumer confidence to plunge to an all-time low in January 2009, as shown in Figure 3.20.

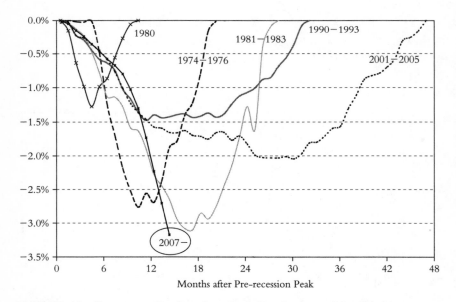

Figure 3.19   Percentage Decline from Peak Employment (Nonfarm)
SOURCE: Bureau of Labor Statistics.

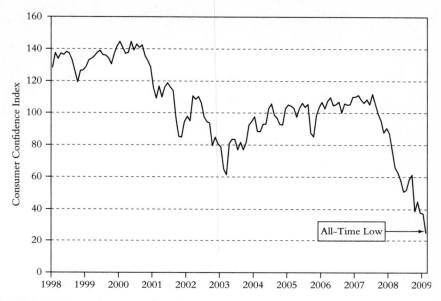

Figure 3.20   Consumer Confidence
SOURCE: The Conference Board.

Conclusion

The bursting of the housing bubble has wreaked havoc not only in the U.S. housing market, but also in the broader U.S. and world economic and financial system. Unfortunately, as we discuss in the next two chapters, the bubble has not finished deflating.

Chapter 4

What Are the Problem Areas?

I f the problems in the mortgage market were limited to subprime loans, then the carnage would mostly be behind us and this would be a history book, useful only in learning the mistakes of the past so they won't be repeated. Unfortunately, however, the bubble infected nearly every area of the mortgage market, and things got crazy not just in subprime but also in a number of other areas. Thus, the problems in the housing market are not over by any means.

To see what is coming, let's start with an overview and then analyze the different areas of the mortgage market one by one, starting with the best prime loans and then continuing into the sewer of subprime, Alt-A, option ARMs, jumbo prime, and second liens/home equity loans, which will cause most of the trouble going forward.

Overview

Figure 4.1 shows the total volume of mortgages written each year from 1999 to 2008 by product type. Note the enormous surge in nonconforming mortgages, which accounted for more than half of the volume in the 2004–2007 period.

Figure 4.2 shows the default rates for different types of mortgages. Subprime is the worst category, but Alt-A and option ARMs aren't far behind, and even prime and jumbo loans will continue to see a surge in delinquencies (all delinquency figures are 60+ days, meaning the borrower has missed two payments, unless otherwise noted).

Now let's take an in-depth look at each type of mortgage.

From the Top: Prime/Conforming Loans

The highest-quality loans are called prime or conforming, terms that are used interchangeably, though they don't have quite the same meaning: conforming describes a loan that meets Fannie Mae and Freddie Mac guidelines and is typically sold to these GSEs. It can't exceed $417,000 (except in certain high-cost areas, where the limit is

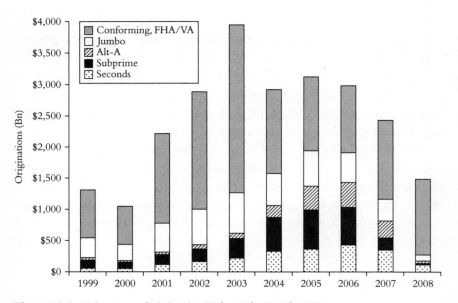

Figure 4.1 Mortgage Origination Volume by Product Type
SOURCE: *Inside Mortgage Finance*, Inside Mortgage Finance Publications, Inc. Copyright 2009. Reprinted with permission.

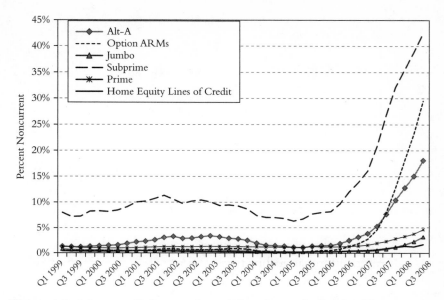

Figure 4.2 Mortgage Delinquencies and Foreclosures by Product Type.
SOURCE: Amherst Securities, LoanPerformance; National Delinquency Survey, Mortgage Bankers Association; FDIC Quarterly Banking Profile; T2 Partners estimates.
NOTE: Home Equity Lines of Credit are 90+ days delinquent. Prime is seasonally adjusted.

$729,750) and the borrower must make a substantial down payment and have a good credit history (usually a FICO score above 740).

As shown in Figure 4.3, conforming loans that went to Fannie and Freddie peaked at 62 percent of the market in 2003 but then declined to only 33 percent in 2006 as Wall Street ramped up its purchases of nonconforming loans, especially subprime and Alt-A.

Overall, the delinquency rate for prime loans is quite low, but has quadrupled from 1 percent to 4 percent in the past two years, as shown in Figure 4.4.

Lending standards for even prime loans deteriorated at the peak of the bubble in 2006 and early 2007, leading to delinquency and default rates far above historical norms for those two years. Figure 4.5 shows Fannie Mae's single-family cumulative default rate (meaning the loan was "terminated without full satisfaction").

For each type of loan, we are using vintage charts like this one, so allow us a moment to explain: Rather than show the total delinquency rate over time for all loans of a certain type, these charts show the delinquency

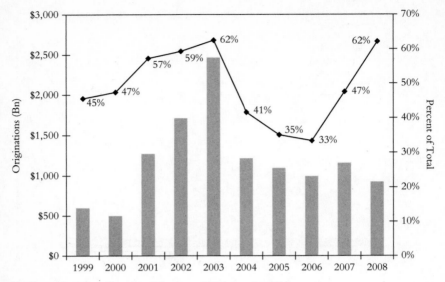

Figure 4.3   Conforming Mortgage Origination Volume

SOURCE: *Inside Mortgage Finance*, published by Inside Mortgage Finance Publications, Inc. Copyright 2009. Reprinted with permission.

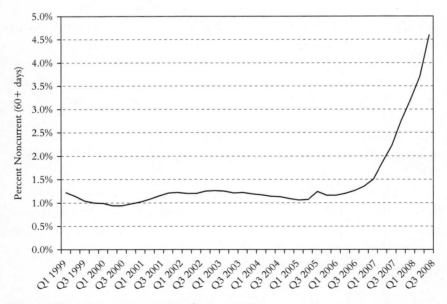

Figure 4.4   Prime Mortgage Delinquency Rate

SOURCE: National Delinquency Survey, Mortgage Bankers Association.

NOTE: Seasonally adjusted.

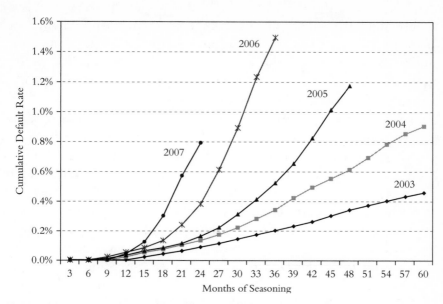

Figure 4.5 Single-Family Cumulative Default Rate by Vintage
SOURCE: Fannie Mae 2008 Credit Supplement (February 26, 2009), T2 Partners estimates.
NOTE: The delinquency rate for all prime mortgages by vintage was unavailable, so we use Fannie Mae data as a reasonable proxy.

rate for loans written during each year, based on how many months elapsed from the time the loans were written. Thus, Figure 4.5 shows that after two years (24 months) of seasoning, only 8 basis points (0.08 percent) of Fannie Mae's prime loans written in 2003 had defaulted. But as lending standards increasingly collapsed in subsequent years, the defaults soar: 8 basis points after two years for 2003 vintage loans, 14 basis points for 2004, 18 basis points for 2005, 38 basis points for 2006, and a horrifying 80 basis points for 2007.

While the default and loss rates for higher-quality prime loans will be much lower than other types, the amount of these loans outstanding, roughly $4.5 trillion, dwarfs that of other types, so even a low percentage loss rate—we estimate 5 to 10 percent—translates into big dollars.

To the Bottom: Subprime Loans

At the opposite extreme from prime loans are subprime ones, which are given to borrowers with very poor credit histories and low FICO scores, typically below 620 to 660, depending on whose definition you want to use (the average FICO score for securitized subprime loans was 617 as of January 2009). Such borrowers are generally poor, aren't well educated, have spotty employment histories, and have frequently been late or defaulted on debts—in short, precisely the people a lender should be very cautious about.

For these reasons, subprime mortgages were only a small part of the market prior to 2002, never far exceeding $100 billion worth per year. But then, amid the madness of the bubble, the volume of subprime loans rose sixfold from 2000 to 2005, peaking at roughly $600 billion worth per year from 2004 through mid-2007, as shown in Figure 4.6.

Approximately $2 trillion worth of subprime mortgages were written from 2000 through 2007, but there is quite a bit less outstanding as of early 2009 because those holding mortgages written prior to 2005 were mostly able to refinance and many subprime mortgages written at the peak have already defaulted. Consequently, there is approximately $700 billion to $800 billion of subprime mortgages currently outstanding (although a Goldman Sachs report puts the figure at $1.4 billion, mostly likely because it counts $515 million of subprime loans at Ginnie Mae, the Federal Housing Administration, and the Department of Veterans Affairs).[1]

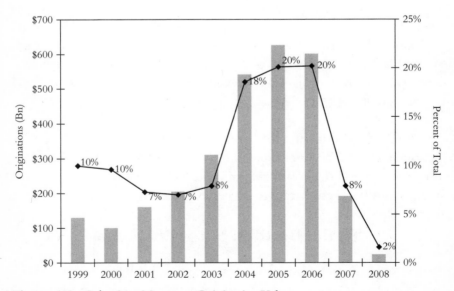

Figure 4.6 Subprime Mortgage Origination Volume
SOURCE: *Inside Mortgage Finance*, Inside Mortgage Finance Publications, Inc. Copyright 2009. Reprinted with permission.

Given the collapse in lending standards, it's not surprising that these loans are suffering catastrophic losses, as shown in Figure 4.7. (Note that all delinquency rate data, both overall and by vintage, in the rest of this chapter, except for Figure 4.27, is for securitized loans—i.e., the loans sent to Wall Street; the data is not available to track delinquencies on loans held by banks and other mortgage lenders.)

Figure 4.8 shows the performance of subprime loans by vintage. It is truly mind-boggling to see that more than 40 percent of the ones written in 2006 and 2007 have defaulted in *less than two years*!

There is no mystery why the housing bubble began to burst in early 2007. In part, it had to do with home prices, which had peaked in mid-2006 and then started to decline, meaning that refinancing was becoming a more difficult option for all types of loans. But the biggest factor was the resetting of subprime loans, most of which had low initial interest rates that reset after two years. Thus, a surge of subprime loans written in early 2005 began to reset beginning in early 2007, an even larger number of subprime loans written in late 2005 reset in late 2007, and so forth, as shown in Figure 4.9. The resets taper off only in mid-2009, two years after subprime lending dried up in mid-2007.

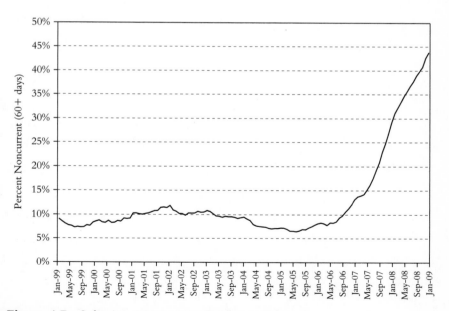

Figure 4.7 Subprime Mortgage Delinquency Rate
SOURCE: Amherst Securities, LoanPerformance.

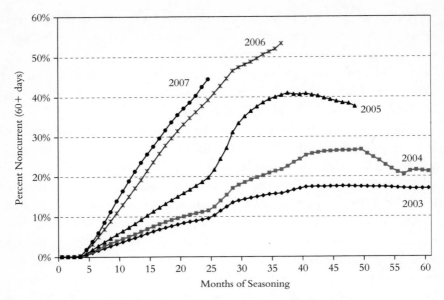

Figure 4.8   Subprime Mortgage Delinquency Rate by Vintage
SOURCE: Amherst Securities, LoanPerformance.

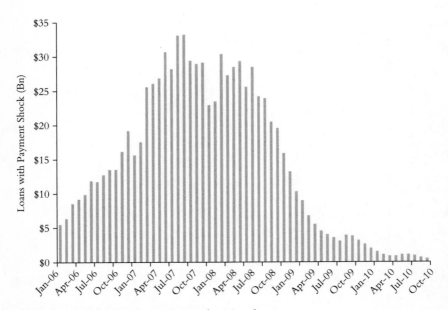

Figure 4.9   Subprime Loan Resets by Month
SOURCE: Amherst Securities, Credit Suisse, LoanPerformance.

Upon reset, the monthly payment for most borrowers jumps because the interest rate rises and/or the loan becomes amortizing, causing payment shock and triggering a wave of defaults. Figure 4.10 shows the monthly default rate for securitized subprime loans with two-year resets of different vintages. A few months after the reset date (months 27 to 29; a default here is three missed payments), defaults skyrocket and then stay at a permanently higher level. What's especially shocking is that 12/2006 and 06/2007 subprime loans are defaulting at more than 8 percent per *month*—before they've even reset!

Anticipating the end of the wave of subprime loan resets, in late 2008 some pundits were starting to get bullish on the outlook for the mortgage crisis. Unfortunately, they missed two things. First, there's a big lag effect since it's not resets but rather homes being sold off that has an impact on the housing market. Resets often lead to default, which usually leads to foreclosure, but this takes a long time. It varies greatly by state, but on average it takes 15 months from the date of the first missed payment to the home being sold, and going forward this will likely take even longer

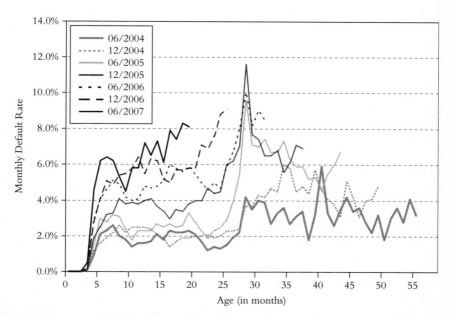

Figure 4.10 Monthly Default Rates for Securitized Subprime Loans with Two-Year Resets by Vintage
Source: Amherst Securities, LoanPerformance.

given the glut of homes on the market and foreclosure moratoriums by many lenders and servicers. Thus, the housing market in early 2009 was feeling the impact of subprime loans that were made in late 2005, reset in late 2007, and defaulted in early 2008. Therefore, the impact of subprime resets tapering off won't be felt until mid-2010.

The second problem with the bullish thesis is that toxic loans weren't limited to the subprime area. Defaults and losses on subprime loans drove the first stage of the mortgage crisis, but another wave of risky loans that had longer reset dates looms.

As for total losses among subprime loans, Goldman Sachs estimates 32 percent, which sounds about right to us.[2]

Alt-A Loans

Alt-A is a catchall category for loans that are typically better than sub-prime but aren't considered prime, most commonly due to:

- Incomplete documentation (stated income, stated assets, low documentation, or no documentation) (73 percent of securitized Alt-A loans).
- Borrower debt-to-income or property loan-to-value ratios too high for the GSEs.
- Non-owner-occupied (27 percent of securitized Alt-A loans).
- Spotty credit history—not bad enough to be considered subprime, but not good enough to be prime (Alt-A FICO scores usually between 660 and 735, with an average of 705 for securitized Alt-A loans).

Historically, Alt-A loans were a small niche, typically covering special cases such as self-employed people who couldn't provide W-2 forms to document their income. But during the bubble, Alt-A became an enormous category, as shown in Figure 4.11.

Because of the fuzzy definition of Alt-A, estimates for the size of the category today vary somewhat, but most are between $1.0 trillion and $1.3 trillion, making it 50 to 100 percent larger than subprime currently, with about half of the loans securitized. (A Goldman Sachs report sizes the Alt-A market at $2.4 trillion because it includes $891 billion of Alt-A loans at Fannie and Freddie and $218 billion held by "finance companies,

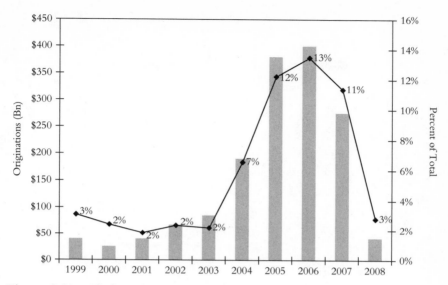

Figure 4.11 Alt-A Mortgage Origination Volume
SOURCE: *Inside Mortgage Finance*, Inside Mortgage Finance Publications, Inc. Copyright 2009. Reprinted with permission.

REITs, insurers and other."[3] Also keep in mind that many banks label certain loans prime that any unbiased analyst would categorize as Alt-A.).

The collapse of lending standards in the Alt-A category rivaled that of subprime, so it's not very surprising that these loans, especially those written from 2005 to 2007, are defaulting at catastrophic rates, as shown in Figures 4.12 and 4.13.

At first glance, Alt-A delinquency rates don't appear to be as bad as subprime, but this has more to do with the structures of the loans: Subprime loans usually reset after only two years, whereas Alt-A loans typically had five-year resets. Thus, as shown in Figure 4.14, Alt-A resets will begin to surge in 2010 (five years after the bubble really started to inflate in 2005) and will continue to rise through 2012.

While Alt-A borrowers generally had higher credit scores than subprime ones, lenders took false comfort in this and thus didn't verify income or assets as often. Figure 4.15 shows that a far higher percentage of Alt-A loans than subprime ones were low- or no-documentation in four bubble states: California, Florida, Nevada, and Arizona.

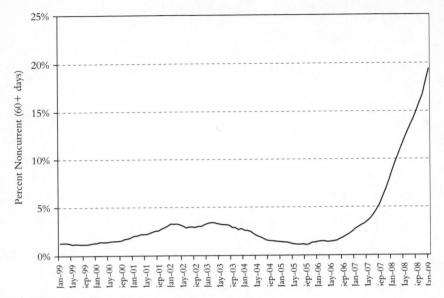

Figure 4.12   Alt-A Mortgage Delinquency Rate
SOURCE: Amherst Securities, LoanPerformance.

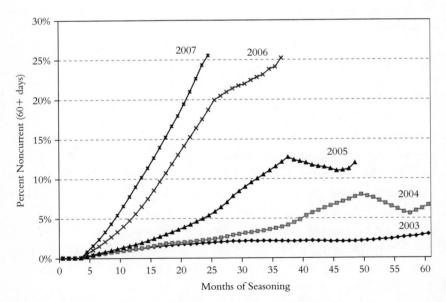

Figure 4.13   Alt-A Mortgage Delinquency Rate by Vintage
SOURCE: Amherst Securities, LoanPerformance.

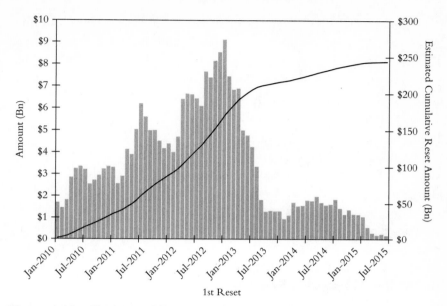

Figure 4.14   Alt-A Monthly Mortgage Rate Resets
SOURCE: Credit Suisse, LoanPerformance.

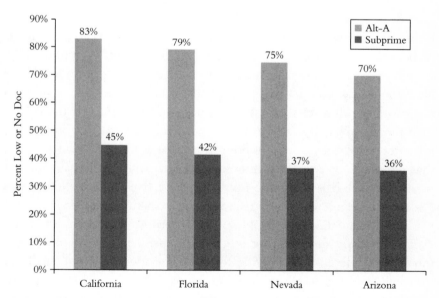

Figure 4.15   Alt-A and Subprime Low-Doc and No-Doc Mortgages by State
SOURCE: Federal Reserve Bank of New York (www.newyorkfed.org/mortgagesmaps),
LoanPerformance.

Contrary to popular perception, it wasn't subprime loans but rather Alt-A ones that brought down Fannie and Freddie. For example, Fannie had $292 billion of Alt-A loans as of December 31, 2008, which accounted for 10.1 percent of its single-family mortgage book of business, but they were responsible for 46 percent of Fannie's total credit losses. Subprime loans, in contrast, were only 0.3 percent of Fannie's book, accounting for 2.0 percent of losses.

The fact that there is greater room for fraud and misrepresentation with Alt-A loans offsets the advantage of higher FICO scores to the point where ultimate losses among Alt-A loans may rival those of subprime, something the market does not yet seem to have factored in. For example, Goldman Sachs estimates that losses among subprime loans will be 32 percent versus only 11 percent for Alt-A loans.[4] While some Alt-A loans are of somewhat higher quality—whereas pretty much all bubble-era subprime loans are toxic—we expect Alt-A losses to be at least double what Goldman Sachs is projecting.

Option ARMs

If one were to design a loan that would blow up the maximum number of borrowers the moment home prices stopped rising, an option ARM would be it. Also known as a pay-option ARM and sold under names like Pick-A-Pay and Pick-A-Payment, this is a 30- or 40-year adjustable-rate mortgage that, for the first five years, gives the borrower the option each month of paying: (1) the fully amortizing interest and principal, (2) full interest only, or (3) an ultralow teaser rate (typically 2 to 3 percent) that doesn't even cover the interest, in which case the unpaid interest is added to the balance of the mortgage. After five years, the loan resets ("recasts"), the interest rate floats, and it becomes fully amortizing.

As many as 80 percent of option ARM borrowers use the third option because it results in the lowest monthly payment or, said another way, a much higher level of borrowing for the same monthly payment. Thus, the rapid spread of option ARMs was the result of—but also fueled—the steep rise in home prices in bubble markets, especially California.

Lenders also loved this product because they could lend a lot of money to seemingly safe borrowers, the amount outstanding would grow every year without any effort due to negative amortization, and—this is key—they could book profits based on the full interest amount owed rather than on the much smaller amount actually paid by borrowers. This was yet another example of how bad accounting can lead to foolish behavior.

Option ARMs are toxic in so many ways it's hard to know where to begin. First, almost all of them were written during the peak bubble years in the peak bubble states, especially California, as shown in Figures 4.16 and 4.17. As with subprime and Alt-A loans, option ARMs had at one time been specialty products but then became widespread during the bubble years. A total of $749 billion of option ARMs were written from 2004 through 2007, about half of which were securitized, with the balance held by lenders. And while some borrowers have been able to refinance, $628 billion of option ARMs are left.[5]

Second, option ARMs often had multiple risk factors, such as being used for a cash-out refinancing, having a simultaneous second lien, and being low- or no-doc (more than 70 percent of option ARMs were

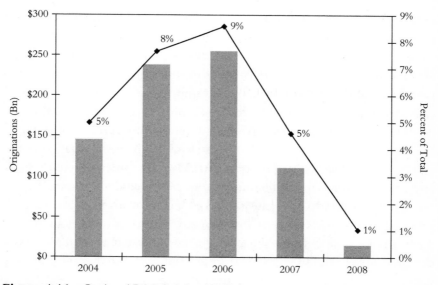

Figure 4.16   Option ARM Origination Volume

SOURCE: *2008 Mortgage Market Statistical Annual*, Inside Mortgage Finance Publications, Inc. Copyright 2008. Reprinted with permission. T2 Partners estimates.

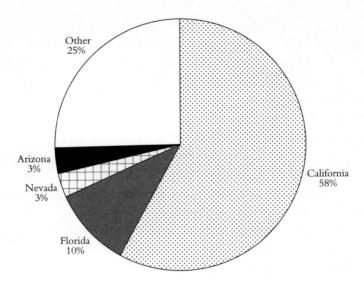

Figure 4.17   Option ARM Originations by State
SOURCE: Amherst Securities, LoanPerformance.

liar's loans; for this reason, most are categorized at Alt-A rather than prime loans). Option ARMs were typically sold to borrowers with good credit—it was the affordability product used by many higher-income/ higher-FICO-score households to buy their dream home—so banks were lending based on FICO scores, the appraised value of the home, and the belief that home prices would keep rising forever, rather than on a borrower's ability to pay the fully amortizing amount after the loan reset. Such loose lending standards are coming back to haunt banks.

Third, because an option ARM is interest-only and has an ultralow teaser interest rate that nearly all borrowers choose to pay, there is severe payment shock when option ARMs reset, much worse than for any other type of mortgage. For example, one study showed that, on average, the monthly payment jumps 63 percent from $1,672 to $2,725 when an option ARM resets.[6] "Payment shock" is a particularly apt name in this case because the jump in monthly payments comes as a shock to many borrowers, who were told only about the low monthly payments by unscrupulous mortgage brokers.

Finally, a mortgage in which the loan balance is going up (called negative amortization) is extremely dangerous, especially in an environment of declining home prices, because borrowers become more indebted every month and so go underwater faster. As a result, nearly three-fourths of option ARM borrowers are now underwater faster, a higher rate than for any other type of loan.

One would rightly conclude, then, that most option ARMs will default, given all of the risk factors, but you don't even need to know all this—all you really have to understand is what the borrowers told you based on their behavior. Figure 4.18 shows interest rates from 2001 to 2008 for a standard 30-year fixed-rate mortgage (FRM) (the jagged line in the middle) and the typical option ARM (the dashed line that curves below the fixed-rate line until early 2005, when it rises above it).

Figure 4.18 shows that from mid-2005 onward, during the period when the majority of all option ARMs were written, an option ARM had a higher interest rate—by mid-2006, nearly 2 percentage points higher—than a fixed-rate loan. Given that most option ARM borrowers had good credit histories and could have qualified for fixed-rate loans,

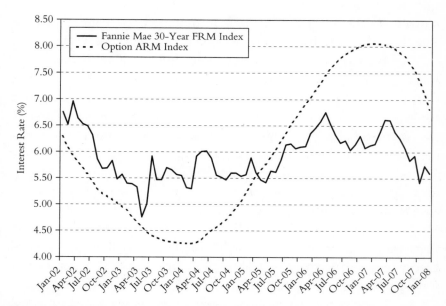

Figure 4.18 Interest Rates for Conforming 30-Year Fixed-Rate Mortgage vs. Option ARM

Source: Bloomberg Finance L.P., Amherst Securities.

why on earth would they take on the risk of an adjustable-rate loan *and* pay a much higher interest rate? (Typically, adjustable-rate mortgages such as option ARMs have *lower* interest rates than fixed-rate loans due to the risk of rising interest rates.)

The answer is simple: For the same loan size, option ARMs initially had much lower monthly payments—or, said another way, for the same monthly payment, a borrower could take out a much bigger mortgage with an option ARM. That's what borrowers cared about during the bubble, and it had the effect of fueling home price increases. Standard fixed-rate loans require the borrower to not only pay full interest but also pay down some principal every month, so even at significantly lower interest rates, they have higher monthly payments. Thus, in doing something that appears to be very irrational (taking out an 8 percent option ARM rather than a 6 percent fixed-rate mortgage), option ARM borrowers were saying that they couldn't afford the full-interest-rate, fully amortizing loan, even at lower interest rates.

Therefore, the only hope for most of these option ARM borrowers is rapid home price appreciation. But now that the reverse has occurred, a significant majority of them are sure to default—we'd guess 70 to 80 percent—in the absence of major loan modifications. Figures 4.19 and 4.20 show that option ARMs are well on their way to this level.

The only apparent good news about option ARMs is that recasts aren't scheduled to hit until five years after the peak of the bubble, or in 2010–2012. But, alas, the wave is already upon us, because an option ARM can recast prior to five years if it negatively amortizes to 110 to 125 percent of the original balance, depending on the terms of the loan. For example, let's say a particular option ARM loan with a 120 percent trigger had a $500,000 balance at inception. If the borrower pays only the minimum, the balance will negatively amortize and within, say, three years the loan balance will have ballooned to $600,000 (hitting the 120 percent trigger) and the loan will reset two years early. This is precisely what is happening, so the option ARM train wreck is starting to hit right now, rather than in 2010 or 2011 as some analysts have projected.

Goldman Sachs estimates that losses among option ARM loans will be 27 percent.[7] We expect a number above 40 percent, based on 70 percent of these loans defaulting with 60 percent average severity.

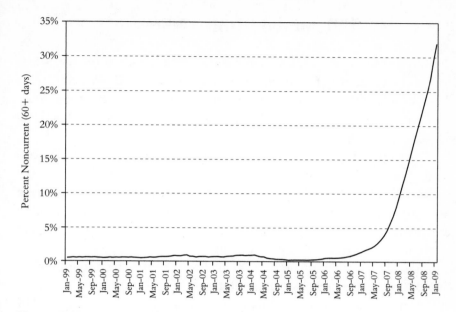

Figure 4.19 Option ARM Mortgage Delinquency Rate
SOURCE: Amherst Securities, LoanPerformance, T2 Partners estimates.

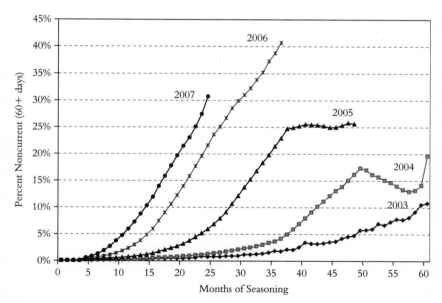

Figure 4.20 Option ARM Mortgage Delinquency Rate by Vintage
SOURCE: Amherst Securities, LoanPerformance.

Jumbo Prime Loans

Jumbo prime loans are those made to borrowers with good credit histories, but which are too big to be sold to the GSEs, which have a limit of $417,000 (in some areas, $729,750). In many ways, these loans have the same problems as option ARMs, the only difference being no negative amortization.

Averaging $750,000, jumbo loans are most common in areas with high home prices like California and Florida—in other words, the areas where the bubble inflated the most and that are now suffering the greatest collapse. Also, some lenders were making jumbo loans to borrowers with FICO scores as low as 620 and calling them prime, but such loans are most certainly not prime.

There are approximately $1.0 trillion to $1.5 trillion of prime jumbo mortgages currently outstanding.

Figure 4.21 shows originations of jumbo prime mortgages by year.

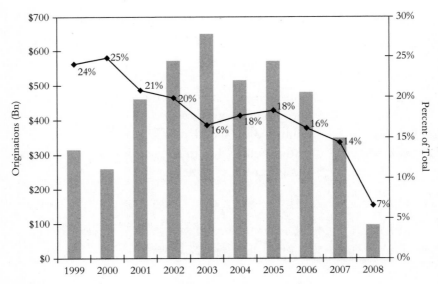

Figure 4.21   Jumbo Prime Mortgage Origination Volume
SOURCE: *Inside Mortgage Finance*, Inside Mortgage Finance Publications, Inc. Copyright 2009.
Reprinted with permission.

During the bubble years, jumbo prime loans typically had a fixed interest rate, usually 1.5 percent below a 30-year fixed rate, which then reset after five, seven, or ten years (called 5/1, 7/1, or 10/1). Such loans were available to borrowers with little money down and with little or no documentation.

Mark Hanson of the Field Check Group explains what's happening to these loans today:[8]

> Jumbo prime are high-leverage programs that allowed borrowers to buy much more home than they should have. Because jumbo prime borrowers had better credit overall, banks were very easy on the qualifying. For example, with full documentation, a 620 credit score [borrower] could get an 80% $750,000 first mortgage that allowed a 15% second [lien] on top of that for a 95% loan.
>
> These loans typically qualified at interest-only payments. For stated income, the fee was very small, typically 0.125% in [increased interest] rate, with allowable credit scores around the 660 level. A 50% debt-to-income ratio was typical. THESE ARE NOT PRIME LOANS. This goes to show how distorted risk management became.
>
> This entire mortgage and housing blowup is very linear. . . . subprime to Alt-A to jumbo prime then prime conventional. Home equity lines of credit blow the entire way up the chain. The defaults in jumbo prime have to do with: a) the way they were structured with longer teasers such as 5, 7, or 10 years; b) the high leverage allowing up to 50% debt-to-income ratios on full-doc and unlimited on stated, no ratio and no doc; [and] c) the massive negative equity due to median home prices falling in the biggest Jumbo regions by 25 to 70%.

Hanson then gives an example of a typical jumbo prime loan:

BUYING A $650K HOME WITH $85K PER YEAR INCOME—MOST POPULAR IN CALIFORNIA

A 5/1 interest-only [loan] at 5% . . . means that a $520,000 loan carried a payment of only $2,166 per month. Add in $650 per month for taxes and insurance, and the total is roughly $2,825.

With a 15% second [lien] of $97,500 at prime [interest rate] carrying payments of $325 per month and reasonable "other debt" at the time of $400 per month, the total payment out the door would be $3,541 approximately.

This means a household income of $7,082 per month could buy a $650,000 home with 5% down. This is not out of the realm of hourly workers or moderate-income single-worker families.

Now the same home is worth $450,000, the borrowers added debt after the loan was funded and all of their after-tax income is going out to [service the] debt each month. They can't save a penny and are going broke just to live in this underwater house.

They can rent the same house for $2,500 per month. The best decision is to walk.

Nowadays, the same income buys a $275,000–$300,000 mortgage with 10% down. This shows why housing prices keep falling.

Interest rates also aren't helping jumbo prime borrowers. Figure 4.22 shows that as Treasury rates have fallen, interest rates on conforming 30-year fixed-rate mortgages that can be sold to Fannie and Freddie have fallen to near all-time lows just above 5 percent, but fixed-rate jumbo mortgage rates are around 7 percent and even jumbo ARMs are at 6 percent. This 163-basis-point spread (as of late February 2009) between conforming and jumbo fixed-rate mortgages was more than six times wider than the average spread of 25 basis points from 2004 to 2007.

Finally, it's important to note that the Obama administration's new Homeowner Affordability and Stability Plan will do little to help the majority of jumbo mortgage holders, since it doesn't apply to any mortgages with a balance above $729,750.

Figures 4.23 and 4.24 show overall delinquencies and delinquencies by vintage for jumbo prime loans. Overall delinquencies were quite low until 2008, and the current trend is alarming.

Figure 4.24 shows jumbo prime mortgage performance by vintage.

In February 2009, Standard & Poor's estimated that losses on jumbo prime loans backing 2006 securitizations will reach an average of 3.65 percent, while losses for similar 2007 bonds will hit 4.5 percent. On March 19, 2009, Moody's one-upped S&P by revising its loss projections

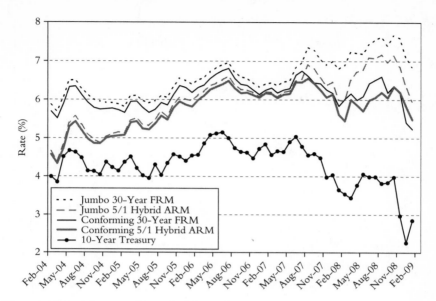

Figure 4.22 Mortgage Rates by Type of Loan
SOURCE: HSH Associates, Yahoo! Finance (http://finance.yahoo.com).

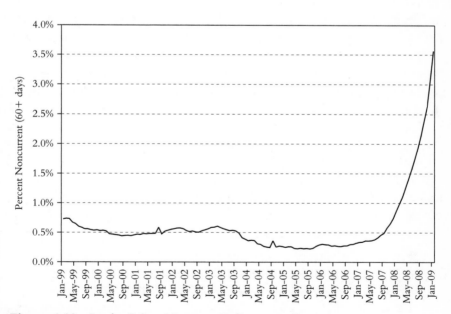

Figure 4.23 Jumbo Prime Mortgage Delinquency Rate
SOURCE: Amherst Securities, LoanPerformance.

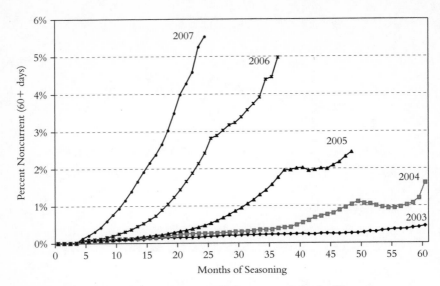

Figure 4.24   Jumbo Prime Mortgage Delinquency Rate by Vintage
SOURCE: Amherst Securities, LoanPerformance.

for RMBSs backed by jumbo prime loans, saying that it "is now projecting cumulative losses of about 1.70 percent for 2005 securitizations, 3.55
percent for 2006 securitizations, 5.05 percent for 2007 securitizations and
6.20 percent for 2008 securitizations." Meanwhile, a Goldman Sachs report
estimated 4.7 percent losses and JPMorgan's analysts doubled their estimates of losses to 8 to 10 percent.[9] We think overall losses will likely be in
the 7 to 12 percent range—and even higher in California, for reasons best
explained by Mark Hanson:[10]

> All over the nation, especially in California, there are millions
> of high-value homes in which the homeowners are trapped,
> unable to sell due to lack of equity or refinance due to the lack
> of financing. I have been watching mid-to-upper-end proper-
> ties in California teetering on the verge of a major fall for a
> year now—they have held better than the lower end, but in
> 2008 everything changed, as subprime loan defaults waned and
> higher grade defaults (Alt-A, option ARM and jumbo prime)
> attached to higher home values look the lead. Now the lion's
> share of defaults is everything but subprime.
>
> The higher grade default wave intensified mid-2008 and
> now those houses have been foreclosed upon and are coming to

market fast, in large quantities. Bottom line: the mid-to-upper-end housing collapse—which has largely been avoided to date, mostly due to better borrowers coupled with higher-leverage and longer-teaser-term loan programs—is upon us.

With all of these foreclosures coming to market and very little financing available to purchase all of the high-end homes available, the supply factor is going to bring down values rapidly—and this does not even count Ma and Pa Homeowner who want to sell. Based upon what I see so far in 2009 prior to the spring and summer selling season, my best forecast is that homes with present values over $750,000 will lose at least 30% in 2009 and those currently worth over $1.5 million will likely decline even more.

Second Liens and Home Equity Loans

All of the mortgages we've looked at so far, as toxic as they might be, are at least first mortgages (or first liens), meaning that if the borrower defaults, the lender can foreclose on the house and sell it, thereby recouping some of the loss. But this isn't so in the case of a home equity line of credit (HELOC) or a home equity loan, (these loans are also known as a second lien, second mortgage, closed-end second (CES), junior lien, or closed-end junior lien).

A HELOC is a line of credit that a lender extends to a homeowner based on the supposed equity in the home. There's a cap on the amount that the homeowner can borrow and the interest fluctuates, usually based on the prime rate plus a certain margin. A HELOC offers the homeowner a great deal of flexibility in terms of the amount borrowed and when to repay the loan—most HELOCs only require that interest be paid until the end of the so-called draw period (typically 5 to 10 years), after which the loan amortizes (i.e., must start to be paid off).

By allowing Americans to borrow against the rapidly rising value of their homes, HELOCs facilitated an orgy of spending. For example, in 2007 30 percent of new car purchases in California and 20 percent in Florida were funded with HELOCs.[11]

A home equity loan differs from a HELOC because it's a one-time, lump-sum loan, often with a fixed rate. It is generally taken out as part of a financing package that includes a first mortgage, in which case it's called a simultaneous second—for example, a first mortgage for 85 percent and a simultaneous second for 15 percent was common during the bubble, meaning the homeowner has no skin in the game and any home price decline puts the second lien underwater.

HELOCs and home equity loans are often lumped together for analytical purposes because they share common risk factors: They are junior not only to first mortgages, but also to accrued interest, foreclosure costs, brokerage commissions, and other expenses in the event of a default. In the current declining home price environment, first mortgages are almost always impaired upon default, meaning HELOCs and home equity loans suffer a total loss—in fact, sometimes even more than 100 percent, since there's a cost to write off the loan.

HELOCs and home equity loans soared in popularity during the bubble, resulting in $900 billion of total exposure by banks by the end of 2008, as shown in Figures 4.25 and 4.26.

In addition to $900 billion held by banks, approximately $100 billion each of HELOCs and home equity loans were sent to Wall Street and securitized, for a total exposure of $1.1 trillion.[12]

Unlike most other types of residential loans, which were sent to the GSEs or Wall Street, banks kept more than 80 percent of HELOCs and home equity loans on the balance sheets, making them especially

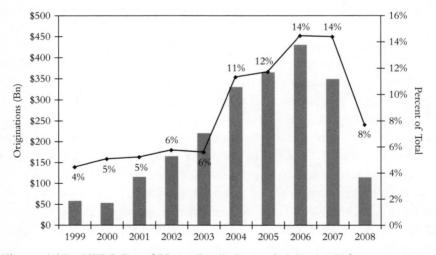

Figure 4.25   HELOCs and Home Equity Loans Origination Volume
Source: *Inside Mortgage Finance*, Inside Mortgage Finance Publications, Inc. Copyright 2009. Reprinted with permission.

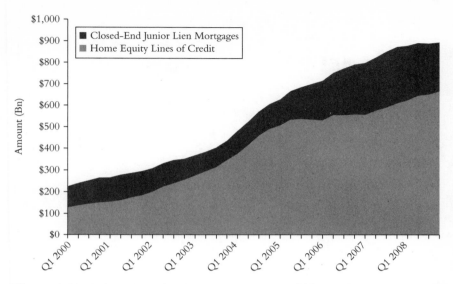

Figure 4.26   HELOCs and Home Equity Loans Held by Banks
Source: FDIC Quarterly Banking Profile.

vulnerable to losses in this area. For example, as of year-end 2008, after acquiring Wachovia, Wells Fargo had $129.5 billion of HELOCs and home equity loans versus only $45.1 billion of common tangible equity.

Delinquencies, while low, are rising rapidly among HELOCs and home equity loans, as shown in Figure 4.27. As of Q3 08, HELOC delinquencies had reached their highest level on record.[13]

Figure 4.28 shows home equity loan performance by vintage (note that very few HELOCs were securitized, so this chart is only for second liens).

To give you a sense of how toxic these loans can be, Figure 4.29 is a chart from the presentation Ambac Financial Group released concurrently with its Q1 2008 earnings report, which shows the monthly losses of a second lien pool securitized by Bear Stearns that closed in April 2007. (Note that these are not delinquencies, but actual losses, though they tend to be identical since there's usually no recovery when a second lien defaults.)

While this is an extreme example of higher-than-average losses due mainly to the 2007 vintage, the rapid implosion of this pool is nevertheless stunning. Ambac projected that the monthly loss rate would peak above

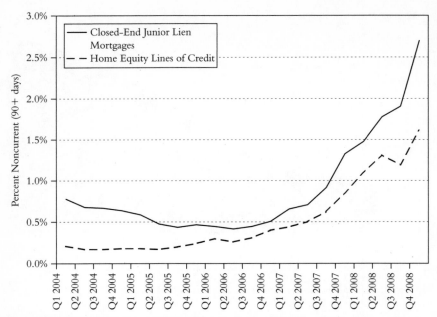

Figure 4.27   HELOCs and Home Equity Loans 90+ Day Delinquency Rate
SOURCE: FDIC Quarterly Banking Profile.

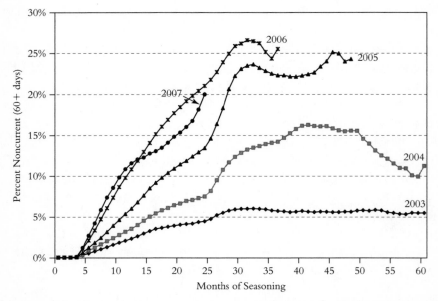

Figure 4.28   Home Equity Loan 90+ Day Delinquency Rate by Vintage
SOURCE: Amherst Securities, LoanPerformance.

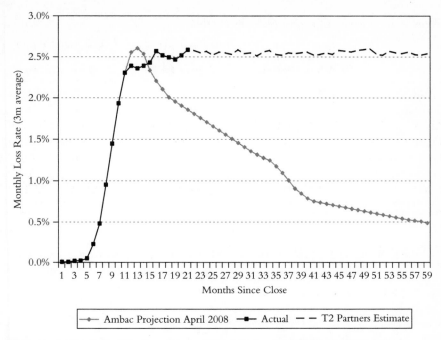

Figure 4.29 Monthly Loss Rate of Bear Stearns 2007 Second Lien Pool
SOURCE: Ambac Financial Group Q1 2008 presentation (April 23, 2008); Amherst Securities.

2.5 percent but then quickly decline thereafter—yet still estimated that total losses to the pool would be 81.8 percent! (This was grim news for Ambac, which guaranteed the senior tranche of this pool thinking that losses might be in the 10 to 12 percent range.) With actual data through the end of 2008, one can see that monthly losses did indeed reach the 2.5 percent level—but have remained at that level rather than declining. At this rate, the pool will be wiped out in a total of five years.

Goldman Sachs estimates that losses among HELOCs and home equity loans will be 11 percent.[14] Yet again, we think losses are likely to be double this.

Conclusion

Table 4.1 summarizes the losses on U.S. mortgages, which we estimate will be between $1.6 trillion and $2.2 trillion.

Table 4.1   Range of Loss Estimates by Product

	Outstanding Balance ($Bn)	Estimated Range of Cumulative Losses (%)	Estimated Range of Cumulative Losses ($Bn)
Prime	$ 4,500	5–10%	$225–$450
Subprime	$ 1,400	30–35%	$420–$490
Alt-A	$ 2,400	20–25%	$480–$600
Option ARM	$ 600	40–45%	$240–$270
Jumbo Prime	$ 1,200	7–12%	$84–$144
Home Equity	$ 1,100	15–25%	$165–$275
Total	**$11,200**	**14–20%**	**$1,614–$2,229**

SOURCE: T2 Partners estimates.

The bubble infected every area of the housing and mortgage markets, which is leading to unprecedented strain and losses. In Chapter 5, we explore what to expect next.

Chapter 5

What's Next?

Having taken a look at what happened and where we are today, let's now turn to what's likely to happen to the U.S. housing market—and the overall economy and stock market—in the future.

The short answer is that we're probably in the late stages of home price declines, in the middle stages of write-downs by the banks and other institutions that are exposed to the U.S. housing market, and, regrettably, in early stages of the overall credit crunch. That said, we think there are great opportunities for savvy and courageous investors, on both the long and short sides, but especially on the long side—not surprising given that the major indexes are down more than 50 percent from their peaks (as of the end of February 2009).

The story over the past two years has been the mortgage meltdown, especially in the subprime area. Going forward, the U.S. mortgage market will continue to be critical—it is the world's largest debt market, after all—but the next wave of defaults will be driven by the other types of creative mortgages. In addition, other debt markets that also got caught up in the bubble—especially commercial real estate, asset-backed securities and loans, consumer loans, and corporate debt—will start to show significant losses, keeping financial institutions, governments, and economies under pressure.

While debt markets of all types are encountering severe distress, we have kept the focus of this book on the U.S. housing market for two reasons: first, it's our area of expertise and we have few insights to add elsewhere; and second, we believe that the U.S. housing market will continue to be the driver of the entire credit crunch and recession. Only when housing prices stop falling and appropriate write-downs are taken will the overall economy rebound in a meaningful way.

That said, the housing market doesn't exist in a vacuum. We are currently in a vicious circle in which the mortgage meltdown has driven the broader credit crunch and severe economic decline worldwide, which in turn is exacerbating the problems in the mortgage market. For example, if a business has difficulty borrowing money or refinancing its debt, it most likely has to downsize by laying off employees. These employees, in turn, are much more likely to default on their mortgages, triggering more losses to financial institutions, which are then even less likely to lend, and so on. . . .

Prospects for Home Prices

To estimate how much further home prices will fall, let's look at some data. First, let's turn back to a chart from Chapter 1 (repeated as Figure 5.1), which shows inflation-adjusted home prices going back to 1950. We can see that home prices had fallen most of the way back to the long-term trend line by the end of 2008 and that prices need to fall another 13 percent or so to reach it.

Other metrics of home prices are based on the relationships among home prices, mortgage payments, rents, and income. According to one measure, mortgage payment as a percentage of income, homes are downright cheap today, as shown in Figure 5.2.

Before you conclude that houses are cheap, however, there are three big caveats: First, low rates are available only to those who qualify for conforming mortgages, which doesn't help the millions of homeowners or potential homeowners who have spotty credit histories or are underwater on their current mortgages. Second, with low-enough

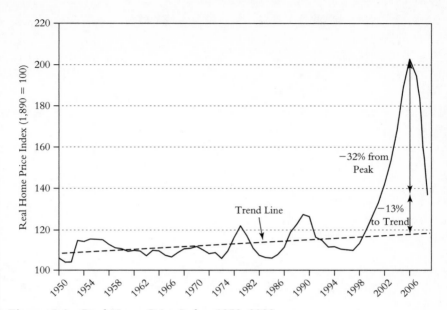

Figure 5.1   Real Home Price Index, 1950–2008
SOURCE: Robert J. Shiller, Professor of Economics, Yale University, *Irrational Exuberance: Second Edition*,
Princeton University Press, 2005, as updated by the author.

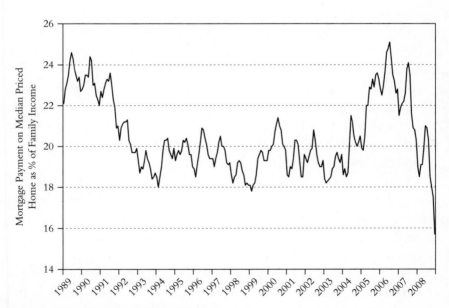

Figure 5.2   Housing Affordability Index
SOURCE: NATIONAL ASSOCIATION OF REALTORS® Housing Affordability Index.

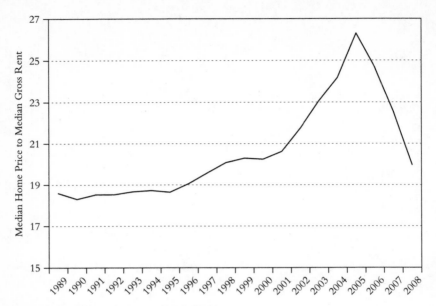

Figure 5.3 Home Price-to-Rent Ratio
SOURCE: NATIONAL ASSOCIATION OF REALTORS® Existing Home Sales data series, U.S. Census Bureau, T2 Partners estimates.

interest rates, almost anything looks affordable, but if rates rise, houses won't look so reasonably priced based on these metrics. Finally, in light of the severe economic downturn, average income may fall for quite some time.

Now let's examine home prices relative to rents. One metric simply divides the median home price by the median gross annual rent, which is similar to calculating the price-to-earnings ratio for a stock. Figure 5.3 shows that this ratio, after peaking above 26, is now back to around 20, near its level during the 1990s.

A final measure compares the average mortgage payment to the average rent payment. Historically, people have paid on average 36 percent more per month to own a house; this rose to over 50 percent more during the bubble and has now fallen back to less than 20 percent more, as shown in Figure 5.4.

Based on all of these analyses—and taking rising unemployment and the weak economy into consideration—we estimate that home prices as of the end of 2008 were within a 10 to 15 percent further

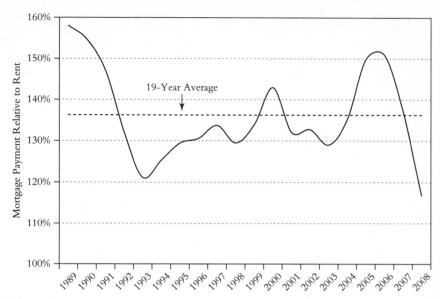

Figure 5.4 Mortgage Payment-to-Rent Ratio
SOURCE: NATIONAL ASSOCIATION OF REALTORS® Existing Home Sales data series, U.S.
Census Bureau, T2 Partners estimates.

decline of reaching fair value, down about 40 percent from the peak
based on the S&P/Case-Shiller national index.

Home prices are almost certain to reach these levels, if past bubbles
are any guide. GMO LLC, a well-respected global investment management firm, has studied every bubble in history—including stocks, cur-
rencies, and commodities worldwide—and found that in every case,
without exception, prices eventually returned to the long-term trend
line. GMO's research also reveals a major risk, however: When bubbles
burst, prices often go crashing through the trend line and fair value.
Consider the two examples shown in Figures 5.5 and 5.6, in which
prices didn't stop falling until they were 45 to 59 percent below the
trend line and then took many years to recover.

How likely is it that U.S. housing prices will go crashing through the
trend line and fall well below fair value? Very likely. In the long term, housing prices will likely settle around fair value, but in the short term prices
will be driven both by psychology as well as by supply and demand. The
trends in both are very unfavorable. Regarding the former, national home

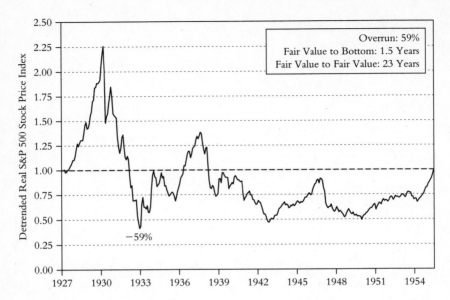

Figure 5.5   S&P 500, 1927–1954
SOURCE: GMO LLC.

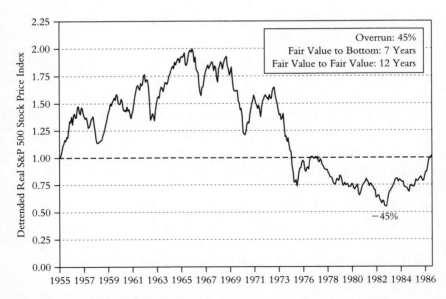

Figure 5.6   S&P 500, 1955–1986
SOURCE: GMO LLC.

prices declined for 29 consecutive months from their peak in July 2006 through December 2008 and there's no end in sight, so this makes buyers reluctant—even when the price appears cheap—and sellers desperate.

Regarding the latter, there is a huge mismatch between supply and demand, due largely to the tsunami of foreclosures. In January 2009, distressed sales accounted for 45 percent of all existing home sales nationwide—and more than 60 percent in California.[1] As noted in Chapter 3, the shadow inventory of foreclosed homes already probably exceeds one year, and there will be millions more foreclosures over the next few years, creating a large overhang of excess supply that is likely to cause prices to overshoot on the downside, as they are already doing in California, as shown in Figure 5.7.

Therefore, we expect home prices (using the S&P/Case-Shiller national index) to decline below fair value, which is roughly a 40 percent drop from the peak, and only bottom after a 45 to 50 percent decline.

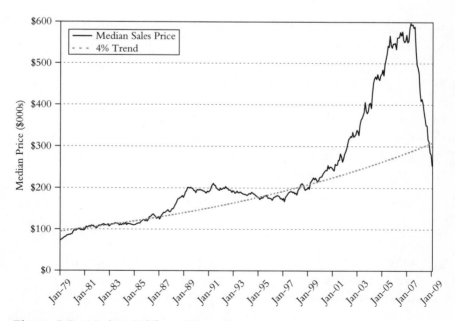

Figure 5.7   Median California Home Prices

We are also quite certain that wherever prices bottom, there will be no quick rebound. There's too much inventory to work off quickly, especially in light of the millions of foreclosures over the next few years. In addition, while foreclosure sales are booming in many areas, regular sales by homeowners have plunged, in part because people usually can't sell when they're underwater on their mortgages and in part due to human psychology: People naturally anchor on the price they paid or on what something was worth in the past and are reluctant to sell below this level. We suspect that there are millions of homeowners like this who will emerge as sellers at the first sign of a rebound in home prices. Finally, we don't think the economy is likely to provide a tailwind, as we expect it to contract over the rest of 2009, stagnate in 2010, and only grow only tepidly for some time thereafter.

The Homeowner Affordability and Stability Plan

To some extent, all of our forecasts regarding the future of the housing market depend on what the government does. If the government wanted, it could borrow a few trillion dollars and save every troubled mortgage in the country. While this would be foolish from a policy perspective, it would make our estimate of future foreclosures look silly.

After a series of ineffective attempts to address the tidal wave of foreclosures under the Bush administration, the Obama administration on March 4, 2009, unveiled the final details of the Homeowner Affordability and Stability Plan (HASP).[2] This $275 billion plan has three primary components:

1. *Loan refinancing.* The 56 percent of the 55 million homeowners with mortgages that are owned or guaranteed by Fannie and Freddie can now refinance to current ultralow interest rates, even if they don't have 20 percent equity in the home, the old test (as long as they are current on their mortgage payments, haven't been more than 30 days delinquent on their mortgage in the previous 12 months, and can prove their ability to afford the new debt). Now, the loan-to-value (LTV) ratio can be as much as 105 percent and still qualify for refinancing by the government-sponsored

enterprises (GSEs), which could help millions of homeowners save hundreds of dollars per month in interest—and probably help many hundreds of thousands avoid default and foreclosure.

2. *Fannie and Freddie.* It increases the government's financial commitment to Fannie and Freddie from $100 billion each to $200 billion each—a necessary step given the GSEs' accelerating losses, and likely future losses from the looser loan refinancing terms (a 105 percent LTV loan is obviously much more risky than an 80 percent LTV loan).

3. *Loan modifications.* HASP provides $75 billion to help certain homeowners whose debt-to-income (DTI) ratio exceeds 31 percent (meaning their housing payments exceed 31 percent of their pretax income), as long as the home is owner-occupied and the loan balance is under $729,750. Under this controversial part of HASP, if a homeowner's DTI is, say, 45 percent, then the mortgage holder or servicer would have to lower the interest rate for five years to get the DTI down to 38 percent and then the government would match the cost dollar for dollar to lower the DTI to 31 percent. There are also various financial incentives to servicers, mortgage holders, and homeowners.

This plan is more comprehensive and thoughtful than previous ones, although the Obama administration's claims that it "will offer assistance to as many as seven to nine million homeowners"—four to five million who might be able to refinance with the GSEs and three to four million who might avoid foreclosure by having their DTIs reduced—is mostly hyperbole, especially the latter.

While the requirements and financial incentives associated with HASP's loan modification plan will surely lead to a better success rate than previous loan modification attempts, that may not be saying much given the dismal prior experience. Wells Fargo's experience trying to modify loans and reduce the number of foreclosures is illustrative.[3] Wells Fargo was unable to reach 20 percent of homeowners at all, 25 percent were not interested in discussing debt relief, and 13 percent were investors or were delinquent on second homes. Thus, the bank could begin a conversation with only 42 percent of homeowners. Of these, it was able to reach agreement with half of them—representing only about 20 percent of troubled mortgages—and most of these quickly redefaulted.

The hard reality is that millions of homeowners can't be saved and will lose their homes for a variety of reasons: they lost their jobs and can't afford even the lower payments; they they're too far underwater; the loan balance is above $729,750; or they don't live in the home. Thus, we estimate that HASP, if it's very successful (and we think it will be), might help two to three million families avert foreclosure and another one to three million refinance into lower rates over the next few years. This is a step in the right direction, but given that Credit Suisse estimated prior to HASP that there would be eight million foreclosures from 2009 to 2012,[4] it is likely HASP will reduce the number of foreclosures by only 25 to 35 percent. If we're wrong and the plan is more widely adopted than we anticipate, that would be good news—but it would also probably mean that its cost would be far more than the projected $75 billion.

In addition while the Obama administration talks about helping only "responsible homeowners" (whatever that means) who have been victimized by "subprime and exotic loans with exploding terms and hidden fees," the reality is that HASP will inevitably help many homeowners who knowingly stretched (even to the point of lying about their income) to buy houses they really couldn't afford because they thought they would be good investments. They were counting on home price appreciation and, when the reverse happened, they were in trouble. This plan will bail out many of these buyers and somewhat insulate them from their bad investment decisions. Given the societal cost of the foreclosure wave, however, we think bailing out a moderate number of homeowners is a reasonable price to pay—though we're aware that others vehemently disagree with our assessment.

All in all, the Homeowner Affordability and Stability Plan is a step in the right direction, but it is likely there will be many improvements over time—and it will probably cost far more than $75 billion to make even a dent in slowing the foreclosure tsunami, given that roughly $30 billion worth of mortgages are defaulting *every month*!

Other Problem Areas

The credit bubble was not limited to the U.S. housing market—the same loose lending standards infected nearly every other debt market

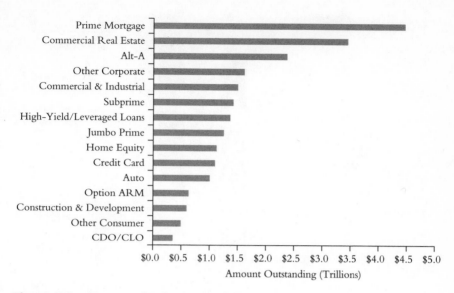

Figure 5.8 Amount of Debt Outstanding by Type
SOURCE: Federal Reserve Flow of Funds Accounts of the United States, IMF Global Financial Stability Report October 2008, Goldman Sachs Global Economics Paper No. 177, FDIC Quarterly Banking Profile, OFHEO, S&P Leveraged Commentary & Data, T2 Partners estimates.

in the world to one degree or another, and the size of these markets dwarfs the U.S. subprime market that has caused so much pain, as shown in Figure 5.8.

So what might the total losses be? Nobody knows for sure, but Figure 5.9 has some estimates, including our own. Both Goldman Sachs and the International Monetary Fund in January 2009 estimated that total losses to the worldwide financial system will be $2.1 trillion to $2.2 trillion; New York University Stern School of Business Professor Nouriel Roubini, who has been more prescient than anyone, recently upped his estimate to almost $3.6 trillion, and our own estimate as of early March 2009 is nearly $3.8 trillion. Note that the world's financial institutions have taken write-downs of only $1.1 trillion to date, so they are likely to experience much more pain.

Figure 5.10 shows our loss estimate, broken down by category. Please keep in mind that there are dozens of variables that will determine what actual losses end up being for each of these categories, so our forecasts are inherently uncertain.

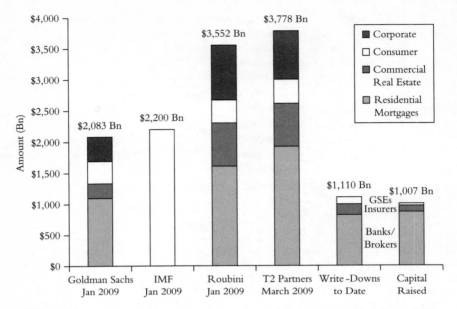

Figure 5.9   Loss Estimates vs. Write-Downs and Capital Raised by Financial Institutions Worldwide
SOURCE: IMF, Goldman Sachs, RGE Monitor, T2 Partners estimates, Bloomberg Finance L.P.

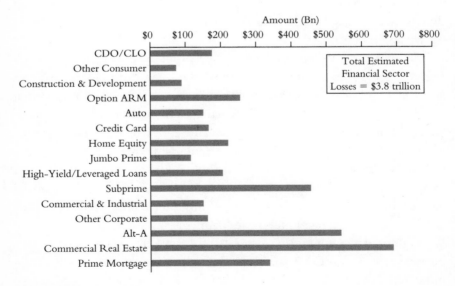

Figure 5.10   Loss Estimates
SOURCE: T2 Partners estimates.

These losses will not be borne solely by banks, but will be shared among other financial institutions, including insurance companies, pension funds, endowments, and sovereign wealth funds. We (and others) estimate that banks will bear approximately half the losses, or $1.1 trillion to $1.9 trillion, based on the range of estimates shown in Figure 5.9.

Can banks around the world absorb losses of this magnitude? If they come in at the low end of this range, then it's possible, given that they've already raised $1 trillion. So far, the world's financial institutions have been able to raise enough capital to nearly offset the write-downs taken through the end of February 2009, as shown in Figure 5.11.

But if losses are at the high end of the range, then banks will need an extra $500 billion to $900 billion, and it's hard to see how they could raise even a small fraction of that in current markets. In this scenario, the world financial system is effectively insolvent, and a large number of the world's banks will need to be bailed out—or go bankrupt. This wouldn't be true for every bank, of course, but $500 billion to $900 billion is the rough size of the hole that governments would need to fill, beyond what has already been injected to date. (This

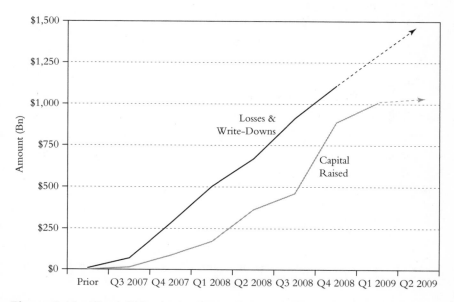

Figure 5.11 Financial Institution Write-Downs and Capital Raised over Time
SOURCE: Bloomberg Finance L.P.

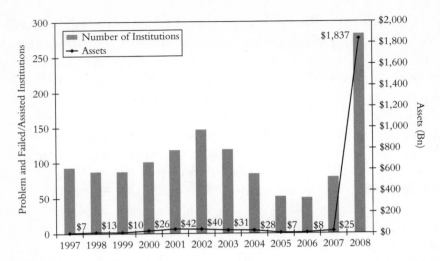

Figure 5.12   FDIC-Insured Institutions Labeled "Problem" or "Assisted/Failed"
SOURCE: FDIC Quarterly Banking Profile.

somewhat optimistically assumes that no government bailout would be needed to cover the other $1.1 trillion to $1.9 trillion of losses that will be borne by institutional investors around the world.)

Many financial institutions have already run into trouble. Figure 5.12 shows the skyrocketing number that the Federal Deposit Insurance Corporation (FDIC) has declared as "problem" or "assisted/failed" and their assets.

It's critical to understand that nearly all of the financial sector's losses are not short-term, mark-to-market losses that will someday be reversed, but *permanent* losses. Many companies complain that mark-to-market accounting rules have forced them to take big write-downs on assets that are not really impaired, but this is almost entirely self-serving nonsense. We struggle to think of a single case in which a company took big mark-to-market write-downs and then reversed them when actual losses came in lower than expected.

To understand why the losses are real, consider this simple example: Imagine a bank that lent someone $750,000 via an option ARM mortgage to buy a McMansion in California at the peak of the bubble less than three years ago. Virtually all homeowners with this type of loan will default for reasons discussed in the prior chapter, and, after foreclosing on the house, the bank will be lucky to sell it for $400,000. Thus, there's been an *actual loss* of $350,000. That money will *never be recovered*.

Multiply this by the millions of toxic loans made during the bubble—both in the housing market and beyond—and it's clear that there will be huge additional very real losses that have not yet been recognized.

Prospects for the Economy

The outlook is grim for the U.S. economy, which led the Federal Open Market Committee (FOMC) on February 24, 2009, to reduce its 2009 projections for the country's economic performance.[5] Its prior forecast, issued in mid-November 2008, predicted the jobless rate would rise to 7.1 to 7.6 percent in 2009, but it now expects it to rise to 8.5 to 8.8 percent. As for 2009 economic growth, the prior forecast was a range of −0.2 percent to +1.1 percent, which the FOMC updated to −0.5 percent to −1.3 percent. This would be the worst year since the 1.9 percent decline in 1982.

Ominously, the FOMC also noted:

> Given the strength of the forces currently weighing on the economy, [FOMC] participants generally expected that the recovery would be unusually gradual and prolonged: All participants anticipated that unemployment would remain substantially above its longer-run sustainable rate at the end of 2011, even absent further economic shocks; a few indicated that more than five to six years would be needed for the economy to converge to a longer-run path characterized by sustainable rates of output growth and unemployment and by an appropriate rate of inflation. . . . Nearly all participants viewed the risks to the growth outlook as skewed to the downside.[6]

Federal Reserve Chairman Ben Bernanke tried to sound a positive note in his report to Congress on February 24, 2009, saying that while the Fed expected a "significant contraction in the first half of" 2009, it also "anticipated gradual resumption of growth in the second half" and said "there is a reasonable prospect that the current recession will end in 2009 and that 2010 will be a year of recovery." He also admitted, however, that this forecast depended on "actions taken by the Administration, the Congress, and the Federal Reserve [being] successful in restoring some measure of financial stability" and noted that "the downside risks probably outweigh those on the upside."[7]

What Should the U.S. Government Do to Save the Financial System?

There's universal agreement that putting the U.S. financial system on a sound footing is necessary to restore economic growth and improve employment, but there's little agreement on exactly how to do this.

We've long been believers that the only solution is for the U.S. government to assume temporary receivership of the many zombie banks in the system—a view that became more mainstream in February 2009, though it remains unclear whether this course of action will be adopted. If it is we believe that it's critical that debt holders—not just stock/equity holders—take a share of the losses.

To save our financial system, somebody is going to have bear big losses—the only question is, who? Some fraction of it will certainly have to be taxpayer money, but all of it needn't be if the government would stop bailing out all of the debt holders, which include other financial institutions such as insurance companies, pension funds, endowments, and sovereign wealth funds.

Government policy has been all over the map. Among the large financial institutions that have run into trouble (in chronological order: Bear Stearns, IndyMac, Fannie and Freddie, Lehman Brothers, American International Group (AIG), Washington Mutual, Citigroup, and Bank of America), in some cases the equity was somewhat protected, while in others it was wiped out, and likewise with the debt, as shown in Figure 5.13.

Most likely due to the chaos that ensued after Lehman Brothers filed for bankruptcy, the current policy, as reflected in the most recent cases of Citigroup and Bank of America, is to at least partially protect the shareholders and, incredibly, fully protect *all* debt holders, even junior, unsecured, and/or subordinated debt holders.

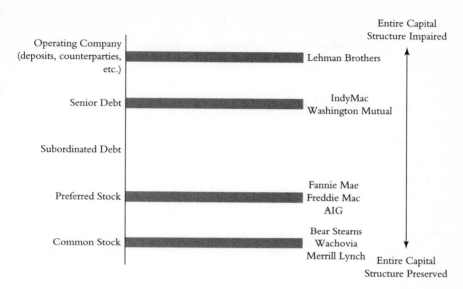

Figure 5.13 Capital Structure Impairment for Various Financial Institutions
SOURCE: T2 Partners.

The result is at least a $1 trillion transfer of wealth from taxpayers to debt holders. This makes no sense from a financial, fairness, or moral hazard perspective. While there's an argument that the government should protect senior debt holders to preserve confidence in the system (even though they knowingly took risk—after all, they could have bought Treasuries), the junior debt holders got paid even higher interest in exchange for knowingly taking even more risk by being subordinate in the capital structure (of course, equity and preferred equity holders are the most junior). These investors made bad decisions, buying junior positions in highly leveraged companies that made bad decisions, so why should they be protected?

Moreover, the reckless behavior of debt investors was a major contributor to the bubble. Remember, it was low-cost debt with virtually no strings attached that allowed borrowers, especially the world's major financial institutions, to become massively overleveraged, which both fueled the greatest asset bubble in history and set the banks up to fail if they incurred even modest losses. This was not an equity bubble—unlike with the Internet bubble, for example, stock market valuations even at the market peak in October 2007 weren't crazy—it was a debt bubble, so it would be particularly perverse and ironic if government bailouts allowed equity holders to take a beating, yet fully protected debt holders at the expense of taxpayers.

Case Study: Bank of America

Let's look at Bank of America (disclosure: we were short the stock as of mid-March 2009). Had the government not stepped in, it almost certainly would have had to file for bankruptcy in January 2009, when it announced that Merrill Lynch, which it had just acquired, suffered a $15.8 billion loss in the fourth quarter of 2008. The cost to taxpayers of avoiding this outcome wasn't the headline $20 billion, but far more—the government is going to take a bath on the $118 billion that it guaranteed (Bank of America takes the first $10 billion in losses, but the government takes 90 percent thereafter)—and it's likely that this is just the beginning of the losses.

Consider this: As of the end of 2008, Bank of America had $1.82 *trillion* in assets ($1.72 trillion excluding goodwill and intangibles), supported by a mere $86.6 billion in tangible equity—5 percent of tangible assets, or 20:1 leverage—and $48.9 billion of tangible common equity—2.8 percent of tangible assets or 35:1 leverage (common equity excludes the TARP injection of capital in the form of preferred stock, which has characteristics of both debt and equity).[8]

At such leverage levels, it takes only tiny losses to plunge a company into insolvency. It's impossible to know with precision what Bank of America's ultimate losses will be, but among the company's loans are many in areas of great stress, including $342.8 billion of commercial loans ($6.5 billion of which is nonperforming, up from $2.2 billion a year earlier); $253.5 billion of residential mortgages ($7.0 billion of which is nonperforming, up from $2.0 billion a year earlier); $152.5 billion of home equity loans and HELOCs (about $33 billion of which were Countrywide's); and $18.2 billion of option ARMs (on top of the $253.5 billion of residential mortgages, all of which were from Countrywide, which reported that as of June 30, 2008, 72 percent were negatively amortizing and 83 percent had been underwritten with low or no documentation).

Bank of America is acknowledging a significant increase in losses, but its reserving policies have actually become *more* aggressive over the past year, as evidenced by the fact that during 2008 nonperforming assets more than tripled (from \$5.9 billion to \$18.2 billion), yet the allowance for credit losses didn't even double (from \$12.1 billion to \$23.5 billion). As a result, the allowance for loan and lease losses as a percentage of total nonperforming loans and leases declined from 207 percent to 141 percent.

So Bank of America had big problems on its own and then made two very ill-advised acquisitions (of Countrywide and Merrill Lynch), the result of which effectively wiped out the company, causing the government to come in and bail it out at a huge cost to taxpayers. So what price is being paid? *None!* The architect of this debacle, Ken Lewis, is still in place, as is the board that approved everything he did. Ditto with Citigroup. These banks are just getting do-overs, with their managements, boards, and debt holders not being touched. The only losers here the common shareholders (to some extent) and taxpayers (to a *huge* extent).

As for Merrill Lynch, its huge, unexpected fourth-quarter loss triggered the bailout by Bank of America, so why are all of its debt holders (\$5.3 billion of junior subordinated notes, \$31.2 billion of short-term debt, and \$206.6 billion of long-term debt) being protected 100 percent, while taxpayers are taking a bath on Merrill's losses from its reckless, greedy behavior? This is madness.

A Better Solution

So what's a better solution? We're not arguing that Bank of America (or Citi, WaMu, Fannie, Freddie, AIG, or Bear) should have been allowed to go bankrupt—nobody wants to repeat the chaos that ensued when Lehman Brothers went under. Rather, if a company blows up (and can't find a buyer), the following four things should happen:

1. The government seizes it and puts it into temporary receivership (as Fannie, Freddie, IndyMac, and AIG effectively were, to one degree or another).
2. Equity is effectively wiped out (again, as with Fannie, Freddie, IndyMac, and AIG).
3. However, unlike Fannie, Freddie, and AIG (and certainly Citigroup and Bank of America), *everything* in the capital structure except *maybe*

the senior debt is put at risk and absorbs losses as they are realized; the government would provide a backstop only above a certain level. This is what happened in the Resolution Trust Corporation (RTC) bailout of failed savings and loans in the 1980s and early 1990s.

4. Over time, in receivership, while the businesses continue to operate (no mass layoffs, distressed sales, etc.), the government disposes of each company as quickly as possible in a variety of ways (just as the RTC did via runoff, selling the entire company or selling it piece by piece), depending on the circumstances (as it's doing with AIG and IndyMac, for example—these are good examples, except that the debt holders were protected).

Counterarguments

One counterargument to this proposal is that the government nationalizing banks smacks of socialism. We disagree. Putting a bank into conservatorship, removing senior management and the board, wiping out the equity, and putting the debt at risk is simply one variation of bankruptcy—and nothing is more fundamental to capitalism than letting failing companies go bankrupt. In contrast, what we've been doing to date *is* socialism: The government is injecting hundreds of billions of dollars of taxpayer money into failing companies, but is *not* taking control; it is protecting managements, boards, and debt holders, and effectively giving the companies a do-over.

Another counterargument is that hitting debt holders might trigger a return to the panic we saw after Lehman Brothers collapsed. But we would argue that the mistake with Lehman wasn't the failure to protect the debt, it was allowing the company to go bankrupt, which not only impacted its equity and debt holders, but also stiffed Lehman's countless clients and counterparties. It's the latter that caused the true chaos. Instead, the company should have been seized and put into receivership, so that all of its clients and counterparties could have relied on it (as was done with AIG)—but debt holders would have taken losses as they were realized (which is not being done with AIG).

Upon further analysis, it's not even clear if senior debt holders needed to take any losses at all. If Lehman had been put into receivership and its $17.6 billion of junior debt converted into equity, the company would have been the best capitalized of any major Wall Street firm and might have weathered the crisis.

A final argument for protecting the debt is the fear of contagion effects: For example, other financial institutions that own the debt might become insolvent (this was probably why Fannie's and Freddie's subordinated debt was saved). Also, debt markets might freeze up such that even currently healthy banks might not be able to access debt and thus collapse.

Regarding the first contagion effect mentioned, the debt is owned by a wide range of institutions all over the world: sovereign wealth funds, pension funds, endowments, insurance companies, and, to be sure, other banks. Some of them would no doubt be hurt if they took losses on the debt they hold in troubled financial institutions—but that's no reason to fully protect all of them with taxpayer money.

As for the concern that debt markets might freeze up, causing even healthy banks to collapse, it's important to understand that right now there is no junior debt available to any financial institution with even a hint of weakness—there's only very high-cost equity and government-guaranteed debt. And neither of these will be affected if legacy debt holders are forced to bear some of the cost of the failure of certain institutions.

Conclusion

Having analyzed the grim housing market and overall macroeconomic environment, let's now turn to how one might profit in these bad times.

Part Two

Profiting from the Meltdown

Chapter 6

Advice for All Investors

The second half of this book shares detailed analyses of six positions that we held in funds we manage as of mid–March 2009. In presenting them, we hope to teach others how to better analyze companies and become better investors, *not* give hot stock tips. We would be disappointed if readers went out and copied any of our positions without doing their own extensive work.

Before we dive into some fairly advanced case studies, however, we'd like to share some thoughts about the current environment and review some value investing fundamentals.

Perils and Profits in the Market

The most pressing question we hear is: "Is it safe to go back into the market?" We wish we knew the answer. But even if we claimed to know, you would be well advised to ignore us because we're no good at timing the market—and are skeptical that anyone else can consistently do so, either.

Our analysis suggests that there is both good news and bad news for investors. First the bad news: As we discussed in the first half of this book, we think that the mortgage meltdown and credit crunch are so severe that both the U.S. and world economies are likely to be weak for a number of years, making it hard to imagine either corporate earnings or the multiples investors are willing to place on those earnings going up for quite some time. Thus, in spite of the devastation visited on equity markets over the past year, we do not think a sustained, meaningful comeback in overall share prices over the next year or two is likely.

Now for the good news: We think a severe, extended economic downturn is priced into the market, so we don't think more major market declines are likely, either. As Warren Buffett noted in his 2008 annual letter, "The economy will be in shambles throughout 2009—and, for that matter, probably well beyond—but that conclusion does not tell us whether the stock market will rise or fall."

There are certainly good reasons to believe that U.S. stocks are cheap. As of the end of February 2009, the Dow Jones Industrial Average and the S&P 500 had both tumbled by more 50 percent from their peaks—the largest drop since the Great Depression—and were at lows not seen since 1997. Specifically, on March 2, 2009, the Dow hit a 12-year low, an extremely rare event that had occurred only twice before, on April 8, 1932, and December 6, 1974. In both prior cases, the economy and unemployment were still four to nine months away from reaching their worst points (in 1974, the unemployment rate was only 6.6 percent and it peaked at 9 percent six months later), yet it was still an excellent time to invest. In 1932, the market was up 5 percent six months later (though it fell 34 percent in the interim). In 1974, December 6 marked the exact day the market bottomed and it was up 45 percent six months later.[1]

Valuation measures also indicate that stocks are cheap. Based on data from Yale economist Robert Shiller, U.S. stocks on March 3, 2009, were trading at a cyclical price-earnings (P/E) ratio of 12.3, their lowest level since 1986 and well below their historical average, dating back to 1870, of 16.3.[2] (The cyclical P/E compares stock prices to average earnings over the previous 10 years in an attempt to smooth out booms and busts.) Over the past 125 years, when stocks have traded at this level, they have doubled on average over the next decade.

So stocks certainly appear cheap, but that doesn't make it an easy time to invest. Many value investors, ourselves included, have lost a lot of money buying stocks that appeared attractive based on a low multiple of earnings or book value—and then seeing the earnings or book value disappear thanks to the terrible macro environment. In fact, traditional value stocks have done even worse than the overall market, thanks largely to the financial sector, as measured by the iShares S&P 500 Value ETF (IVE), which declined 56 percent from the market's peak in October 2007 through February 2009, versus a 53 percent decline for the S&P 500.

Oaktree Capital Management chairman Howard Marks captures the dilemma nicely:

> In my opinion, there are two key concepts that investors must master: value and cycles. For each asset you're considering, you must have a strongly held view of its intrinsic value. When its price is below that value, it's generally a buy. When its price is higher, it's a sell. In a nutshell, that's value investing.
>
> But values aren't fixed; they move in response to changes in the economy. Thus, cyclical considerations influence an asset's current value. Value depends on earnings, for example, and earnings are shaped by the economic cycle and the price being charged for liquidity.[3]

To summarize, in spite of how far the markets have fallen, this is by far the most difficult investing environment we've ever encountered, one filled with both peril and promise, because the range of potential outcomes—for the economy and for individual companies—is so wide.

So how should you invest in such an uncertain and perilous environment? If you know what you're doing and have courage and the ability to hedge, you could follow our path: invest with conviction on the long side, but hedge aggressively on the short side. Our positioning in the hedge funds we manage is roughly 100 percent long, but also 55 percent short, resulting in a net long exposure of about 45 percent. In other words, for every $100 of capital we have, we've invested all of it and, in addition, have shorted $55 worth of stocks, which generates cash since shorting involves selling a stock, holding the cash, and hoping to buy the stock back at a lower price later.

What this means is that we're finding enough incredible bargains to be fully invested on the long side, but are nervous enough that we want to protect our downside as well, because as bad as things are, they could get worse. How much worse? Consider that the cyclical P/E ratio, while below its historical average, is well above previous bear market lows of 6—meaning stocks could almost get cut in half again. We don't think this is at all likely, but we can't rule it out, either.

We tend to agree with Oaktree's Marks, who has argued that there are three stages of a bear market. In the first stage, just a few prudent investors recognize that the still-prevailing bullishness is likely to be unfounded. In the second stage, the market drifts down in an orderly fashion. By the third stage, everyone is convinced things can only get worse, volatility increases sharply, and the collective herd exits.

Marks pegged October 2008 as the point at which the current bear market entered its third phase. As he said at the time: "That doesn't mean [the market] can't decline further, or that a bull market's about to start. But it does mean the negatives are on the table, optimism is thoroughly lacking, and the greater long-term risk probably lies in not investing."[4]

In our view, the most likely scenario is that the markets will muddle along, trading in a range, for quite some time. This is the type of environment when good stock picking, rooted in company-specific and industry-specific analyses, will shine—in marked contrast to the past year-and-a-half, when portfolio positioning, long and short, as well as industry exposure mattered far more than bottom-up analysis.

If we're right, this is great news for value investors, as we are currently finding the greatest number of cheap stocks in our careers. With fear running rampant, some of the best businesses are priced today as if their earnings will never rise again, and many lesser businesses are priced as if they might go out of business entirely. While we profess no great insight into calling the bottom of the market, we have never felt greater certainty that with patience and perseverance we will be well rewarded by the stocks we own at current prices.

We won't be greedy, however. In light of our macro concerns, we are now generally quicker to take profits on winning positions. Historically, we would try to buy 60-cent dollars (i.e., stocks trading at a 40 percent discount to our estimate of intrinsic value) and sell 90-cent dollars, but today we are more likely to be buying 30-cent dollars and selling 75-cent dollars. This is not a market in which to be holding out for the last dollar of value.

We'd also suggest that, if you're fortunate enough to be on the sidelines holding cash, you average into the market slowly over the course of 2009.

Perspectives from Buffett and Klarman

For further perspectives on this treacherous environment, let's turn to two of the greatest investors of all time: Berkshire Hathaway's Warren Buffett and Seth Klarman of the Baupost Group. On October 16, 2008, Buffett published an Op-Ed in the *New York Times* in which he highlighted the perils facing investors:

> The financial world is a mess, both in the United States and abroad. Its problems, moreover, have been leaking into the general economy, and the leaks are now turning into a gusher. In the near term, unemployment will rise, business activity will falter and headlines will continue to be scary.[5]

Yet Buffett was aggressively buying stocks. Why?

> A simple rule dictates my buying: Be fearful when others are greedy, and be greedy when others are fearful. And most certainly, fear is now widespread, gripping even seasoned investors. To be sure, investors are right to be wary of highly leveraged entities or businesses in weak competitive positions. But fears regarding the long-term prosperity of the nation's many sound companies make no sense. These businesses will indeed suffer earnings hiccups, as they always have. But most major companies will be setting new profit records 5, 10 and 20 years from now. Equities will almost certainly outperform cash over the next decade, probably by a substantial degree.[6]

In his 2008 annual letter, Buffett expanded on why he's bullish on America:

> Amid this bad news, however, never forget that our country has faced far worse travails in the past. In the 20th Century alone, we dealt with two great wars (one of which we initially

appeared to be losing); a dozen or so panics and recessions; virulent inflation that led to a 21½% prime rate in 1980; and the Great Depression of the 1930s, when unemployment ranged between 15% and 25% for many years. America has had no shortage of challenges.

Without fail, however, we've overcome them. In the face of those obstacles—and many others—the real standard of living for Americans improved nearly seven-fold during the 1900s, while the Dow Jones Industrials rose from 66 to 11,497. Compare the record of this period with the dozens of centuries during which humans secured only tiny gains, if any, in how they lived. Though the path has not been smooth, our economic system has worked extraordinarily well over time. It has unleashed human potential as no other system has, and it will continue to do so. America's best days lie ahead.[7]

Seth Klarman sees opportunity as well:

In the past 15 months we're starting to see stocks trade at whatever price. There's a much higher probability that fundamental value investors in this type of period will be able to add value with specific stock selection. . . . The chaos is so extreme, the panic selling so urgent, that there is almost no possibility that sellers are acting on superior information. Indeed, in situation after situation, it seems clear that investment fundamentals do not factor into their decision-making at all. . . . The ability to remain an investor (and not become a day-trader or a bystander) confers an almost unprecedented advantage in this environment.[8]

Yet Klarman also offers words of caution:

The investor's problem is that this perspective will seem a curse rather than a blessing until the selloff ends and some semblance of stability is restored.

The greatest challenge of investing in this environment is neither the punishing price declines nor the extraordinary volatility. Rather, it is the sharply declining economy, which makes analysis of company fundamentals extremely difficult. When securities decline, it is crucial to distinguish, as possible causes, legitimate reaction to fundamental developments from extreme overreaction. . . .

In today's market, however, where almost everything is down sharply, distinguishing legitimate reaction from emotional overreaction is much more difficult. This is because there is a vicious circle in effect (the reverse of the taken-for-granted virtuous circle that buoyed the markets and economy in good times). This vicious circle results from the feedback effects on the economy of lower securities and home prices and a severe credit contraction, and, in turn, effects of a plunging economy on credit availability and securities and home prices. . . .

Ultimately, this vicious cycle will be broken and neither securities prices nor the economy will go to zero, just as they did not go to infinity when the virtuous cycle was in place. But throughout 2008, prudent investors sifting through the rubble for opportunity were repeatedly surprised by the magnitude of the selling pressure, and, in many cases, by the extent to which the deterioration in business fundamentals has come to justify the lower market prices. Many forced sellers, through their early exits, inadvertently achieved better outcomes than the value-oriented bargain hunters who bought from them. . . .

Buying early on the way down looks a great deal like being wrong, but it isn't. It turns out you won't be able to accurately tell who's been swimming naked until after the tide comes back in.[9]

Why Not Go to Cash?

Having suffered along with almost all other investors during the severe market decline that began in September 2008 (which showed no signs of abating by early March 2009), we'll admit to having two feelings just about every day that we suspect are widely shared by other investors: First, we berate ourselves for being such idiots for not having foreseen the meltdown and gone to 100 percent cash or at least fully hedging our long positions. How did we miss something that seems 100 percent obvious (with the benefit of hindsight, of course, which is always 20/20)? Second, we want to stop the pain—and it's very painful losing money seemingly every day, month after month, especially when it's not only your own money but, more importantly, also the savings of many friends and family members who have put their trust in you.

There's an easy way to stop the pain and prevent future losses, of course sell everything and sit in cash until the situation stabilizes and stocks have started to recover. Surely there will be plenty of time to get back in, right? This is the approach being taken by more and more investors every day, which is contributing to the market meltdown. But while we certainly wish we'd been smart enough to do this many months ago, it's not what we're doing today. Why? There are two reasons.

First, when we look at our portfolio and evaluate every stock we own, trying to find something to sell, we can't find a single appropriate candidate. For each stock, we've carefully evaluated the underlying businesses, come up with what we believe is a conservative estimate of its intrinsic value (making no optimistic assumptions; we think the economy will be in dire straits for the foreseeable future), and then compared this value to the current stock price. In each case, the stock is trading at a huge discount—anywhere from 35 percent to 80 percent—to its intrinsic value.

Benjamin Graham, widely considered to be the father of value investing (he taught Warren Buffett), once said, "In the short run, the market is a voting machine but in the long run it is a weighing machine."[10] By this, he means that over short periods of time stocks can trade almost anywhere depending on the whims, fear, and greed of investors, but over time they will trade based on the earnings and financial fundamentals of the underlying businesses. We're convinced that the market today (early March 2009) has become almost entirely a voting machine. We're also convinced that someday—we can't predict when—it will again become a weighing machine, and we will be well rewarded for our patience.

One might agree with this, but still want to sit in cash until the market stops acting like a voting machine, so why don't we recommend this approach? Buffett and Klarman provide the answer. Buffett writes:

Let me be clear on one point: I can't predict the short-term movements of the stock market. I haven't the faintest idea as to whether stocks will be higher or lower a month—or a year—from now. What is likely, however, is that the market will move higher, perhaps substantially so, well before either sentiment or the economy turns up. So if you wait for the robins, spring will be over. . . .

Today people who hold cash equivalents feel comfortable. They shouldn't. They have opted for a terrible long-term asset, one that pays virtually nothing and is certain to depreciate in value. . . .

Those investors who cling now to cash are betting they can efficiently time their move away from it later. In waiting for the comfort of good news, they are ignoring Wayne Gretzky's advice: "I skate to where the puck is going to be, not to where it has been."[11]

And Klarman adds:

While it is always tempting to try to time the market and wait for the bottom to be reached (as if it would be obvious when it arrived), such a strategy has proven over the years to be deeply flawed. Historically, little volume transacts at the bottom or on the way back up and competition from other buyers will be much greater when the markets settle down and the economy begins to recover. Moreover, the price recovery from a bottom can be very swift. Therefore, an investor should put money to work amidst the throes of a bear market, appreciating that things will likely get worse before they get better.[12]

It's a fatalistic attitude—"I fully expect that the stock or mutual/ index fund I'm buying today will be lower in the future"—but it's the only alternative to complete paralysis in this terrible market.

Where Are the Opportunities?

In light of our dour macro view, we've sold or trimmed significantly many of the positions that we owned based on a multiple of earnings for the simple reason that, with few exceptions, we are in an environment in which it's difficult to have confidence in earnings estimates. Instead, most of our portfolio is invested in what we think are better and safer alternatives, including asset plays, turnarounds, and special situations. The stocks in our portfolio fall into six broad categories, listed in increasing level of risk:

1. *Blue-chip stocks.* The stocks of some of the greatest businesses, with strong balance sheets and dominant competitive positions, are trading at their cheapest levels in years—due primarily to the overall market decline and weak economic conditions rather than any company-specific issues. In this category, we'd put Coca-Cola, McDonald's, Wal-Mart, Altria, Exxon Mobil, Johnson & Johnson, and Microsoft. They're not as cheap as many other stocks we're finding, which is why we don't own a material position in any of them, but if one wants to buy a handful of great companies and sleep well at night, these stocks would be good candidates.

2. *Out-of-favor blue-chip stocks.* For somewhat more adventurous investors looking to buy great companies in the most out-of-favor sectors like financials and retailers, we own Berkshire Hathaway, American Express (both discussed later), and Target. All are great businesses, but their stocks have suffered mightily thanks to the economic downturn. We think they're good bets to rebound when things stabilize—but in the meantime, their stocks seem to have no bottom.

3. *Balance sheet plays.* For investors who are comfortable with lower-quality businesses but want downside protection, there are many companies trading near or even below net cash on the balance sheet. Examples in our portfolio include digital media equipment company EchoStar Corp. and clothing retailer dELiA*s. Berkshire Hathaway is the best of both worlds: a premier company but also a balance sheet play.

4. *Turnarounds.* There are countless companies that have gotten clobbered by the economic downturn and are reporting dismal results—with stock prices to match. Investors in those that survive and return to anything close to former levels of profitability will be well rewarded—but picking these stocks isn't easy. Among our

holdings in this category are Wendy's restaurants; Winn–Dixie supermarkets; Huntsman, a specialty chemical maker; Crosstex, a pipeline company; and Resource America, a specialty finance company (discussed later).

5. *Special situations.* This is somewhat of a catchall category that, for us, includes Contango Oil & Gas, a stock that has declined due to an aborted attempt to sell the company and the sharp drop in the price of natural gas, and Rohm & Haas, which Dow Chemical, as we write, is trying to weasel its way out of buying. Significant capital has left the risk arbitrage business, so spreads are unusually wide.

6. *Mispriced stocks.* On occasion we take a tiny position in a highly speculative situation—often when the stock price is below $1—in which there's a real chance that the outcome will be zero, but also a decent chance, in our opinion, of making many multiples of our money. On an expected value basis, therefore, a small portfolio of such investments is attractive. Our holdings here include General Growth Properties, TravelCenters of America, Ambassadors International, Borders Group, and PhotoChannel. But do not buy stocks like these unless you really know what you're doing and have nerves of steel!

Let's now turn from stocks to general advice for investors.

Don't Swing for the Fences

We hesitate to even mention the mispriced stocks, because we don't want to encourage anyone to take excessive risk, a particularly strong inclination given the losses most of us have taken in our portfolios. In *Roughing It*, Mark Twain described feeling "as if an electric battery had been applied to me" when he thought he'd struck a huge lode of silver in Nevada in 1862.[13] Although the claim was denied within days, Twain often referred to this euphoric episode in later writings.

Neuroscientists have found that the high Twain described at the prospect of sudden wealth has a biological origin. As Jason Zweig explained in his book *Your Money and Your Brain*, the expectation of making money causes the release of dopamine, which fires up the emotional circuitry located in the lower front region of the brain.[14]

Anticipation of such basic pleasures as food, drink, and sex triggers a similar response.

For investors, the unfortunate side effect of this natural response is that the fired-up parts of the brain that anticipate a reward—in this case, a rapidly increasing stock price—are much more sensitive to the size of the potential gain than to the likelihood of it actually occurring.

Because so many stocks have fallen so far, you might imagine now is an opportune time to swing for the fences in your investment portfolio. But we strongly caution against succumbing to such natural inclinations. Given the economic uncertainty, now is not the time to try to take fliers on speculative stocks, of which there are many, in an attempt to quickly dig yourself out of the hole in your portfolio. The odds are heavily stacked against this type of approach, dopamine notwithstanding.

Be Courageous and Resolute, but Show Humility

Rather than swinging for the fences, this environment is one in which to make smaller bets and keep more cash on hand than usual. Jeremy Grantham of investment manager GMO LLC put it well recently in an interview with *Value Investor Insight*: "Now we have to earn our living the usual way. The probabilities of things we're looking at today are 60/40 or 55/45. Most of the near certainties are gone."[15]

As Seth Klarman notes, we're in a time that requires resolve, but he also cautions against being overly certain and instead calls for "flexibility and open-mindedness" and "a large dose of humility":

> Successful investing requires resolve. When taking a contrary approach, one has to be able to stand one's ground, be unwavering when others vacillate, and take advantage of others' fear and panic to pick up bargains. But successful investing also requires flexibility and open-mindedness. Investments are typically a buy at one price, a hold at a higher price, and a sale at a still higher price. You can never be sure if the economy will grow or shrink, whether the markets will rise or sink, or whether a particular investment will meet your expectations. Amidst such uncertainty, people who are too resolute are hell-bent on destruction. Successful investors must temper the arrogance

of taking a stand with a large dose of humility, accepting that despite their efforts and care, they may in fact be wrong.

Robert Rubin once observed that some people are more certain of everything than he is of anything. We feel the same way. One can see the investment universe as full of certainties, or one can see it as replete with probabilities. Those who reflect and hesitate make far less in a bull market, but those who never question themselves get obliterated when the bear market comes. In investing, certainty can be a serious problem, because it causes one not to reassess flawed conclusions. Nobody can know all the facts. Instead, one must rely on shreds of evidence, kernels of truth, and what one suspects to be true but cannot prove. . . .

It is much harder psychologically to be unsure than to be sure; certainty builds confidence, and confidence reinforces certainty. Yet being overly certain in an uncertain, protean, and ultimately unknowable world is hazardous for investors. To be sure, uncertainty breeds doubt, which can be paralyzing. But uncertainty also motivates diligence, as one pursues the unattainable goal of eliminating all doubt. Unlike premature or false certainty, which induces flawed analysis and failed judgments, a healthy uncertainty drives the quest for justifiable conviction.[16]

You Don't Have to Pick Stocks

The advice we've given so far is aimed at people who are willing and able to pick stocks. Unfortunately, the number of people who fall into this category is far larger than the number of people who *should* be picking stocks. Allow us to explain.

Investing is challenging even during calm markets and is extraordinarily difficult during times like these. Few people are able to succeed over time—and the penalties for trying can be severe. As Warren Buffett noted in his 1982 annual letter to Berkshire Hathaway shareholders, "the market, like the Lord, helps those who help themselves. But, unlike the Lord, the market does not forgive those who know not what they do."[17]

Author and investing consultant Charles Ellis uses a compelling analogy to underscore the difficulty of being a winning stock picker:

> Watch a pro football game, and it's obvious the guys on the field are far faster, stronger and more willing to bear and inflict pain than you are. Surely you would say, "I don't want to play against those guys!" Well, 90 percent of stock market volume is done by institutions, and half of that is done by the world's 50 largest investment firms, deeply committed, vastly well prepared—the smartest sons of bitches in the world working their tails off all day long. You know what? I don't want to play against those guys either. . . . Stock picking is a loser's game, but Wall Street loves creating the perception that you can win at it.[18]

It may sound arrogant to caution people about doing what we do for a living, but consider the following analogy between picking stocks and piloting a plane:

- Both piloting a plane and stock picking can be enjoyable and exciting.
- Both activities are extremely dangerous without the right skill set. Some people with inadequate skills or bad judgment die piloting. Similarly, some people with inadequate skills or bad judgment lose a lot of money picking stocks.
- In both cases, by investing enough time, one can generally become proficient enough to undertake the activity safely.
- However, many people—perhaps not a majority, but certainly a large minority—should not undertake either activity, regardless of how much training they have. People who are easily frightened shouldn't try piloting, because if you panic you can die. Similarly, those who are predisposed to follow the herd, or who lose their heads when a stock they own declines, shouldn't be picking stocks.
- In both cases, there is no substitute for experience, so one is generally better off starting slowly in low-risk situations.
- There's no shame in deciding you don't enjoy—or don't have the time for—either activity and calling it quits.

There's one big difference between the two activities, however, that explains why so many people get into trouble picking stocks, while far fewer do so piloting: Anyone can open a brokerage account and start trading, while one must undertake lengthy training and pass a test before being allowed to fly. We're certainly not advocating that similar certification be required before one can begin picking stocks, but investors would be well-served to act as if this were the case.

In so many aspects of life, we face decisions about whether to do something ourselves or get a professional to do something for us: painting a house, teaching our children, drafting a will, unclogging a stopped-up pipe, setting a broken bone, and so forth. Most of us could probably learn to do these things adequately, yet we generally hire an expert instead. Why? Partly because we are too busy to do everything ourselves, but also because no matter how hard we tried, we probably wouldn't ever be as good as a professional painter, teacher, lawyer, plumber, or doctor.

As you think about whether you want to be a stock picker, we urge you to do an honest self-assessment. Do you have the time, training, and temperament to succeed? What exactly are your competitive advantages that are going to enable you to beat the smart, "deeply committed, vastly well prepared" people at the top investment firms in the world? If you can't come up with good answers, then invest in index or mutual funds or find a good financial adviser.

Easier said than done, of course, so let's take them in order. Very few mutual funds beat the market, so we'd recommend a few well-diversified, low-cost index funds or exchange-traded funds that track the S&P 500, the Russell 2000, and international stocks.

If you want to try to beat the market with a few mutual funds, we'd suggest choosing from well-established value-oriented funds like (in alphabetical order): Davis, Dodge & Cox; Fairholme; First Pacific Advisors/FPA; Legg Mason; Longleaf; Oakmark; Sequoia; Third Avenue; and Tweedy Browne. Many of these funds had a terrible year in 2008 and some of their managers have become media punching bags, but we don't think they've suddenly become stupid. Just as the time to buy good companies is when their stocks are beaten down and out of favor, the same is true of mutual funds.

Finally, with regard to financial advisers, we can't recommend any particular firm because what's most important is the individual you're working with, so talk to your friends and get many recommendations.

Our bias would be to find a fee-only adviser, so there's no incentive to make money by encouraging heavy trading, and be sure to understand if your adviser is getting paid to recommend certain funds. Most important, look for an adviser who is a true value investor, who has read Graham and Buffett and uses terms like Mr. Market, intrinsic value, and margin of safety, as we discuss next.

The Fundamentals of Value Investing

What is value investing? No, it's not some strange church in Omaha with a pope named Warren Buffett and a cardinal in Pasadena named Charlie Munger, though you might think you were at a revival meeting if you attended (as we always do) the Berkshire Hathaway annual meeting in Omaha the first Saturday in May every year.

Value investing is simply trying to buy an asset such as a stock, bond, or business for less than it is worth—that is, for less than its so-called intrinsic value, which is defined in two ways: first, the value of all the future free cash that can be taken out of the business or asset over its life, discounted at an appropriate rate; or as the price a rational, cash-paying buyer would pay for the entire business or asset. Intrinsic value is never a precise number, but rather a range of possible values based on conservative estimates.

Benjamin Graham is widely considered to be the father of value investing—he taught Warren Buffett, and Buffett has called Graham's book *The Intelligent Investor* "by far the best book about investing ever written."[19] In particular, Buffett recommends Chapters 8 and 20 of the book, in which Graham explores the concepts of "Mr. Market" and "margin of safety," respectively.

In light of the recent chaos in the market, now is an excellent time for a Graham refresher course. In Chapter 8, Graham makes a distinction between trying to profit by "timing" and by "pricing." He likens making bets on the anticipated direction of the overall market (timing) to speculative folly, providing "a speculator's financial results." The true opportunity presented by volatility, he writes, is simply to take advantage of the resulting price changes "to buy stocks when they are quoted below their fair value" and to sell them when they rise above that value. Graham adds:

The investor who permits himself to be stampeded or unduly worried by unjustified market declines in his holdings is perversely transforming his basic advantage into a basic disadvantage. That man would be better off if his stocks had no market quotation at all, for he would then be spared the mental anguish caused him by other persons' mistakes of judgment. . . . [20]

Graham explains the fundamental importance of not taking signals from the market with his famous parable of "Mr. Market," the investor's manic–depressive, but very accommodating, business partner:

Imagine that in some private business you own a small share that cost you $1,000. One of your partners, named Mr. Market, is very obliging indeed. Every day he tells you what he thinks your interest is worth and furthermore offers either to buy you out or to sell you an additional interest on that basis. Sometimes his idea of value appears plausible and justified by business developments and prospects as you know them. Often, on the other hand, Mr. Market lets his enthusiasm or his fears run away with him, and the value he proposes seems to you a little short of silly.

If you are a prudent investor or a sensible businessman, will you let Mr. Market's daily communication determine your view of the value of a $1,000 interest in the enterprise? Only in case you agree with him, or in case you want to trade with him. You may be happy to sell out to him when he quotes you a ridiculously high price, and equally happy to buy from him when his price is low. But the rest of the time you will be wiser to form your own ideas of the value of your holdings, based on full reports from the company about its operations and financial position. . . .

. . . Basically, price fluctuations have only one significant meaning for the true investor. They provide him with an opportunity to buy wisely when prices fall sharply and to sell wisely when they advance a great deal. At other times he will do better if he forgets about the stock market and pays attention to his dividend returns and to the operating results of his companies. [21]

In Chapter 20, Graham writes about the other key concept of value investing: "Confronted with a challenge to distill the secret of sound investment into three words, we venture the motto, Margin of Safety."[22] By this, he simply means that, given how uncertain the future is and therefore how hard it is to accurately value a company, one should buy a stock only when the price is far below even a very conservative estimate of intrinsic value. That way, even if your analysis is wrong or there are unexpected external shocks to the market or the company, you won't lose very much money.

Here are seven other core principles of value investing:

1. *A share of stock is a share of a business.* Lost at times in the breathless tracking of daily highs and lows is the fact that the value of a company's shares is ultimately tied to the free cash flow it can generate over time. That means you should put considerable emphasis on researching a company's strengths and weaknesses, the competitive dynamics of its industry, and the likelihood that in 10 years its business will not be truly different than it is today.

2. *Stick to what you know.* Buffett often speaks of the importance of staying within your circle of competence when investing. "They don't give bonus points for difficulty," he says, so if you don't understand how a company makes money—or what could cause a company to stop making money—go elsewhere.

3. *Ignore the "cheery consensus."* Independent thinking is not just helpful in becoming a successful investor, it's required. Conventional wisdom is already built into a stock's price, so if you find yourself agreeing with it, your upside will be limited. Or, as Buffett puts it: "You pay a very high price in the stock market for a cheery consensus."[23]

4. *Avoid losses.* Value investors first focus on avoiding losses—defined as a permanent loss of capital—before thinking about possible gains.

5. *Value can mean many things.* By his own admission, early in his career Buffett focused much more on quantitative measures of a stock's cheapness—a low price-earnings or price-to-book-value ratio, for example. Over time (and with the prodding of partner Munger), he also came to recognize the tremendous value inherent in a company's ability to generate sustainable growth—insight that helped lead him to the likes of Coca-Cola and Gillette.

6. *Don't swing often—but when you do, swing hard.* The market is very efficient, so it's rare to find a stock that is truly deeply undervalued. Buffett points out that there are no called strikes in investing and says to swing only at the "fat pitches" and ignore the rest. When you are certain you've found a fat pitch, invest a meaningful amount of your capital. Different value investors define *meaningful* in different ways, but in this environment we'd suggest 5 to 7 percent of your portfolio. You can't beat the market by mirroring it, so don't hide behind the supposed safety of closet indexing.

7. *Never stop learning.* What's both fascinating and challenging about investing is that the changing nature of business and finance means you can never have it all figured out. Those who stop learning get passed by. We'd argue that never succumbing to hubris and constantly challenging himself to learn new things are primary reasons why Buffett has stayed at the top of his game so long. We suggest reading the *Wall Street Journal*, the business section of the *New York Times, Fortune, Forbes, BusinessWeek, Barron's*—and, of course (warning: shameless self-promotion), subscribing to *Value Investor Insight* and *SuperInvestor Insight* and attending the Value Investing Congress twice a year.

Why Isn't Everyone a Value Investor?

If value investing sounds perfectly sensible (which it is), you might wonder why everyone isn't a value investor. A simple explanation is that you must be able to estimate the value of a business, which requires a great deal of skill and experience to do with reasonable accuracy.

There are other explanations as well. James Montier has studied the subject and finds the reasons are deeply rooted in human nature—and, therefore, unlikely to ever change.

The first reason he cites is aversion to loss. Research shows that people perceive the pain of a loss about twice as strongly as the pleasure of a comparable gain. With its decidedly contrarian bent, value investing can sometimes fail to work for long periods of time, causing plenty of pain. To avoid such an outcome, investors get drawn into a sucker's game of rapidly trading their portfolios rather than waiting out the inevitable periods when they don't perform well.

A second reason investors don't embrace value investing is that it's a get-rich-slowly approach. We are all hardwired to pursue actions that offer immediate gratification. But stocks that are cheap often offer the greatest long-term rewards precisely because they have no short-term catalyst.

A final reason for the dearth of value investors is the human desire to be part of the crowd. If you didn't own Internet stocks during the late 1990s or weren't buying property in 2006, not only did you leave a lot of money on the table, but you also felt excluded. As Montier points out, "Contrarian strategies are the investment equivalent of seeking out social pain."[24] That's not easy to do.

There's one more reason that value investors probably aren't at risk of being overrun by too many like-minded competitors: Value investing lacks drama. Poring over numbers and digging for deeper insight into a company or industry don't exactly produce an adrenaline rush. To that, we'd suggest an alternative view of excitement: Sleeping well at night and compounding your money safely and at a decent clip over time seem like fun to us.

The Threat of Premature Accumulation

Investing too early is one of the more common sins of value investors. Watching as that well-researched idea you loved a few months ago falls 20 percent to 30 percent can be painful and nerve-racking. Fairholme's Bruce Berkowitz calls it "premature accumulation."[25]

Getting your timing wrong to some extent is inevitable—especially in current markets, in which stock prices continue to plumb new depths in a wide variety of industries. Value investors like us can be particularly susceptible to bad timing because we often buy on bad news or bet on turnarounds, both of which have the unfortunate habit of dragging on much longer than expected, often causing share prices to continue to decline.

So while the pursuit of perfect investment timing is laudable, a more realistic goal is to respond smartly when your timing isn't so perfect. If a stock you bought declines, there are three options. You can throw in the towel, promising to get back in when the company's situation starts to improve. You can sit tight, comfortable that the stock remains undervalued but not undervalued enough to add to the position. Or you can buy more, in the belief that the stock is now even more undervalued than before.

Your choice among these is one of the most important, yet difficult decisions you'll make as an investor, as Richard Pzena, of Pzena Investment Management, points out: "I believe the biggest way you add value as a value investor is how you behave in those down-25% situations. . . . We probably hold tight 40% of the time, and split 50/50 between buying more and getting out. Making the right decisions at those moments adds more value, in my opinion, than the initial buy decision."[26] When we asked Pzena what he most often does in such cases, he estimated that he buys more, sells, and does nothing in roughly equal proportions.

Each situation is unique, but if you're able to look beyond near-term trouble, you have an advantage over many professional investors. The Wall Street trading mentality and pressures on money managers to put up strong quarterly or even monthly performance numbers can make it hard for them to own obviously beaten-down stocks. Bosses may not want to hear why something looks attractive two years out if it might not go anywhere in the next six months. Investors see holdings of unpopular stocks and call managers to ask, "Don't you read the newspaper?" But it's precisely such negativity that creates bargains for investors with the patience and resilience to endure cheap stocks becoming even cheaper.

Sidestepping Mental Mistakes

The field of studying the mental mistakes investors make is called behavioral finance, and understanding it is critical to investment success. As Warren Buffett once said, "Investing is not a game where the guy with the 160 IQ beats the guy with the 130 IQ. . . . Once you have ordinary intelligence, what you need is the temperament to control the urges that get other people into trouble in investing."[27]

In a perfectly efficient market, stock prices and company intrinsic values would move in lockstep. Thankfully, the real market is not so efficient, giving smart investors the opportunity to take advantage when a stock price diverges markedly from its underlying value. Panic and fear create buying opportunities; euphoria and complacency deliver great opportunities to sell.

Prudently acting on these opportunities, however, is much easier said than done. One key problem is no less than the hard-wiring of the brain: "The 100 billion neurons that are packed into that three-pound clump of tissue between your ears can generate an emotional tornado when you think about money," writes Jason Zweig.[28] As you can imagine, emotional tornadoes are not conducive to rational decision making.

When confronted with a potential risk, two small knobs of tissue deep in our brains, the amygdalae, generate immediate hot emotions like fear and anger that help us address those risks. Our pulse quickens, our muscles tense, and our brains center nearly full attention on the threat. All of this makes perfect evolutionary sense, helping our ancestors respond to natural threats to life and limb.

The problem for investors, though, is that this same natural, reflexive response mechanism is triggered by losing money, or believing that you might. However, says Zweig, "When a potential threat is financial instead of physical, reflexive fear will put you in danger more often than it will get you out of it. A moment of panic can wreak havoc on your investing strategy."[29] This helps explain why investors frequently sell when they should be buying or sit on the sidelines out of fear for much longer than is advisable.

So taking a proverbial deep breath before responding to short-term market moves will go a long way toward avoiding panic-induced mistakes. This gives our reflective brain time to kick in and enable a more objective decision. Also important are regular disciplines or checklists to follow in making any buy or sell decision. Many investors institute formal reviews of any holding whose value falls a given percentage, asking what—other than the share price—has fundamentally changed in the investment thesis. This doesn't guarantee that the right decision is made, but it does increase the likelihood that the decision is made for the right reasons.

Avoiding Overconfidence

There are dozens of behavioral finance traps, but the single biggest one is overconfidence. One can't be a successful investor without a healthy dose of confidence. To commit your own and others' hard-earned capital requires conviction, and conviction requires confidence. But as with fine brandy or coffee ice cream, too much of a good thing can be problematic.

Social scientists have confirmed time and again that people generally overestimate their abilities and knowledge. More than 80 percent of drivers think they're among the safest 30 percent of those driving. When asked at conferences to write down how much money they will have at retirement versus the amount the average person in the room will have, money managers and business executives consistently judge that they'll end up with about twice the average—also an impossibility, of course.

In life, an abundance of confidence gives us higher motivation, persistence, and optimism and can allow us to accomplish things we otherwise might not have undertaken. But overconfidence can hurt investors in a variety of ways, leading to too much trading, sloppy analysis, and excessive risk taking. Brad Barber and Terrance Odean of the University of California, Davis, in extensive studies of individual trading behavior, have found that investors generally overestimate the precision of their knowledge about a security's value and the probability that their assessment is more accurate than that of others. The result, Barber and Odean say, is more active trading—"I've got to act on the advantage I have"—but not better performance. They conclude that "those who trade the most realize by far the worst performance."[30]

Another academic study, by Lin Peng of Baruch College and Wei Xiong of Princeton University, has found that overconfident, time-pressed investors put too much weight on market-level or sector-level information and not enough on company-specific data. The authors argue that this sloppiness was a key contributor to the Internet stock bubble, as investors ignored company specifics and made broadly positive judgments about entire industry sectors—much to their eventual chagrin.[31]

The Dangers of Following the Herd

In *Irrational Exuberance*, Yale economics professor Robert Shiller defined a speculative bubble as "a situation in which temporarily high prices are sustained largely by investors' enthusiasm rather than by consistent estimation of real value."[32] Such phenomena have become all too familiar in the past decade as markets have lurched from bubble to bubble, in Internet stocks, housing, and commodities.

Because human nature plays such a central role in speculative excesses, it is inevitable that such manias will recur. This inevitability makes it important for investors to understand why bubbles happen—if for no other reason than to limit the damage inflicted on their portfolios by the next one.

One psychological underpinning of bubbles is the desire to conform. "Humans have a strong desire to be part of a group. That desire makes us susceptible to fads, fashions, and idea contagions," says Michael Mauboussin, equity strategist at Legg Mason. People actually have a "preference for being an accepted part of a majority over being part of the correct minority."[33]

Herd members frequently fall victim to the common investor mistake of overweighting recent experience. Behavioral scientists have shown that individuals are more likely to judge recent events as more numerous and predictive of the future than those less recent. After four years of 20+ percent overall market returns, investors in a December 1999 Gallup survey of investor optimism were still predicting a 15.3 percent average return over the following 12 months.

Humans also suffer from an illusion of control that can cause them to ignore evidence of irrationality. Montier cites one academic study that found subjects were willing to pay four-and-a-half times more for a lottery ticket that contained numbers they chose rather than for a ticket with randomly generated numbers. Participants also bet more on a coin toss before the coin was tossed rather than after—"as if they could influence the spin of the coin in the air," Montier notes.[34] This perception of control can fuel speculation, as investors riding a swelling wave assume they will get to the shore well before it breaks.

The crucial lessons in all this are: make your own decisions independent of what the crowd is doing; rely on your own estimate of intrinsic value rather than a stock's current price to tell you what it is truly worth; frequently challenge your investment assumptions, and enlist others you respect to do the same; and learn from your mistakes.

Never Fall in Love

Another common mental mistake is to fall in love with the stocks you own. (In the never-ending quest for the next great idea, however, investors also often give short shrift to their existing investments.) While everyone would love to have that perfect portfolio of stocks that can be bought and held forever, things usually don't work out that way. Markets, technology, and businesses change too quickly these days to put portfolios on autopilot.

Successful investing, then, requires that difficult decisions be made all the time about what one already owns. This is not an argument for rapid-fire trading, as the right decision is often to do nothing. But it does require a conscious effort on the investor's part to constantly "re-buy" his or her portfolio every day. As Lee Ainslie of Maverick Capital described it to *Value Investor Insight*: "One thing I learned from Julian Robertson [Ainslie's former boss at Tiger Management] is the concept that there are no 'holds.' Every day you're either willing to buy more at the current price or, if you aren't, you should redeploy the capital to something you believe does deserve incremental capital. I sometimes hear: 'If my target price is $45, why should we sell at $43?' The answer is simple: I believe we have better uses for that capital than getting the last few percentage points in the move from $43 to $45."[35]

Such vigilance is equally important in cases—often faced by value investors—when a laboriously researched stock proceeds to plunge after its purchase. Making such decisions is hard to do on a purely rational basis, however. Numerous studies have shown that investors tend to disregard any information that challenges their investment thesis. As Robert Cialdini summarized in his fabulous book, *Influence*, humans have a "nearly obsessive desire to be (and to appear) consistent with what we have already done. Once we have made a choice or taken a stand, we will encounter personal and interpersonal pressures . . . [that] will cause us to respond in ways that justify our earlier decision."[36]

Even Buffett, in his 2003 annual letter, acknowledged falling into the commitment trap. Referring primarily to Coca-Cola and Gillette—companies that he had earlier labeled as "inevitables"—he wrote: "I made a big mistake in not selling several of our larger holdings during The Great Bubble. If these stocks are fully priced now, you may wonder what I was thinking four years ago when their intrinsic value was lower and their prices far higher. So do I."

Other common mental mistakes include loss aversion (studies show that investors feel the pain of loss twice as much as they feel pleasure from an equal gain) and anchoring on the price paid for a stock. These two mistakes often result in a refusal to sell at a loss, even if the original investment thesis is in tatters. As the investment legend Philip Fisher wrote in *Common Stocks and Uncommon Profits*, "More money has probably been lost by investors holding a stock they really did not want until they could 'at least come out even' than from any other single reason."[37]

Even the most experienced investors can fall into these traps, so what do they do to avoid them? Benjamin Graham's discipline of investing with a significant margin of safety is a great start. The consequences of overestimating a company and your ability to analyze it are greatly diminished when you pay a lot less for it than your analysis shows it is worth.

Maverick's Ainslie distributes to his analysts every day a "Sheet of Shame," which shows the firm's 10 largest losses since original purchase, year-to-date, month-to-date, and for the previous day. "There are only two ways to get something off the Sheet of Shame—which people are eager to do: either eliminate the position or increase the position and be right, earning some of the losses back," he says.[38]

Another technique is used by Greenlight Capital's David Einhorn: If he's thinking he should trim or sell a position entirely, he sells a few shares, sleeps on it, and then sees how he feels about it the next day. Often, he finds, he feels great about the sale, which is a strong sign that he should keep selling.[39]

We use a disciplined investing approach and stick with it. Our checklist includes answering the following four questions affirmatively for any investment we make: Is it well within our circle of competence? Is it a good business? Do we give management high marks on operations, capital allocation, and integrity? And, most important, is the stock really, really cheap?

Finally, it's important to test your thinking on as many informed and dispassionate listeners as possible. In addition to the benefits of hearing alternative viewpoints, the simple act of articulating an idea is a powerful check on the thoroughness of your analysis. In the end, inaction is a viable alternative. Don't pretend you have your brain fully around an idea when you don't. Save your money for later—there will always be other things to invest in.

Conclusion

We wish we could give clear advice—"Stocks are cheap, so it's time to go all in" or "The economy is getting worse, so sit in cash"—but we can't because we don't have a strong feeling about what the market's going to do. We're finding quite a few exceptionally cheap stocks to buy and we obviously have a great deal of conviction about what we own, but we've had so many unpleasant surprises that we've become very cautious. It's very hard to differentiate between the handful of genuine, safe, profitable value opportunities and the many deadly value traps in today's markets.

We think this economic crisis is unlike any we've experienced in our lifetimes and it will turn out to be the most severe economic down-turn since the Great Depression (though we don't think things will get anywhere near that bad, so let's call this one the Great Recession). Thus, while we wouldn't bet on much more downside for U.S. stocks in general, we wouldn't bet on much of a recovery, either, for quite some time.

In light of this uncertainty, our main advice is that you don't have to be a hero by calling the bottom on the market or a particular stock. Pretty much everyone who has tried to do so has been taken out on a stretcher by this brutal market. Instead, be cautious and humble, make smaller bets than usual, and be ready to admit mistakes and change your mind.

To repeat what we wrote earlier, if you know what you're doing and have courage and the ability to hedge, you could follow our path: invest with conviction on the long side, but hedge aggressively on the short side. In the rest of this book, we show you how we're doing this.

Chapter 7

A False Alarm on Derivatives

Case Study: Berkshire Hathaway

Before we share our analysis of the six stocks we either own or are short, we want to repeat that our goal in writing about these companies is not to give hot stock tips.* By the time you read this book, these stocks might have moved dramatically and we might not have positions in any of them anymore—or we might even have switched positions. In fact, as we discuss in the Wells Fargo chapter, in the weeks

---

*This book is not a solicitation to invest in any investment product, nor is it intended to provide investment advice. It is intended for information purposes only and should be used by sophisticated investors who are knowledgeable of the risks involved. All data and comments herein are believed to be correct, but there are no guarantees and readers should do their own work. Please refer to the relevant Confidential Private Placement Memorandum for full details on the investment products and strategies of T2 Partners LLC.

before we submitted the manuscript for this book to our publisher, we covered our Wells Fargo short and went long the stock. Our goal in sharing our work on these six stocks is to help you become a better analyst, and we hope these case studies will be valuable even to people reading them many years later.

With that, let's turn to Berkshire Hathaway (BRK), currently our largest long position and the only stock we've owned continuously since we started our original hedge fund on January 1, 1999.

We've seen a lot of crazy things in our investment careers, but struggle to think of anything that tops this: Berkshire Hathaway's five-year credit default swap (CDS) spreads went up *10 times* from June 2008 through March 4, 2009 to stand at an all-time high of 514 basis points above the risk-free rate, as shown in Figure 7.1.

To get some perspective on what this means, the median CDS spread for companies with the lowest investment-grade bond rating (BBB–) is around 350 basis points, so the CDS market is indicating that Berkshire's bonds are junk, 11 notches lower than its actual AAA rating! Or consider Figure 7.2, which shows that Berkshire's CDSs are higher

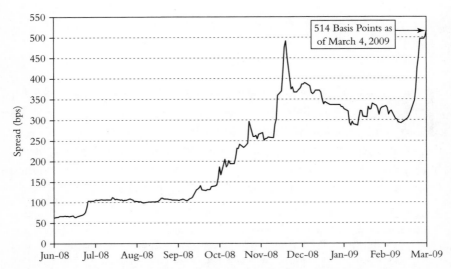

Figure 7.1 Berkshire Hathaway Five-Year Credit Default Swap Prices, March 4, 2009
Source: Bloomberg Finance, L.P.

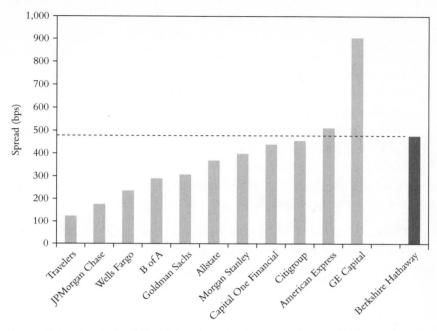

Figure 7.2 Credit Default Swap Prices for Various Financial Companies, March 4, 2009
Source: Bloomberg Finance, L.P.

than a wide range of other financial companies, not one of which is even close to Berkshire's financial strength.

We struggle to think why anyone would pay such an absurd price for protection against Berkshire defaulting on its debt, given that Berkshire has $100 billion of equity, more than any other company in the United States except Exxon Mobil (excluding the doubtful equity numbers of Citigroup and Bank of America). We can think of two reasons:

1. *American International Group (AIG) flashbacks.* Superficially, there are some parallels between Berkshire today and AIG when it was collapsing in 2008: a massive, complex, global insurance company built over decades by a revered and legendary man, with a rapidly falling stock price, rapidly rising CDS spreads, and exposure to derivatives. But as we discuss later, these similarities mean nothing once one does a bit of homework—though we question how many people are in fact doing much homework in this sell-first/ask-questions-later environment.

2. *Hedging.* Berkshire sold 15- and 20-year index put options to certain companies (most likely life insurers that have sold annuities that guarantee the principal in 15 or 20 years) that are now sitting on paper gains of more than $10 billion. However, these companies can't collect for more than a decade, so nervous risk managers may be forcing them to buy CDSs as protection against Berkshire not being able to pay when the puts expire. This raises two questions, however: (1) What good is a five-year CDS against the possibility that Berkshire doesn't pay in 10 to 20 years? and (2) If the world has collapsed to such a degree in 10 to 20 years that Berkshire can't pay, exactly which counterparty is going to be able to pay off on the CDSs?

There is no rational explanation for Berkshire's CDSs trading where they are—they are certain to expire worthless—but during market panics lots of crazy things happen. We wish we were set up to sell CDSs, but it's not easy and we're content to own the stock.

Why Are Investors Panicked about Berkshire Hathaway?

Perhaps in part due to investors getting spooked by the widening CDS spreads, Berkshire's stock tumbled to a six-year low of $70,050 in early March 2009 before rebounding to $84,844 on March 10. Berkshire is our largest position, so the decline has been painful, but we're delighted to have the opportunity to add to our largest investment at such attractive prices, and have been doing so aggressively.

Beyond the dreadful economy, the market's recent concerns appear to revolve around four things: the pounding Berkshire's stock portfolio has taken, earnings, the exposure to derivatives, and Buffett's age, all of which are raising questions as to whether Buffett has lost his touch. Before we address each of these, let's step back and provide some background.

Background

Berkshire Hathaway is an unusual company and possibly the most talked-about yet least understood business in the world. It is a diversified conglomerate whose chairman is the world's most famous and success-ful investor. The company employs more than 246,000 people world-wide (only 19 of whom are at the headquarters) and is ranked second, fourth, and eleventh in equity, market capitalization, and sales, respec-tively, among U.S. companies. Finally, it is one of only seven AAA-rated corporations in the United States and, according to *Fortune* magazine, was the second most admired company in the world in 2008.

Berkshire Hathaway has been one of the most extraordinary invest-ments of all time. Buffett took control what was then a New England textile company on May 10, 1965, when it had a market cap of $18 million and equity (book value) of $22 million, equal to $19.46 per share (he bought his first shares at $7.50).[1] It was a classic Ben Graham cigar-butt stock, trading below its liquidation value. The stock closed that year at $19.02 and now sits at nearly $85,000, approximately *4,500 times higher.* As late as 1983, both the Dow Jones Industrial Average and Berkshire Hathaway were trading at 1,000. The Dow on March 10, 2009, closed at 6,926 and Berkshire closed at $84,844.

The company's performance has been extremely consistent: In the 44 years under Buffett, it has grown its book value per share, a good proxy for the growth in intrinsic value per share, in all but two years (its worst year was −9.6 percent in 2008). In addition, book value has grown each year by more than the S&P 500 index in all but six years (the last time Berkshire trailed was in 2003).

Market Inefficiencies

In spite of this extraordinary track record and Buffett's fame, Berkshire Hathaway is not well understood for a number of reasons:

- It is a very complex company, operating in a wide range of busi-nesses with many sources of value.
- Earnings can be volatile. Buffett doesn't try to manage them so that they increase smoothly and steadily. In fact, he highlights the fact that one of the company's competitive advantages as an insurer is Berkshire's willingness to accept the risk of periodic large claims in exchange for a higher level of overall profitability over a long period of time.[2]

- Berkshire Hathaway's shares trade at high prices, which intimidates many buyers and makes it impossible for small investors to purchase the stock.
- There is very little coverage of the stock by Wall Street firms because Buffett does not try to promote it, refuses to play the quarterly earnings game, and has little need for investment banking services. Also, the stock's high price and low turnover discourage brokers from promoting the stock since their commissions are based on the number of shares traded. In fact, Berkshire, which has the eighth largest market capitalization of any U.S. company, isn't even a part of the S&P 500 index.

These factors (and others) lead to severe mispricing at times, including the current one, from which savvy investors can profit.

Overview of Berkshire's Businesses: Insurance

Berkshire's single most important business is insurance, consisting of Government Employees Insurance Company (GEICO), General Re, Berkshire Hathaway Reinsurance Group, and Berkshire Hathaway Primary Group. These four generated $58.5 billion in float as of year-end 2008 and during the year earned $25.5 billion in premiums and $2.8 billion in pretax profits.

In general, insurance companies make money in two ways. First, like any other business, they can make an operating profit by charging more than they pay out in expenses (in this case, claims plus overhead). Over time, the best insurance companies are lucky to break even on their operations. Second, and this is where insurance companies can become fabulous businesses (and investments), they can invest the float—the premiums charged to customers, but which have not yet been paid out in claims—and pocket the returns as profit.

Berkshire Hathaway's returns over time have been driven by extraordinary success in both areas. First, Berkshire's insurance operations, over time, have been consistently profitable, meaning the cost of float has been *negative*. In other words, Berkshire has effectively been able to borrow money at a cost significantly *below* that of the U.S. government. That's quite remarkable.

At year-end 2008, Berkshire had $58.5 billion in float, up from $22.8 billion 10 years earlier, after the acquisition of General Re (that's 9.9 percent compound annual growth). The growth and negative cost of float—coupled with Buffett's superior investment talent—have had the effect of turbo charging Berkshire's results over time.

GEICO sells auto insurance directly to consumers, cutting out the brokers and other intermediaries used by almost all of its competitors, and thus it can offer lower prices while making higher profits. It was founded in 1936 and was one of Warren Buffett's first major stock purchases in 1951. It is the third largest auto insurer in the United States, having grown its market share from 2.0 percent in 1993 to 7.7 percent in 2008, and is poised to continue this growth. In his 2008 annual letter to Berkshire Hathaway shareholders, Buffett wrote: "As we view GEICO's current opportunities, Tony and I feel like two hungry mosquitoes in a nudist camp. Juicy targets are everywhere."[3] (Tony Nicely has been at GEICO for 48 years and has been CEO since 1993.)

Berkshire Hathaway's reinsurance business includes both General Re and Berkshire Hathaway Reinsurance Group, which specializes in "super cat" policies ("cat" stands for catastrophe). A typical super cat policy might be written when, say, Allstate insures homes on the Florida coast against hurricane damage. Allstate's total exposure could be billions of dollars, so it will sell some of its exposure to reinsurance companies like Berkshire's.

The economics of the reinsurance business are volatile: A reinsurer might pocket hefty profits in years with few claims, but will have to pay out very large claims in some years, such as 2005 when hurricanes Katrina and Rita hit. The competitive advantages of Berkshire Hathaway's reinsurance businesses are its willingness to write very large policies, unsurpassed capitalization to back up them up, long-standing presence and unsurpassed reputation in the market, global reach, and the ability to make quick underwriting decisions. It also has the singular ability to withstand long periods of declining business activity if pricing isn't commensurate with the risks taken. Buffett doesn't care about market share or business volume; he cares about being properly compensated for the risks taken. Very few reinsurers have this type of discipline.

Given Berkshire's success, why don't other insurers use their float to buy companies and stocks rather than mostly bonds? The reason is that the float is needed to pay claims, so insurance regulators, rating agencies, and investors will not allow most insurance companies to invest more of their float in equities, which can be quite volatile (as we've certainly seen recently!). But Berkshire Hathaway is an exception, for reasons explained by then-PaineWebber analysts Alice Schroeder and Gregory Lapin in a January 1999 research report:[4]

> Berkshire is the only insurer with an unlimited investment universe and maximum flexibility to allocate capital. Thanks to its track record of superb investing and superior capitalization, the Nebraska insurance department, the rating agencies and investors give Berkshire Hathaway investing latitude not granted to any other insurer. This enables Berkshire to invest for an equity return any capital that it is not using in the insurance business, eliminating the "burden" of subpar returns on excess capital. Because no competitor has, or could develop in a reasonable time horizon, an investment record similar to Berkshire's, we believe that this is an overwhelming and practically permanent competitive advantage.

Overview of Berkshire's Businesses: Utilities and Other

Berkshire's second most important business is utilities, which includes a wide variety of operations, which Buffett described as follows in his 2008 annual letter to shareholders:

> The largest of these are (1) Yorkshire Electricity and Northern Electric, whose 3.8 million end users make it the U.K.'s third largest distributor of electricity; (2) MidAmerican Energy, which serves 723,000 electric customers, primarily in Iowa; (3) Pacific Power and Rocky Mountain Power, serving about 1.7 million electric customers in six western states; and (4) Kern River and Northern Natural pipelines, which carry about 9% of the natural gas consumed in the U.S.
>
> Somewhat incongruously, MidAmerican also owns the second largest real estate brokerage firm in the U.S., HomeServices

of America. This company operates through 21 locally-branded firms that have 16,000 agents.

Collectively, these businesses had $14.0 billion of revenues and $2.2 billion of pretax operating earnings in 2008.

Beyond insurance and utilities, Berkshire Hathaway owns a wide range of more than 60 manufacturing, service, and retailing businesses, including NetJets, FlightSafety, Iscar, Shaw carpets, Marmon, McLane, Dairy Queen, Borsheim's jewelry, Clayton Homes, See's Candies, Benjamin Moore paints, and a number of furniture stores. In 2008, these businesses had $66.1 billion in revenues and $4.0 billion in pretax profits.

As a group, Berkshire's businesses have shown very healthy long-term growth, generate high returns on capital, and produce prodigious amounts of free cash flow, which Buffett and longtime investing partner and Berkshire Vice Chairman Charlie Munger invest wherever it will generate the highest returns. Figure 7.3 shows the billions of dollars they've put to work over the past 13 years acquiring businesses outright and purchasing stocks.

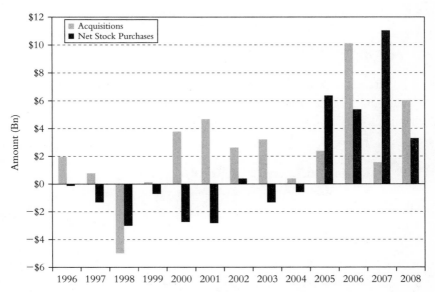

Figure 7.3   Berkshire Hathaway: Net Acquisitions and Stock Purchases and Sales
SOURCE: Berkshire Hathaway annual reports.
NOTE: Acquisitions were negative in 1998 due the purchase of General Re and the liquidation of its investment portfolio.

Table 7.1   Berkshire Hathaway: Investments and Commitments in 2008

Investment/Commitment	Amount (Bn)	Comment
Mars/Wrigley	$6.5	
Auction rate securities	$6.5	Q2 event; sold much in Q3
Goldman Sachs (GS)	$5.0	Plus $5Bn to exercise warrants
Constellation Energy stock and preferred	$5.7	Sold for a $1.1Bn gain including breakup fee
Marmon	$4.5	The remaining 34.6% not owned by BRK will be purchased from 2011 to 2014
General stock purchases	$3.3	Full year; net of sales
Dow/Rohm & Haas	$3.0	
General Electric (GE)	$3.0	Plus $3Bn to exercise warrants
Federal Home Loan Discount Notes	$2.4	Q2 event; sold much in Q3
Tungaloy	$1.0	Iscar acquisition
Swiss Re unit	$0.8	Plus sharing agreement
ING reinsurance unit	$0.4	
Other businesses purchased	$3.9	
Total	**$46.0**	Plus $8Bn to exercise GS and GE warrants

SOURCE: Berkshire Hathaway press releases, T2 Partners estimates.

As shown in Table 7.1, Berkshire also put approximately $46 billion to work in 2008 as prices tumbled—in some cases too early, but we think it's likely that these purchases will work out well over time.

Investments

Buffett and Munger have invested very successfully over time both the float from the insurance operations and the high levels of excess cash generated by Berkshire's many businesses (approximately $10 billion in 2008), buying all of the companies that make up Berkshire and also accumulating large holdings in such blue-chip companies as Coca-Cola, Procter & Gamble, Kraft Foods, American Express, Washington Post Company, and Wells Fargo. Though these stock holdings are substantial, they represent only 31 percent of Berkshire Hathaway's market capitalization, so

Berkshire Hathaway is not, as many people think, similar to a closed-end mutual fund.

Table 7.2 shows Berkshire's 11 U.S. stock positions that are larger than $800 million, based on values as of March 10, 2009.

One of the major drivers of Berkshire's recent stock price decline is the massive decline in the company's U.S. stock portfolio from roughly $70 billion at the end of Q3 2008 to $34 billion as of March 6, 2009. This $36 billion drop, after adjusting for taxes, is equal to $15,000 per share, which sounds like a lot until you consider that the stock has fallen $58,200 per share.

Does this decline indicate that Buffett is starting to lose it and/ or is out of touch with the realities of the postbubble world? One critic even went so far as to say that while Buffett is the Willie Mays of investing, over the past three years he's been the aging, over-the-hill Willie Mays who hit .250, .250, and .211 in his last three seasons. We remember well similar nonsense at the peak of the Internet bubble, when critics said Buffett just didn't get it and that his investing principles no longer worked.

It's absurd and unfair Monday morning quarterbacking, in the midst of the most severe market downturn since the Great Depression, to compare Buffett to an aging athlete in the twilight of his career. On the

Table 7.2   Eleven Largest U.S. Stock Positions of Berkshire Hathaway as of March 10, 2009

Company	Shares	Price	Value ($Bn)
Coca-Cola	200.0	$39.16	$7.8
Procter & Gamble	91.9	$45.17	$4.2
Burlington Northern Santa Fe	70.1	$54.87	$3.8
Wells Fargo	304.4	$11.81	$3.6
ConocoPhillips	84.9	$38.00	$3.2
Kraft Foods	130.3	$21.80	$2.8
American Express	151.6	$12.17	$1.8
Johnson & Johnson	30.0	$47.78	$1.4
Wal-Mart	19.9	$48.67	$1.0
Moody's Investors Service	48.0	$18.04	$0.9
U.S. Bancorp	75.1	$11.40	$0.9

SOURCE: Berkshire Hathaway 10-K, 2008.

contrary, we think Buffett is still at the peak of his game, though by his own admission he has made some mistakes—nobody claims he's perfect.

Regarding the recent losses in Berkshire's stock portfolio, some of the things that look like mistakes might end up turning out okay. We recall that earlier in this decade he bought USG Corporation in the high teens and it soon plunged to around $3—yet by 2006, the stock was above $120. We think most of the stocks in Berkshire's portfolio are likely to eventually return to their former highs.

The financial stocks Berkshire has large positions in—Wells Fargo, American Express, and U.S. Bancorp—have declined significantly during the crisis, but long-term the jury is still out. As we discuss later, we recently covered our short position in Wells Fargo because if it survives without a bailout or a highly dilutive equity raise, the stock could skyrocket once things improve. Ditto for U.S. Bancorp. And as we discuss in the next chapter, we're long American Express because we think it's likely to recover in a huge way.

Even if some of these stocks end up being permanent losses, this has been a brutal, once-or-twice-in-a-century bear market that has clobbered just about everybody, making it really easy for critics to throw stones.

Financial Performance

If the decline in Berkshire's equity portfolio doesn't explain the stock's decline, what about its financial performance? When the company released its annual report on February 28, 2009, the headlines in the newspapers highlighted that Q4 2008 net income was down 96 percent year over year and that it was Berkshire's worst year ever in terms of book value, which declined 9.6 percent (since 1965, it has declined only once before, by 6.2 percent in 2001). But we view 27.4 percentage points of outperformance relative to the S&P 500, which declined 37.0 percent, as remarkably strong. In fact, it was the third-best outperformance in the past three decades.

Berkshire's operating profits also are remarkably strong in light of the weak economy, setting a new record in 2008. Table 7.3 shows Berkshire's annual operating profit over the past five years. Note the losses for the reinsurers in 2005 due to hurricanes Katrina and Rita and the skyrocketing profits of MidAmerican.

Table 7.3   Berkshire Hathaway's Annual Operating Profits, 2004–2008

	2004	2005	2006	2007	2008
Insurance Group					
GEICO	$ 970	$1,221	$ 1,314	$ 1,113	$ 916
General Re	$ 3	–$ 334	$ 523	$ 555	$ 342
Berkshire Reinsurance Group	$ 417	–$1,069	$ 1,658	$ 1,427	$ 1,324
Berkshire H. Primary Group	$ 161	$ 235	$ 340	$ 279	$ 210
Investment income	$2,824	$3,480	$ 4,316	$ 4,758	$ 4,722
Total Insurance Operating Income	**$4,375**	**$3,533**	**$ 8,151**	**$ 8,132**	**$ 7,514**
Non-Insurance Businesses					
Finance and financial products	$ 584	$ 822	$ 1,157	$ 1,006	$ 787
Marmon					$ 733
McLane Company	$ 228	$ 217	$ 229	$ 232	$ 276
MidAmerican/Utilities/ Energy	$ 237	$ 523	$ 1,476	$ 1,774	$ 2,963
Shaw Industries	$ 466	$ 485	$ 594	$ 436	$ 205
Other businesses	$ 1,787	$1,921	$ 2,703	$ 3,279	$ 2,809
Total Non-Insurance Operating Income	**$3,302**	**$3,968**	**$ 6,159**	**$ 6,727**	**$ 7,773**
Total Operating Income	**$7,677**	**$7,501**	**$14,310**	**$14,859**	**$15,287**

SOURCE: Berkshire Hathaway annual reports.

Table 7.4 shows Berkshire's quarter-by-quarter performance in 2008. Note that the weak economy hit Shaw Industries and "other businesses" hard in Q4, but that was also Berkshire's best quarter ever for income from both insurance underwriting as well as investments (MidAmerican also reported its best quarter ever, but that was driven by a one-time gain in Constellation Energy).

Most important, Berkshire's main businesses, insurance and utilities, are performing exceptionally well, have bright future prospects, and are not correlated to the general economy, as Buffett writes in his annual letter to shareholders:

> . . . [W]e are fortunate that Berkshire's two most important businesses—our insurance and utility groups—produce earnings that are not correlated to those of the general economy.

Table 7.4 Berkshire Hathaway's Quarterly Operating Profits in 2008

	Q1 2008	Q2 2008	Q3 2008	Q4 2008
Insurance Group				
GEICO	$ 186	$ 298	$ 246	$ 186
General Re	$ 42	$ 102	$ 54	$ 144
Berkshire Reinsurance Group	$ 29	$ 79	–$ 166	$ 1,382
Berkshire H. Primary Group	$ 25	$ 81	–$ 8	$ 112
Investment income	$1,089	$ 1,204	$1,074	$ 1,355
Total Insurance Operating Income	**$1,371**	**$1,764**	**$1,200**	**$3,179**
Non-Insurance Businesses				
Finance and financial products	$ 241	$ 254	$ 163	$ 129
Marmon	$ 28	$ 261	$ 247	$ 197
McLane Company	$ 73	$ 68	$ 68	$ 67
MidAmerican/Utilities/Energy	$ 516	$ 329	$ 526	$ 1,592
Shaw Industries	$ 51	$ 82	$ 49	$ 23
Other businesses	$ 721	$ 874	$ 749	$ 465
Total Non-Insurance Operating Income	**$1,630**	**$1,868**	**$1,802**	**$2,473**
Total Operating Income	**$3,001**	**$3,632**	**$3,002**	**$5,652**

SOURCE: Berkshire Hathaway quarterly and annual reports.

Both businesses delivered outstanding results in 2008 and have excellent prospects.

As predicted in last year's report, the exceptional under-writing profits that our insurance businesses realized in 2007 were not repeated in 2008. Nevertheless, the insurance group delivered an underwriting gain for the sixth consecutive year. This means that our $58.5 billion of insurance "float"—money that doesn't belong to us but that we hold and invest for our own benefit—cost us less than zero. In fact, we were *paid* $2.8 billion to hold our float during 2008. Charlie and I find this enjoyable.

Over time, most insurers experience a substantial underwrit-ing loss, which makes their economics far different from ours.

Of course, we too will experience underwriting losses in some years. But we have the best group of managers in the insurance business, and in most cases they oversee entrenched and valuable franchises. Considering these strengths, I believe that we will earn an underwriting profit over the years and that our float will therefore cost us nothing. Our insurance operation, the core business of Berkshire, is an economic powerhouse.

Charlie and I are equally enthusiastic about our utility business, which had record earnings last year and is poised for future gains. Dave Sokol and Greg Abel, the managers of this operation, have achieved results unmatched elsewhere in the utility industry. I love it when they come up with new projects because in this capital-intensive business these ventures are often large. Such projects offer Berkshire the opportunity to put out substantial sums at decent returns.

Derivatives Exposure

The single biggest area that appears to be causing investors to panic and dump Berkshire's stock is concern over the company's derivatives exposure.

Buffett provided many details in his 2008 annual letter about this exposure, which should put to rest the silly rumors that we heard about possible liquidity risk. Here are the highlights:

- "Berkshire is a party to 251 derivatives contracts."
- There is no counterparty risk. ("Our derivatives dealings require our counterparties to make payments to us when contracts are initiated. Berkshire therefore always holds the money, which leaves us assuming no meaningful counterparty risk.")
- Berkshire's derivatives provided $8.1 billion of float ("the payments made to us less losses we have paid") as of year-end 2008.
- There is no liquidity risk. ("Only a small percentage of our contracts call for any posting of collateral when the market moves against us. Even under the chaotic conditions existing in last year's fourth quarter, we had to post less than 1% of our securities portfolio." Later, when commenting on why he was not writing more

credit default swaps, Buffett added: "We are unlikely to expand this business to any extent because most buyers of this protection now insist that the seller post collateral, and we will not enter into such an arrangement.")

Buffett then went into even more detail about the four types of derivatives he has written. The equity puts have gotten the most attention because of the large potential exposure ($37.1 billion), so let's review what Buffett had to say about them (emphasis added):

We have added modestly to the "equity put" portfolio I described in last year's report. Some of our contracts come due in 15 years, others in 20. We must make a payment to our counterparty at maturity if the reference index to which the put is tied is then below what it was at the inception of the contract. *Neither party can elect to settle early; it's only the price on the final day that counts.*

To illustrate, we might sell a $1 billion 15-year put contract on the S&P 500 when that index is at, say, 1300. If the index is at 1170—down 10%—on the day of maturity, we would pay $100 million. If it is above 1300, we owe nothing. For us to lose $1 billion, the index would have to go to zero. In the meantime, the sale of the put would have delivered us a premium—perhaps $100 million to $150 million—that we would be free to invest as we wish.

Our put contracts total $37.1 billion (at current exchange rates) and are spread among four major indices: the S&P 500 in the U.S., the FTSE 100 in the U.K., the Euro Stoxx 50 in Europe, and the Nikkei 225 in Japan. Our first contract comes due on September 9, 2019 and our last on January 24, 2028. We have received premiums of $4.9 billion, money we have invested. We, meanwhile, have paid nothing, since all expiration dates are far in the future. Nonetheless, we have used Black-Scholes valuation methods to record a year-end liability of $10 billion, an amount that will change on every reporting date. The two financial items—this estimated loss of $10 billion minus the $4.9 billion in premiums we have received—means that we have so far reported a mark-to-market loss of $5.1 bil-lion from these contracts.

We endorse mark-to-market accounting. I will explain later, however, why I believe the Black-Scholes formula, even though it is the standard for establishing the dollar liability for options, produces strange results when the long-term variety are being valued.

One point about our contracts that is sometimes not understood: For us to lose the full $37.1 billion we have at risk, all stocks in all four indices would have to go to zero on their various termina-tion dates. If, however—as an example—all indices fell 25% from their value at the inception of each contract, and foreign-exchange rates remained as they are today, we would owe about $9 billion, payable between 2019 and 2028. Between the inception of the contract and those dates, we would have held the $4.9 billion premium and earned investment income on it.

Berkshire has reported a loss of $5.1 billion on these equity puts, which has likely risen to between $8 billion and $9 billion in light of what markets have done through early March 2009. So was this a mis-take? We think not, for two reasons. First, even if Berkshire ends up los-ing money on these puts, it doesn't mean Buffett made a mistake. This is an important concept to understand: Sometimes you make money on bad bets and lose money on good bets, so it's critically important to learn the right lessons.

For example, if you gave us a 2:1 payoff if we threw anything but a pair of ones on one throw of two six-sided dice, we'd bet a lot of money (not more than we could safely afford to lose, however, because no matter what the odds might be, we'd never risk losing what we have). Why? Because the expected value is very favorable: there's a 35 in 36 chance of doubling our money and only a 1 in 36 chance of los-ing all of our money. But if by chance snake eyes came up and we lost our money, would you say we'd made a bad bet? Of course not.

Buffett's index put bet is similar. When he wrote the contracts, the odds were extraordinarily favorable. Consider that March 2009 was only the third time *ever* that the Dow was flat compared to 12 years earlier, so a 17-year period where any of the major indexes have been even flat, much less down, is an extremely rare event (the only exception has been the Nikkei over the past 20 years, but that peak in 1989 was a far bigger bubble by any measure than our market when it peaked in October 2007).

The second reason we don't think Buffett made a mistake is that Berkshire's actual losses will likely be much lower than currently reported or may even end up being none at all—in stark contrast to most mark-to-market losses, which turn out to be very real. Why?

First, Berkshire's losses are calculated by the Black-Scholes formula, which has major flaws when valuing long-dated options. In fact, in his 2008 letter Buffett gave a detailed example to prove this, showing that the Black-Scholes model would allow you to borrow money at 0.7 percent for 100 years on an equity index put on the S&P 500 index. Note that this is *exactly* what Buffett has been doing in his insurance businesses: generating float at very low, or negative, cost. He then concluded:

> Though historical volatility is a useful—but far from foolproof—concept in valuing short-term options, its utility diminishes rapidly as the duration of the option lengthens. In my opinion, the valuations that the Black-Scholes formula now places on our long-term put options overstate our liability, though the overstatement will diminish as the contracts approach maturity.
>
> Even so, we will continue to use Black-Scholes when we are estimating our financial-statement liability for long-term equity puts. The formula represents conventional wisdom and any substitute that I might offer would engender extreme skepticism. That would be perfectly understandable: CEOs who have concocted their own valuations for esoteric financial instruments have seldom erred on the side of conservatism. That club of optimists is one that Charlie and I have no desire to join.

In addition, there is a very strong likelihood that the indexes Buffett sold puts on will rebound before the expiration of the puts, such that Berkshire will have to pay out little or nothing on them. The average strike price of the puts has not been disclosed, but let's assume the worst case that these indexes are down by 40 percent on average from their strike prices (the major indexes are down more than 50 percent from their peaks, but Buffett wrote the puts over the past few years). If the indexes rebound by 67 percent over the next 13.5 years (the average remaining duration of the puts), a mere 3.9 percent annually, then the puts will expire worthless and Buffett can pocket the entire $4.9 billion.

Berkshire's maximum exposure is $37.1 billion if all four indexes go to zero, but this isn't going to happen, so let's look at more likely scenarios. Imagine that the indexes are down 50 percent from the puts' average strike price 13.5 years from now, an additional 17 percent below today's levels. This would require Berkshire to pay out $18.5 billion (half of the $37 billion maximum). This would be a painful loss, to be sure, but one that Berkshire could easily afford: The company's earning power today exceeds $10 billion per year and, even factoring in Berkshire's losses this year, its net worth is approximately $100 billion—and both figures will be *much* higher more than a decade from now.

It's also important to understand that the loss in this doomsday scenario would not be $18.5 billion minus $4.9 billion, because Buffett can invest the $4.9 billion for the entire period. If he earns a mere 7 percent return for 13.5 years, $4.9 billion becomes $12.2 billion, making Berkshire's break-even point on this investment a 34 percent decline in the indexes from the point at which the puts were written. This, in turn, means the indexes would only have to increase less than 1 percent annually over the next 13.5 years to reach this from today's level (down 40 percent).

We believe it's very likely that the indexes will compound in excess of 4 percent annually from today's depressed levels, if only simply from inflation (consider all the money governments around the world are currently printing), retained earnings, and survivorship bias (the indexes remove failing/failed companies every year and replace them with thriving companies). Thus, we think it's unlikely that Berkshire will have to pay out a single dollar on these contracts. And given how much Buffett was paid to write them and his ability to invest the premium he was paid in any way he chooses, it's even more unlikely that this will be a losing investment.

In conclusion, even knowing what we know today, we think Buffett was wise to have sold these index puts—and we very much hope he's writing more of them today, because the odds are even more favorable now that the markets have fallen so much.

Hypocrisy or Style Drift?

Some critics have accused Buffett of hypocrisy or style drift because he exposed Berkshire to derivatives after repeatedly warning about their dangers, famously calling them "financial weapons of mass destruction" in his 2002 annual letter to shareholders:[5]

> The derivatives genie is now well out of the bottle, and these instruments will almost certainly multiply in variety and number until some event makes their toxicity clear. . . . Central banks and governments have so far found no effective way to control, or even monitor, the risks posed by these contracts. . . . In our view . . . derivatives are financial weapons of mass destruction, carrying dangers that, while now latent, are potentially lethal.

These critics have little understanding of Buffett, what he's said about derivatives, or the natures of the derivatives he's written. If one takes the time to read all three pages he wrote on derivatives in his 2002 annual letter, for example, it's clear that he doesn't think all derivatives are inherently evil or dangerous and even notes that he sometimes engages in "large-scale derivatives transactions":

> Many people argue that derivatives reduce systemic problems, in that participants who can't bear certain risks are able to transfer them to stronger hands. These people believe that derivatives act to stabilize the economy, facilitate trade, and eliminate bumps for individual participants. And, on a micro level, what they say is often true. Indeed, at Berkshire, I sometimes engage in large-scale derivatives transactions in order to facilitate certain investment strategies.

In fact, Buffett's remarkably prescient point was that derivatives, as they were being used by a wide range of companies, especially financial institutions, were subject to all sorts of problems like accounting issues and counterparty risk, and were morphing into a monster that created systemic risk:

> Charlie and I believe, however, that the macro picture is dangerous and getting more so. Large amounts of risk, particularly credit risk, have become concentrated in the hands of relatively few derivatives dealers, who in addition trade extensively with one other. The troubles of one could quickly infect the others. On top of that, these dealers are owed huge amounts by non-dealer counterparties. Some of these counterparties, as I've mentioned, are linked in ways that could cause them to contemporaneously run into a problem because of a single event (such as the implosion of the telecom industry or the precipitous decline in the value of merchant power projects). Linkage, when it suddenly surfaces, can trigger serious systemic problems.

Buffett elaborated during an interview with CNBC on March 9, 2009:[6]

> We've used derivatives for many, many years. I don't think derivatives are evil, per se. I think they are dangerous. I've always said they're dangerous. I said they were financial weapons of mass destruction. But uranium is dangerous, and I just went through a nuclear electric plant about two weeks ago. Cars are dangerous.
>
> A lot of things can be dangerous, but generally we regulate how they're used. I mean, there was a guard up there with a machine gun on me, you know, when I was at the nuclear plant the other day. So we use lots of things daily that are dangerous, but we generally pay some attention to how they're used. We tell the cars how fast they can go.

The derivatives Buffett has written are far different from the ones he warns about, because he has no counterparty or liquidity risk. Buffett acknowledges and addresses his apparent inconsistency in his 2008 annual letter to shareholders:

> Considering the ruin I've pictured, you may wonder why Berkshire is a party to 251 derivatives contracts (other than

those used for operational purposes at MidAmerican and the few left over at Gen Re). The answer is simple: I believe each contract we own was mispriced at inception, sometimes dramatically so. I both initiated these positions and monitor them, a set of responsibilities consistent with my belief that the CEO of any large financial organization *must* be the Chief Risk Officer as well. If we lose money on our derivatives, it will be my fault.

As for accusations of style drift, this is nonsense. Buffett has been in the insurance business for more than 40 years, and all he's doing with the derivatives is selling insurance. The fact that the insurance is structured in the form of a derivative is irrelevant. He is simply making a probabilistic bet, like the countless others he makes every day—and has made so successfully over the years. He has written insurance on all sorts of things, including a major California earthquake and a terrorist attack that results in the cancellation of the National Collegiate Athletic Association (NCAA) Final Four basketball tournament. In fact, the index puts he's sold are among the simpler types of insurance he has written.

Buffett himself makes no apologies for his derivatives bets. He concluded the discussion of derivatives contracts in his 2008 annual letter by writing:

> We have told you before that our derivative contracts, subject as they are to mark-to-market accounting, will produce wild swings in the earnings we report. The ups and downs neither cheer nor bother Charlie and me. Indeed, the "downs" can be helpful in that they give us an opportunity to expand a position on favorable terms. I hope this explanation of our dealings will lead you to think similarly.

When pressed on CNBC on March 9, 2009, about whether this was one "of the investments maybe you regret," he replied:[7]

> Well, the S&P has to end up 15 or 20 years from the time we did the deals at the price at which we did them. Although, if the S&P actually ends up, you know, 15 percent below or so, we still break even and we've had the use of the money for 15 or 20 years. So we're holding about $4.8 billion. The first one

comes due in the latter part of 2019. And obviously I would rather put those positions on now than having put them on a few years ago. But if you—if you gave me the choice of not having the positions at all, and not being able to put them on or sticking with the positions we have, I would stick with the positions we have. I think—I think we will—the odds are good we will make money. And the thing I know for sure is we'll hold almost $5 billion for between 15 and 20 years in conjunction with it.

Succession

The most common question we get these days is: "What happens when Buffett is gone?" Let's start with the facts: Buffett turned 78 on August 30, 2008, and is in excellent health. We expect that he'll be running Berkshire for at least another decade. We watch closely for any signs that his age is catching up with him—we're not oblivious to his age and obviously nobody can go on forever—but so far his mind actually seems to be getting even sharper with age. It's really quite remarkable.

The answer to what will happen when he is gone depends on where the stock price is and how unexpected his departure is. If he died suddenly today, that would be an unexpected, negative surprise to the market (not to mention Buffett!), so the stock would go down, but probably not by very much since it's currently trading right around cash and investments and therefore it's hard to argue there's much of a Buffett premium in the stock. (Heck, if you read some of the articles being written, some might say there's a Buffett discount!) But most people don't die suddenly. They get older, their minds and bodies start to fade, they retire, and eventually they pass away—hopefully with many loved ones around them. Why should it be any different for Buffett?

In fact, it's very likely that there will be a smooth transition as Buffett passes the reins to his successors, so his age and the succession plan are not things we spend much time worrying about. (Buffett's job will be split into two roles: a CEO to run the businesses and a chief investment officer to handle investing. The CEO has been identified, but his name hasn't been revealed because it would create unwanted pressure and publicity and the choice might change, in part depending on how long Buffett remains CEO. As for the CIO, Buffett and Munger are currently evaluating four people—again, unidentified—by giving them a bit of Berkshire's money to manage.)

Valuation

We value Berkshire the same way Buffett has indicated he does: value the investments (cash, bonds, and stocks) at market prices and then add the value of the operating businesses by putting a conservative multiple on their earnings.

How do we know this is how Buffett values Berkshire? He's never come out and said it explicitly, but he's given clues in some of his annual letters to shareholders:

> Over the years we've . . . attempt[ed] to increase our marketable investments in wonderful businesses, while simultaneously trying to buy similar businesses in their entirety.
>
> **—1995 Annual Letter**

> In our last two annual reports, we furnished you a table that Charlie and I believe is central to estimating Berkshire's intrinsic value. In the updated version of that table, which follows, we trace our two key components of value. The first column lists our per-share ownership of investments (including cash and equivalents) and the second column shows our per-share earnings from Berkshire's operating businesses before taxes and purchase-accounting adjustments, but after all interest and corporate expenses. The second column excludes all dividends, interest and capital gains that we realized from the investments presented in the first column.
>
> **—1997 Annual Letter**

In effect, the columns show what Berkshire would look like were it split into two parts, with one entity holding our investments and the other operating all of our businesses and bearing all corporate costs.

—1997 Annual Letter

The cash and investments are easy to value, but what multiple should one use to value the operating businesses? Again, Buffett has provided clues over the years that lead us to believe he uses a 12 multiple of pretax earnings, equal to about an 18 P/E multiple, which until the recent market meltdown was roughly the market multiple. But it's no longer 18. With the cyclical P/E around 12, that translates into an 8 pretax multiple for the average large U.S. company. While we think Berkshire's collection of businesses is *far* above average, let's be conservative and use this.

One final (and somewhat controversial) adjustment: In his 2008 annual letter, Buffett said that Berkshire's pretax earnings for the year were $3,921 per share (after minority interest). It is important to note that Buffett *excludes* the earnings of Berkshire's insurance businesses, which earned an additional $1,807 per share. Given the unparalleled quality of these businesses, their consistent profitability, and Buffett's prediction that they will continue to be profitable, we think these earnings should be included, which brings the total to $5,728 in pretax earnings per share last year. In light of the worsening recession in 2009 and a relatively benign year for super-cat insurance claims in 2008, to be conservative we estimate Berkshire's pretax earnings at $5,000 per share in 2009.

Some would argue that we are double counting because we're including the float from Berkshire's insurance operations in investments, plus we're putting a multiple on the insurance earnings in valuing the operating businesses. Perhaps this is a little aggressive, but to exclude the earnings of Berkshire's superior insurance operations and simply value them at book value is ridiculously conservative. In addition, we don't factor in any value for the fact that Berkshire's float isn't static, but instead has grown at a healthy rate over time and is likely to continue to do so. Finally, the 8 multiple we use is an estimate based on a blend of various businesses, some of which would have a higher multiple and some lower. Given that insurance companies traditionally trade at low multiples of earnings, if we removed Berkshire's insurers from the calculation, one could argue that a 10 multiple would be more appropriate for the remaining businesses, which gets us to the same place (i.e., $5,000 per share times 8 is roughly equal to $3,921 times 10).

Regarding Berkshire's investments, they were valued at $77,793 per share as of year-end 2008, but in the annual report Berkshire disclosed that book value had fallen "approximately $8 billion since the end of 2008." Let's assume this figure was through the third week of February and Berkshire's stocks have fallen since then, so let's say investments are down by $12 billion after tax or $7,700 per share, which would bring the total to approximately $70,000 per share.

Now the math is easy: $70,000 + ($5,000 × 8) = $110,000. With the stock closing at $84,844 on March 10, 2009, Berkshire is trading at a 23 percent discount to its intrinsic value.

Look-Through Earnings

Another way to value Berkshire is to simply put a multiple on its after-tax earnings—the P/E ratio—just as one might do for any company. It's a little complex for two reasons, however: First, Berkshire's earnings need to be adjusted for "investment and derivative gains/losses," which (from the 2008 annual report) have "no predictive value, and variations in amount from period to period have no practical analytical value." For example, in 2008 there were big mark-to-market losses on derivatives, and in 2005 there was a huge gain when Gillette was acquired by Procter & Gamble. So, net earnings for Berkshire in 2008 were $5.0 billion, to which one would add back $7.5 billion in investment and derivative losses, which equals $12.5 billion. However, it was a benign year for super-cat losses and the odds that Berkshire might have to pay out real cash on its derivatives contracts went up, so we haircut the $12.5 billion to $10 billion.

The second adjustment is that Berkshire owns large stakes in many publicly traded companies, but the pro-rata shares of those companies' retained earnings don't appear on Berkshire's income statement, so we need to estimate what Berkshire's shares would be. Our estimate is $2.4 billion of 2008 look-through earnings. Again, now the math is easy: $10 billion of Berkshire's earnings plus $2.4 billion of look-through earnings equals $12.4 billion, or $8,000 per share. With the stock at $84,844,

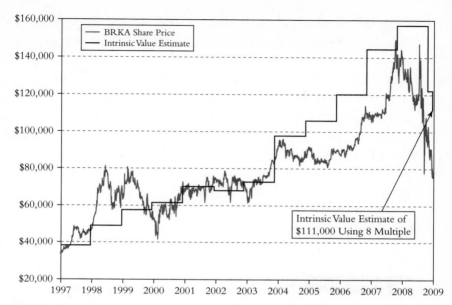

Figure 7.4   Berkshire Hathaway's Share Price vs. Estimated Intrinsic Value
SOURCE: Yahoo! Finance (http://finance.yahoo.com), T2 Partners estimates.

that means Berkshire is trading at only 10.5 times earnings, a very low multiple for such a great business. We think Berkshire warrants a higher-than-market multiple; if we use 14, it translates into $112,000 per share.

Using either valuation method, we come to roughly the same intrinsic value. Figure 7.4 shows Berkshire's stock price from 1997 through early March 2009, along with the intrinsic value each year using the first method: cash and investments plus 12 times pretax earnings until 2008, when 8 times earnings was used. Note that in most years, Berkshire's stock at some point during the year reaches intrinsic value. If Berkshire were to do so this year, it would jump more than 30 percent.

What Could Go Wrong?

It's always a good idea to ask about any investment: What could go wrong? In Berkshire's case, there are a number of possibilities:

- The current recession turns into a depression and impacts Berkshire's earnings materially.

- Berkshire's stock portfolio collapses even further (for example, Wells Fargo, U.S. Bancorp, and American Express all go under, wiping out a portion of Berkshire's investments).
- The recent investments in General Electric, Goldman Sachs, and others turn out badly.
- Losses in shorter-duration derivatives such as credit default swaps are larger than expected and/or mark-to-market losses mount among the equity index puts.
- A major super-catastrophe event occurs that costs Berkshire many billions.
- No catalyst occurs, so the stock sits there and doesn't go up.
- Something happens to Buffett.

We don't think any of these things are likely to happen, but there are indeed many things to worry about in these bad times. If you think the U.S. economy is headed toward something resembling the Great Depression, with unemployment and gross domestic product (GDP) declines exceeding 25 percent, then you probably don't want to own Berkshire—or any other stock, for that matter!

Conclusion

In every investment, we look for securities that we believe are safe, rapidly growing, and cheap—and Berkshire has all three in spades. It has one of the few AAA credit ratings in the world, maintains a Gibraltar-like financial position, and has huge excess liquidity—critical in these troubled times—that increases every day thanks to the enormous profits earned by Berkshire's operating businesses; in addition, the stock trades at more than a 20 percent discount from intrinsic value. In addition, it has exemplary corporate governance and is overseen by Warren Buffett, perhaps the world's greatest capital allocator.

It is only fitting to conclude with a final quote from Buffett's 1998 shareholders meeting:

> You just have to make a few good investment decisions in a lifetime. But the important thing is that when you do find one where you really do know what you are doing, you must buy

in quantity. . . . Charlie and I have made a dozen or so very big decisions relative to our net worth, although not as big as they should have been. And in each of those, we've known that we were almost certain to be right going in. They just weren't that complicated. . . . That's what we look for—a fat pitch.

We believe that we have found a fat pitch in Buffett's own company, and are aggressively taking advantage of the opportunity.

Chapter 8

A Battered Blue Chip

Case Study: American Express

—T2 Partners analyst Christopher D. Woolford

Over the past 159 years American Express (Amex) has grown to be one of the most admired companies in the world and among the most recognized global brands, yet its stock price has plunged more than 80 percent from its peak less than two years ago, hitting a 14-year low below $10 on March 6, 2009, as shown in Figure 8.1.

Is American Express yet another storied financial company doomed to fail amid the worst economic downturn since the Great Depression? Or is it a fabulous investing opportunity: a great company with solvable problems that will someday return to its former glory? In short, is it American International Group (AIG) at $10 in September 2008, on its way to oblivion, or McDonald's near $10 in March 2003, on its way to $60?

We believe it's the latter. While Amex is not immune to the credit crisis—card member spending is slowing, losses are rising, and securitization markets remain closed—we think it's likely to survive the downturn

Figure 8.1   American Express Stock Price, March 6, 2007–March 6, 2009
SOURCE: Yahoo! Finance (http://finance.yahoo.com).

without having to raise capital on onerous terms, and will thrive in the recovery. The possibility of a large equity-destroying loss is remote, and management is focused on remaining both profitable and liquid (with some assistance from the Federal Reserve and Treasury). When a more normal environment returns, Amex's business should rebound significantly. At $10, the stock is dramatically underpriced, as panicky investors focus only on the worst-case scenarios and ignore the enormous long-term franchise value.

History

American Express was established in 1850 to capitalize on the booming express delivery business—transporting financial papers, parcels, and small packages from one town to another. By the turn of the century, Amex also offered consumer financial products like money orders and traveler's checks. Other banking products followed, as well as a travel and tour business, and in the late 1950s Amex entered the credit card business.

Intent on becoming a global conglomerate, in the late 1970s Amex acquired several companies, including First Data, Lehman Brothers, and Investors Diversified Services (rebranded American Express Financial Advisors). But anticipated synergies did not materialize, so between 1985 and 2007, the company shed these and other noncore, low-return businesses to focus on its high-return payments segment.

Today the company's business is organized into two groups: Global Consumer (charge and credit card products for consumers and small businesses worldwide) and Global Business-to-Business (business travel, corporate cards, network services, and merchant services). Its largest shareholder is legendary investor Warren Buffett, who owns a 13.1 percent stake through Berkshire Hathaway.

Credit Card Economics 101

Credit card companies make money from two primary sources: fees and interest income. Fees include annual membership fees, foreign exchange conversion fees, and service fees. In addition, when a card member buys something from a merchant—a pair of jeans, a meal, an airline ticket—the credit card company pays the merchant and pockets a small fee, typically 2.0 to 2.5 percent of the sale, called the merchant discount fee. As detailed later, depending on the network involved, the merchant discount fee may be shared among one or more businesses.

Credit card issuers also earn interest income, which is the difference between the company's financing revenue (the interest charged on loans to card members) and interest expense. At the end of each month, card members decide whether to pay off their balance or "revolve," unless it's a charge card, in which case the balance must be paid in full every month. If they choose to revolve, the issuing bank or credit card network charges interest, often at a very high rate, on the balance due. These card member loans are typically financed using debt, and the issuer earns an interest spread that depends on prevailing interest rates and underwriting discipline (if card members default, the card issuer must absorb the losses).

Credit card networks operate under two frameworks: closed (Amex and Discover) and open (Visa and MasterCard). In a closed network the credit card company incorporates both card members and merchants into its network and generally keeps the entire merchant discount fee. In an open network, the merchant discount fee is divided among multiple parties: the issuer (the bank that owns the card member relationship and finances the transaction), the merchant acquirer (the company that pays the merchant and connects the merchant to the network), and the network. Closed networks have an embedded information advantage over open networks because of their direct relationships with merchants and card members. Open networks, however, do not take on credit risk, a clear benefit in today's environment.

Amex and Discover opened their networks to other issuers in 2004, following a Department of Justice ruling disallowing Visa and MasterCard's long-established practice of barring banks from issuing cards with any other brands. For example, Citibank and Bank of America now issue cards on the Amex network, and this is a rapidly growing, profitable business for all involved. Visa and MasterCard, in turn, have attempted to replicate some of the advantages of the closed network by requesting additional information from their issuers and merchants to help tailor rewards programs.

The Spend-Centric Model

Amex is the world's largest issuer of charge and credit cards as measured by purchase volume, with over 90 million cards in force generating over $650 billion of annual spending. *BusinessWeek* ranks it 15th among the top 100 global brands, and *Forbes* ranks it 17th among the most admired companies in America.

Amex's business model, which the company terms "spend-centric," is focused on attracting premium card members who spend more per card, which in turn allows Amex to charge premium prices to merchants, which Amex then invests in rewards and services for card members. This model contrasts with other "lend-centric" issuers (most of the competition) that rely heavily on growing card member loan balances and maximizing interest income. The result: Amex generates the majority of its revenues and profits from recurring fees, as opposed to interest income.

The model is a virtuous circle that works well:

- *Amex card members spend far more per card than any other network.* Figure 8.2 shows average spending per card. Amex card members spend over three times as much as Visa and MasterCard card members.
- *Merchants pay Amex higher fees than any other network.* Amex's merchant discount rate is about 2.5 percent, versus an estimated 2.2 percent for Visa and MasterCard and below 2 percent for Discover.
- *Amex ranks highest in overall customer satisfaction.* Figure 8.3 shows results from the 2008 J.D. Power and Associates Credit Card Satisfaction Study. As shown, closed networks provide a better customer experience.
- *Amex's model has historically been tremendously profitable.* Over the past 10 years, average return on equity has ranged between 22 percent (2008) and 37 percent (2007), with a 10-year average of over 30 percent.
- *Amex has historically been very shareholder-friendly.* Since 1999, Amex has returned an average of 65 percent of the capital generated by the business to shareholders via dividends and share repurchases.
- *Amex has historically traded at a premium market multiple.* The price-earnings (P/E) ratio has averaged between 14 and 22 times earnings since 1960, as shown in Figure 8.4.

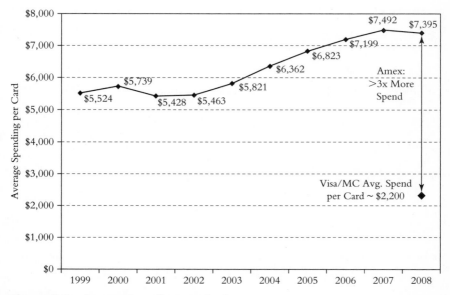

Figure 8.2   Average Spending per Card
SOURCE: SEC filings, T2 Partners estimates.

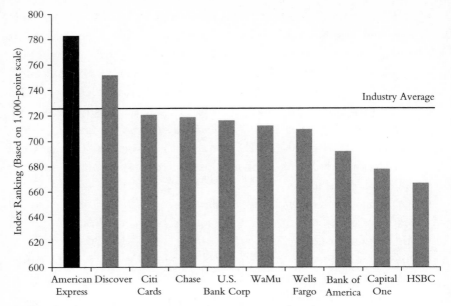

Figure 8.3   J.D. Power and Associates Credit Card Satisfaction Index
SOURCE: J.D. Power and Associates 2008 Credit Card Satisfaction Study.

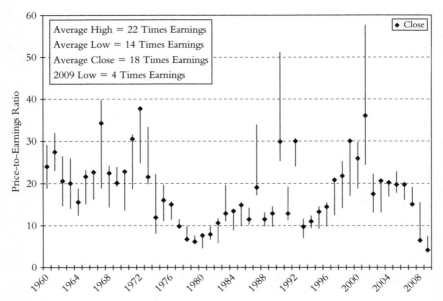

Figure 8.4   Amex Price-Earnings Ratio, 1960–March 6, 2009
SOURCE: American Express, Compustat, T2 Partners.

In summary, Amex is an exceptional company with enduring competitive advantages: its brand, spend-centric model, and closed network information and economics. It's a great business, and one we're delighted to own, especially at today's bargain price.

Why Are Investors So Worried?

With the stock trading at its lowest level in 14 years, investors are obviously panicked about Amex. Here are the top six reasons why.

Liquidity

In October 2008, asset-backed securitization markets ground to a halt. The Federal Reserve estimates that 25 percent of all nonmortgage consumer credit—including auto loans, student loans, and credit card loans—were funded in the securitization markets. For many credit card issuers, including Amex, these markets were a critical source of funding, as shown in Figure 8.5.

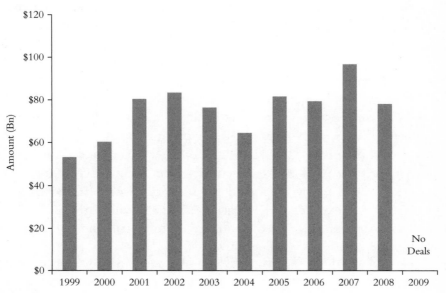

Figure 8.5   Global Issuance of Credit Card Asset-Backed Securities
SOURCE: Asset-Backed Alert (ABAlert.com).

And the problems don't end here. Like all financial institutions, Amex doesn't currently have access to unsecured term debt, and its ability (and desire) to rely on short-term commercial paper markets is also limited. With $20 billion in debt due in 2009, will Amex be able to meet its obligations?

Fortunately, Amex has always had contingency plans in place, and it has acted swiftly amid the current crisis to diversify and safeguard its liquidity. Since the summer of 2008, Amex:

- Issued $6 billion in unsecured debt guaranteed by the Federal Deposit Insurance Corporation (FDIC) Temporary Liquidity Guarantee Program (TLGP).
- Issued $4.5 billion of commercial paper purchased by the Federal Reserve through the Commercial Paper Funding Facility (CPFF).
- Became a bank holding company, which gives it greater flexibility to access government programs.
- Launched a program to gather retail deposits.
- Applied for and received $3.4 billion under the Capital Purchase Program (CPP) run by the Department of Treasury.

Amex's near-term strategy is to maintain cash and readily marketable securities equal to the next 12 months of debt maturities.

Table 8.1 shows that Amex has at least $65 billion in liquidity, which we believe provides an adequate margin of safety against $20 billion in maturities. But what if all these government programs go away?

First, we don't think that they will go away anytime soon. Amex is a major source of consumer credit, and we expect the government to maintain—or even expand—the current funding programs. For instance, in November 2008, the Federal Reserve announced the creation of the Term Asset-Backed Securities Loan Facility (TALF) to help financial institutions by supporting the issuance of asset-backed securities. TALF was expanded in February 2009 and will begin disbursing funds in March; it is expected to finance up to $1 trillion in new lending through at least December 2009.

Second, we think that Amex's direct deposit initiatives will succeed due to the strength of the Amex brand, its history of customer service, and its marketing expertise. Amex is targeting $10 billion to $30 billion in brokered retail certificates of deposit (CDs) and brokerage

Table 8.1 Amex's Funding and Liquidity Sources

Source (Use)	Description	Amount (Bn)
Cash	Cash on hand December 31, 2008	$21
Operating cash	Working capital needs	−$4
Short-term debt	Assumes short-term debt markets are shut	−$9
Liquidity investment portfolio	Readily marketable securities	$5
CPP proceeds	Preferred stock issued to the U.S. Treasury	$3
Subtotal	**Excess cash and readily marketable securities**	**$16**
Unsecured TLGP	Remaining TLGP issuance	$7
Direct deposits	Brokered retail brokerage and CD programs	$10–$30
Asset-backed securities	Securitization market reopens	Market-driven
Unsecured non–TLGP	Unsecured debt markets reopen	Market-driven
Discount window	Secured borrowing from the Federal Reserve under the Term Auction Facility	$20–$30
Bank facilities	Committed lines from 34 financial institutions	$9
Conduit	Financing conduit with six banks to take receivables out of Amex's securitization trust (expires June 2009)	$5
Grand Total		**$65+**

SOURCE: American Express Financial Community Meeting Presentation, February 4, 2009, T2 Partners estimates.

sweep accounts over the medium term. Given that the company raised $2 billion in January 2009 alone, we expect Amex to quickly meet or exceed its targets.

These government programs ultimately will—and should—be phased out, but it won't happen until they have succeeded in reviving the markets they are replacing—in which case, Amex would again have access to the commercial paper, securitization, and unsecured term debt markets.

Credit Losses

Rising unemployment and weak housing prices will probably drive net write-offs above historical peak levels. Investors are particularly worried about Amex's heavy exposure to California and Florida, as well as to small businesses. In addition, Amex rapidly added new card members and grew its loans between 2005 and 2007, and these accounts are defaulting at rates much higher than Amex's historical averages, as shown in Figure 8.6.

Indeed, due to rising losses among newer card members, Amex's write-off rate, after being lower than the industry average, recently surpassed it in Q3 and Q4 2008, as shown in Figure 8.7. We include the unemployment rate to show how correlated it is with credit card write-offs.

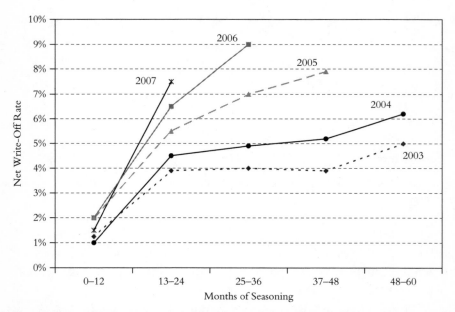

Figure 8.6   U.S. Consumer Lending Managed Net Write-Off Rates by Acquisition Vintage

Source: American Express Q2 2008 earnings presentation, July 21, 2008, T2 Partners estimates.

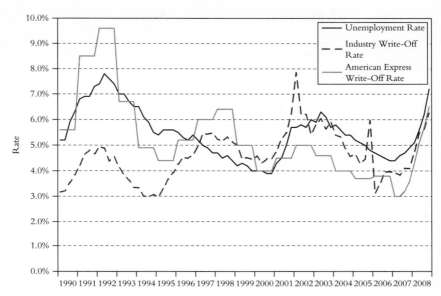

Figure 8.7 Net Write-Off Rates vs. Unemployment Rate
Source: Federal Reserve, American Express, Bureau of Labor Statistics, T2 Partners estimates.

In order to assess what Amex's losses might be, let's review some of the numbers. First, let's take a look at what happened to Amex in prior downturns, as shown in Table 8.2.

Next, let's review Amex's balance sheet. Table 8.3 shows Amex's owned and securitized loan portfolio, with loss provisions through year-end 2008.

How bad does this downturn need to be for us to be worried that Amex will need to raise more capital? A close read of Amex's presentation to investors in February 2009 gives us a hint. While discussing capital ratios, Chief Financial Officer Dan Henry implied that Amex issued $3.4 billion in preferred stock to the Treasury because the company would otherwise not have been considered "well-capitalized" by rating agencies, regulators, and the marketplace. In other words, were Amex to lose $3.4 billion, it would have to raise more capital, which could be very bad for shareholders.

With loss rates growing rapidly, it is reasonable to question why we believe American Express can weather the current storm. It can and will. Our confidence comes from the power of the underlying business, which annually generates $8 billion to $10 billion in pretax profit before

Table 8.2   Amex's Performance in Prior Downturns

Recession	Real GDP Growth	Peak Unemployment Rate	Peak Write-Off Rate for Credit Card Loans
1990–1991	–0.2%	7.8%	9.6%
2001	0.8%	6.3%	6.0%
2007–?	?	?	?

SOURCE: American Express Merrill Lynch Conference, November 13, 2007.

Table 8.3   Amex's Owned and Securitized Loan Portfolio, with Loss Provisions

	December 31, 2008 (Bn)
Gross balance:	
Charge card	$ 33.0
Credit card—owned	$ 42.2
Credit card—securitized	$ 29.0
Total Loans	**$104.2**
Loss provision:	
Charge card	$ 0.8
Credit card—owned	$ 2.6
Credit card—securitized	$ 1.8
Total	**$ 5.2**
Percent of Total Loans	**4.9%**

SOURCE: American Express 2008 Annual Report.

loss reserves. Bear in mind, Amex was profitable during the fourth quarter of 2008, when the banking industry collectively lost $26 billion. This is a testament to the underlying earning power of Amex's spend-centric model.

We are confident that Amex can, in effect, earn its way out of trouble. Its current earnings levels (after deducting normalized loss provisions) will more than cover the growth in loss rates, even assuming they more than double from today's already elevated levels due to the severe recession and unprecedented defaults. To put the losses in perspective, every 100 basis point increase in Amex's overall loss rate equals approximately $1 billion.

We estimate that net write-off rates on Amex's U.S. credit card loans will be in the 10 to 12 percent range, above the peak of 9.6 percent in the early 1990s. But loss rates on Amex's other products will be significantly lower. Charge cards are a pay-in-full-every-month product, so loss rates will be markedly lower than those on credit card loans. For example, write-offs on charge cards issued to multinational corporations should be insignificant, likely in the 2 to 3 percent range.

Based on our analysis, even if losses on U.S. credit card loans reach the 10 to 12 percent level, Amex will not need to raise additional capital. These losses will occur over the next 12 to 18 months and will be more than adequately funded with existing reserves and Amex's ongoing earnings. Even if losses exceed 12 percent, Amex has the flexibility to make further cost reductions or, if necessary, reduce or eliminate its $800+ million annual dividend.

During this period of increasing losses, reported earnings will likely be very weak, and may even go slightly negative. But the losses will eventually peak and start to decline, revealing once again Amex's exceptional profitability.

Cash Trapping / Early Amortization

As an increasing number of Amex card members default, cash flows due to Amex from its securitized loan pools can be diverted into special reserve accounts. This so-called cash trapping occurs if the excess spread—the interest Amex collects after bondholders receive their interest—falls below a certain level (typically 4 to 5 percent). Only $22 million was trapped in Amex's lending trust as of March 2009, but this could rise significantly—to a maximum of $2 billion.

In the event that the excess spread falls below zero, the cash reserve is available to the bondholders in what is called "early amortization." If this occurs, the securitization trust would revert to Amex's balance sheet and Amex would need to find alternate sources of funding for the loans.

Obviously, Amex wants to resume pocketing the trapped cash by restoring the excess spread, which it can do via structural adjustments to the securitization trust and/or actions to improve the trust's performance, which might include reducing credit lines or increasing interest rates and fees to card members. Amex has already taken steps to improve performance and is likely to be considering structural changes as well.

We think Amex will continue to have some cash trapped in its securitization trusts, but that the amounts will be manageable and an early amortization event, although possible, is unlikely.

Spending

Many investors believe that the spending decline we are experiencing is secular, not cyclical. Personal consumption expenditures (PCE) as a percentage of GDP have been increasing for the past two decades, but that trend may be reversing in a big way, as shown in Figure 8.8.

The decline in PCE, which would obviously be bad for Amex, will likely be offset over time by the fact that the world is quickly transitioning away from paper (cash, checks) toward cards (credit, debit) and electronic payments. Amex estimates that approximately one-third of

Figure 8.8   Personal Consumption Expenditures as a Percentage of GDP
SOURCE: Bureau of Economic Analysis.

global consumption is paid with cards and electronic payments, but this number rises to one-half in a mature market like the U.S. market, and the trend is clearly in Amex's favor, as shown in Figure 8.9.

Moreover, Amex has been gaining substantial market share, and industry observers expect that it will continue to so, as shown in Figure 8.10, due to increasing merchant acceptance and new network partnerships.

Profitability

For most of the past decade, Amex established—and met or exceeded—long-term average financial targets that included revenue growth of 8 percent or more, earnings per share (EPS) growth of 12 to 15 percent, return on equity of 33 to 36 percent, and capital returned to shareholders of more than 65 percent.

Clearly, these goals will need to be adjusted downward to reflect not only the current environment but also the likely future one, in which Amex will have higher required capital levels.

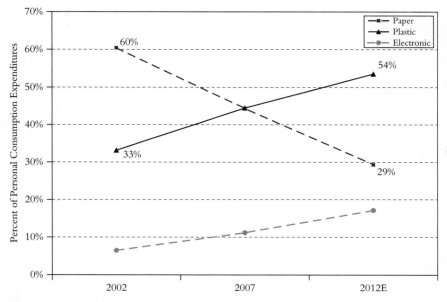

Figure 8.9   Consumer Payment Volume (U.S.)
SOURCE: The Nilson Report.

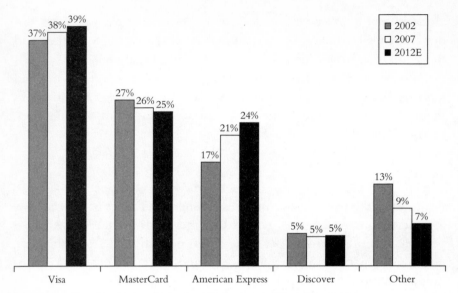

Figure 8.10   Credit Card Purchase Volume Market Share (U.S.)
SOURCE: The Nilson Report.

In the meantime, Amex is focused on staying profitable. The company is reengineering its revenue and expense base by repricing its loan portfolio and cutting costs. Recently, Amex increased interest rates by 200 to 300 basis points on card members who comprise 55 percent of its loan portfolio. And in October 2008, Amex cut 10 percent of its workforce as part of a cost reduction program that will generate $1.8 billion of annual savings.

Amex recently set an objective of earning at least a 20 percent return on equity over time. We suspect that the company will comfortably exceed this level. Even if 20 percent is the "new normal," Amex is still a superb business, as the average company generates a return on equity in the 10 to 12 percent range.

Regulatory Changes

In December 2008, federal bank regulators adopted rules that restrict certain credit and charge card practices. The regulations, which become effective in July 2010, include rules relating to fees and interest rate increases on card member loans. While Amex is less affected than its lend-centric peers, the changes are expected to affect the profitability of the payments industry overall.

The payments industry also faces scrutiny over the merchant discount rate. In 2008, legislation was introduced to give merchants antitrust immunity to negotiate fees collectively with Visa and MasterCard. Future regulation of Visa's and MasterCard's pricing could ultimately affect Amex's network pricing as well.

We also need to consider the impact of possible cram-down legislation, which would allow bankruptcy judges to modify mortgage principal on primary residences. On one hand, if there is mortgage payment relief, consumers will have more available cash flow to pay off credit card loans. On the other hand, the legislation could lead to many more bankruptcy filings in which judges could potentially restructure loans beyond mortgages, including credit card loans, which would obviously be a negative for Amex.

Finally, the Financial Accounting Standards Board (FASB) is considering measures to require financial institutions to bring off-balance-sheet assets like securitized credit card loans back onto their books. If adopted, Amex would have to consolidate the assets and liabilities of its securitized card member loans and reestablish $1.8 billion of reserves, which would reduce Amex's regulatory capital.

On balance, we believe these regulatory risks are real and are monitoring them closely.

Valuation

We think Amex should be valued on a multiple of normalized earnings, which can be estimated by taking shareholders' equity and multiplying it by the company's return on equity.

Amex's equity today is $11.8 billion, and it earned a 22 percent return on equity (ROE) in Q4 and the full year 2008. Due to rising losses and the slowdown in billed business, we expect that ROE will drop to around 5 percent in 2009, which would result in earnings of $600 million or $0.50 per share, just under the $800 million dividend.

(In light of the uncertainty about what losses might be and the difficulty of raising capital in this environment, we think Amex should immediately cut its dividend to virtually nothing to conserve capital until the storm passes, but suspect the company will not do so.) Based on $0.50 per share of earnings, the stock might not appear dramatically undervalued at around $10, but Amex's ROE and earnings are severely depressed.

We think Amex's earnings and ROE will start to recover in 2010 and 2011 and return to normalized levels in 2012, roughly in line with our expectation for the overall economy. We estimate that over the next three years (2009–2011) Amex will earn enough to cover its dividends ($2.4 billion total) and also accumulate enough excess cash to pay off the Treasury's preferred stock investment ($3.4 billion), which would leave shareholders' equity flat at $11.8 billion in 2012. Depending on how the losses occur, the shareholders' equity may need to be adjusted downward due to losses on subordinated tranches in credit card securitizations ($0.8 billion) and/or the establishment of reserves due to early amortization ($1.8 billion). If 2012 is a normal year, we think Amex's ROE will be between 20 percent and 30 percent, which would result in earnings and EPS as shown in Table 8.4.

What are those earnings worth? We believe Amex will still be a world-class business with attractive long-term growth prospects and above-average profitability, so it should trade at a premium valuation. But who knows where the market will be then? So let's apply 12, 15, and 17 multiples, all below Amex's long-term average. This would result in share prices as shown in Table 8.5.

These scenarios are 2 to 5 times today's share price—a very satisfactory return.

Table 8.4 Normalized Earnings Power

Scenario	Return on Equity	Net Income (Bn)	Earnings per Share
Low	20%	$2.4	$2.04
Base	25%	$3.0	$2.55
High	30%	$3.5	$3.06

SOURCE: T2 Partners estimates.

Table 8.5 Valuation Scenarios

Earnings per Share	12×	15×	17×
$2.04	$24.48	$30.60	$34.68
$2.55	$30.60	$38.25	$43.35
$3.06	$36.72	$45.90	$52.02

SOURCE: T2 Partners estimates.

Not Platinum, but Still Gold

Some have speculated that Berkshire Hathaway, Amex's largest shareholder, might be increasing its stake. Unfortunately for Berkshire shareholders, it cannot do so without permission from the Federal Reserve due to ownership limitations of bank holding companies. Nevertheless, Buffett made his views on the company clear in a March 9, 2009, interview when he said: "It's very clear that American Express's losses in 2009 on their receivables will be, you know, considerably higher than last year. And their earnings will suffer to some degree accordingly. But that doesn't mean that American Express isn't a hell of a buy at $10. American Express is going to be around forever. They've got the cream of cardholders. Unfortunately, they have some cardholders that aren't the cream, too."[1]

While we aren't qualified to say whether Amex will be around *forever*, we believe it will survive the Great Recession that we are in the midst of, just as it has survived many other challenges in its history: the Merchants Union Express merger in the 1860s, the express industry consolidation in 1918, the Chase takeover of the 1920s, the salad oil scandal in 1963, the Optima card debacle in the late 1980s, and the events of September 11, 2001. To be sure, there are significant challenges at hand, but we think that Amex will overcome them and long-term shareholders will be richly rewarded.

That said, Amex today is not safe enough to back up the truck, as Buffett did after the salad oil scandal, when he put 40 percent of his portfolio in the stock. As of early March 2009, it was roughly a 5 percent position in the funds we manage.

Chapter 9

Bottom Fishing in Microcaps

Case Study: Resource America

I n sharp contrast to the previous two case studies, in which we analyzed two large, well-known companies, Berkshire Hathaway and American Express, in this chapter we turn to a little-known microcap, Resource America (REXI). Resource America has everything the market hates right now: It's tiny (as of March 10, 2009, the stock was at $3.19, giving it a market cap of $56 million); it has lots of debt ($609 million—more on this later); the stock is illiquid; it's a sum-of-the-parts valuation story; it's complex; and most of the businesses it's in are deeply distressed.

It's no wonder REXI's Q1 2009 earnings conference call had no analysts on it—no analysts cover the company—and the few listeners didn't ask a single question. As of early March 2009, we owned a bit more than 6 percent of the company across the funds we manage (note that positions may change at any time), 17 percent was owned by insiders, and most of the rest was owned by a few other value-oriented funds.

The company has an excellent long-term record of value creation, but has been a complete disaster over the past two years, tumbling nearly 90 percent, as shown in Figure 9.1.

So why would anyone be interested in a stock with these characteristics? Well, we think it's precisely *because* of these characteristics that it's interesting. Generally speaking, the best bargains in the market are not widely followed companies like Berkshire Hathaway, which, as out of favor as it is today, trades "only" at roughly a 25 percent discount to its intrinsic value. In contrast, as we discuss in this chapter, we think REXI trades at a 63 to 86 percent discount to intrinsic value. The crazy cheap stocks—the ones that can go up two, five, or ten times if anything good happens—are the obscure small caps and microcaps that few investors (and no Wall Street analysts) are paying any attention to.

A word of caution, however: Just as these stocks can soar, when they fall, they can fall hard. One forced seller—a hedge fund that is getting hit with redemptions or is going out of business, for example—can crush a stock like REXI.

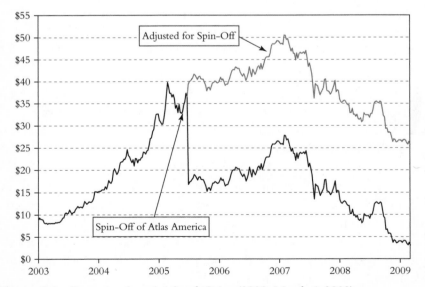

Figure 9.1 Resource America Stock Price (2003–March 6, 2009)
SOURCE: Yahoo! Finance (http://finance.yahoo.com).

We have been embarrassingly wrong on this stock for the past two years, but think it's a steal at today's price. We view this as an opportunity to invest with the Cohen family, which has a proven track record in the type of specialty finance that REXI does. In particular, we believe that the CEO, Jonathan Cohen, is a strong operating manager, very risk-averse, trustworthy, and shareholder oriented. Furthermore, we think today's price is a substantial discount to even a worst-case scenario. The confusion and turmoil in the stock and mortgage markets is giving us a chance to buy high-quality assets with a substantial margin of safety. That said, this is not an ultrasafe stock like Berkshire Hathaway. There are possible bad outcomes here that would result in a permanent loss of capital, so this is the type of stock to keep at 5 percent or less of your portfolio.

Background

Resource America went public in 1986 as a specialty finance company that bought commercial mortgages at a discount. It also held some energy assets like gas wells and pipelines. It built up Fidelity Leasing and in 2000 sold it to ABN Amro for $583 million, approximately twice the net assets of the lease portfolio, a significant premium. Later, REXI IPO'd its energy assets by selling shares of Atlas America in 2004 and then spun off its remaining shares the next year. In 2005, REXI also created Resource Capital Corporation, a real estate investment trust (REIT) that trades separately under the ticker RSO. Overall, REXI has a very good track record of accumulating assets on the cheap and selling them at good prices, with solid gains for shareholders.

Today, REXI manages assets across a broad range of categories and earns attractive spreads on structured finance pools. We believe that while some of these pools may experience problems, REXI has modest liability, which is more than discounted in the stock price. In addition to substantial excess assets outlined later, we estimate that REXI has earnings power of over $1 per share, though it will not reach this level in 2009; the company's guidance is $0.50 to $0.70 per share. REXI operates in three segments: financial fund management (FFM), which manages various types of asset-backed securities; real estate,

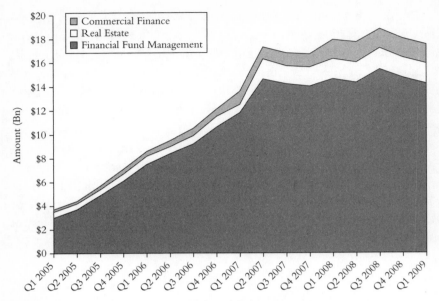

Figure 9.2   Resource America Assets under Management, Q1 2005 to Q1 2009
SOURCE: REXI earnings releases.

which invests in and manages multifamily and commercial real estate; and commercial finance, which is comprised of LEAF Financial, a small equipment leasing business. We believe that the combined value of these businesses, when added to the value of other investments and what's on the balance sheet, is multiples of the current market price. REXI's upside is very high when the markets eventually recover.

Figure 9.2 shows the growth of REXI's assets under management over time. One can see that the company grew its assets rapidly when times were good, and now that capital markets are closed it's managing the funds and earning fees for doing so.

Financial Fund Management

The financial fund management (FFM) business represents the majority of REXI's assets under management and, in this environment, is the most out of favor. It acquires, pools, structures, finances, and manages pools of assets, ranging from collateralized loan obligations (CLOs) and collateralized debt obligations (CDOs), which is essentially a wind-down business (it's cash flow positive, but it will likely have zero terminal value), to real estate and bank loan pools, to pools of trust preferred securities. REXI has a competitive advantage in the fund management business, which is, in normal times, a very attractive area.

As of year-end 2008, the FFM business consisted of 35 CDOs and 13 limited partnerships, as shown in Table 9.1.

REXI earns money in three ways: origination fees, management fees, and returns on the company's own capital that it invests in the funds. Table 9.2 shows the financial statement for FFM for Q1 2009, the quarter ending December 31, 2008 (REXI's fiscal year [FY] ends September 30).

Going from top to bottom, here are the things to notice:

• The fair value adjustments declined markedly from a $6.7 million loss to a $1.2 million loss, reflecting the fact that the CDOs REXI created have done poorly (like most CDOs), so REXI has had to write down the amount it invested in them. Fortunately, nearly all of the write-downs are now behind REXI, as it reported in its Q1 2009 earnings release:

  The Company has reduced to $354,000, net of tax, its balance sheet exposure to future valuation adjustments related to investments in trust preferred securities reported as investments in unconsolidated entities and direct investments in collateralized debt obligations secured by trust preferred securities. The

Table 9.1 Financial Fund Management Assets under Management, December 31, 2008

Name	Asset Class	# of CDO Issuers	Total (Bn)
Trapeza	Trust preferred securities	13	$ 4.8
Apidos	Bank Loans (CLOs)	12	$ 3.9
Ischus	RMBS/CMBS/ABS	9	$ 5.1
Other	Miscellaneous	1	$ 0.5
			$14.3

Source: REXI 10-Q, Q1 2009.

Table 9.2   Financial Fund Management Income Statement (000s)

	Three Months Ended	
	12/31/08	**12/31/07**
Revenues:		
Limited and general partner interests:		
Fair value adjustments	−$1,218	−$6,681
Operations	−$ 31	$1,401
Total limited and general partner interests	−$1,249	−$5,280
Fund and RCC management fees	$6,125	$6,881
Interest income on loans	$3,504	$6,580
Earnings on unconsolidated CDOs	$ 461	$ 813
Introductory agent, due diligence, and placement fees	$ 874	
Earnings of Structured Finance Fund partnerships	$ 158	$ 463
Other	$ 46	$ 165
Total Revenues	**$9,919**	**$9,622**
Costs and expenses:		
General and administrative expenses	$5,711	$6,493
Equity compensation (income) expense—RCC	−$ 4	$ 110
Expenses of Structured Finance Fund partnerships	$ 21	$ 11
Total Expenses	**$5,728**	**$6,614**
FFM Operating Profit	**$ 4,191**	**$3,008**

Source: REXI 10-Q, Q1 2009.

Company has no exposure to valuation adjustments for residential mortgage-backed securities and has reduced its balance sheet exposure to investments in collateralized debt obligations secured by bank loans reported as securities available-for-sale to $3.4 million, net of tax.

- Fund and Resource Capital Corporation (RCC) fees declined a bit due to a reduction in the subordinated fees in a number of the CDO vehicles. We expect the Ischus CDOs, comprised of residential mortgage-backed securities (RMBSs) and commercial mortgage-backed securities (CMBSs), to decline in value quickly, so REXI will lose those management fees, but the Trapeza and Apidos

CDOs should perform well and REXI should continue to collect its management fees for many years.

- The interest income on loans declined because REXI was creating new investment vehicles in 2007 and therefore earned interest on the money it had borrowed to set up these vehicles, but in today's market REXI is not setting up any more vehicles so its interest income fell. We expect REXI to continue earning about $3 million per quarter in interest income. However, this interest income is off-set by approximately $2 million of interest expense that doesn't appear in the segment disclosure, so operating profit was roughly $2.2 million, not $4.2 million.

- General and administrative expenses fell, reflecting cost cut-ting. In its Q1 2009 earnings release, REXI announced that it had "instituted measures in fiscal 2008 to reduce its general and administrative expenses, which it expects will result in savings of approximately $19.5 million on an annualized basis beginning in January 2009, $2.5 million more than previously reported."

Going forward, we expect write-downs to quickly decline to vir-tually nil by the end of FY 2009, fund and RCC management fees and interest income on loans to decline slowly, and general and administra-tive expenses to fall to around $4 million per quarter. The result should be $7 million to $12 million in operating profit for FFM in FY 2009. Thereafter, profits will continue to decline if capital markets remain frozen, but could grow if capital markets open up and REXI can once again resume creating investment vehicles.

Given the uncertainty about the future of this business, it's ulti-mately difficult to value. If it's in runoff, then it's probably worth $40 million. If it can raise a few new funds over time and maintain operat-ing profit of $10 million, then it's probably worth 6 times pretax profits or $60 million.

Real Estate

REXI's real estate portfolio has taken a beating, along with the rest of the real estate market, but the company has real expertise in the dis-tressed real estate business, which is booming in these troubled times.

REXI manages distressed real estate with money raised from others and earns a fee and a carry (percentage of the profits) from that, which is a highly attractive business model.

REXI manages real estate in five areas:

1. A commercial real estate debt portfolio comprised principally of A notes, whole loans, mortgage participations, B notes, mezzanine debt, and related commercial real estate securities.
2. Real estate investment fund assets, primarily multifamily apartments.
3. Portfolios of distressed or value-added real estate assets acquired through joint ventures with institutional investors.
4. Real estate loans, owned assets, and ventures, known collectively as legacy portfolio.
5. A portfolio of distressed real estate loans acquired at a discount, primarily from the Department of Housing and Urban Development (HUD).

Table 9.3 shows the assets under management in each area.

REXI summarized its real estate activities and future plans in its Q1 2009 earnings release. Here are key excerpts:

- The Company, through its distressed real estate joint ventures, has closed on $71.1 million of acquisitions, including committed capital, from September 2007 through November 2008. The Company acquired $13.2 million of these distressed

Table 9.3   Real Estate Assets under Management

	As of Dec. 31	
Assets under Management (millions)	**2008**	**2007**
Commercial real estate debt	$ 888	$ 935
Real estate investment funds and programs	$ 538	$ 448
Institutional portfolios	$ 129	$ 86
Legacy portfolio	$ 96	$ 100
Distressed portfolios	$ 68	$ 75
	$1,719	**$1,644**

SOURCE: REXI 10-Q, Q1 2009.

assets in the first fiscal quarter of 2009 and anticipates using its retail broker–dealer channel to launch a $50.0 million fund to expand its distressed real estate operations.

- Since January 1, 2008, Resource Real Estate has acquired $119.3 million in real estate assets for its investment vehicles including four properties during the first fiscal quarter ended December 31, 2008.
- Resource Real Estate commenced fundraising for Resource Real Estate Investors 7, L.P. ("RREI 7"), a $40.0 million offering that will invest in multifamily real estate assets. Through February 3, 2009, Resource Real Estate had raised $20.4 million through RREI 7. We anticipate closing this fund in late fiscal 2009. In addition, Resource Real Estate intends to launch Resource Real Estate Opportunity Fund L.P., a real estate partnership focused on investing in discounted real estate.
- Resource Real Estate's wholly-owned subsidiary, Resource Residential, a multifamily and commercial property management company, completed its first full year of operations.
- Resource Real Estate increased the apartment units it manages or whose management it supervises to 17,653 at December 31, 2008 from 14,919 at December 31, 2007. This includes a portfolio of 50 multifamily properties representing 12,301 apartment units managed by Resource Residential.

Table 9.4 shows the financial statement for REXI's real estate operations for Q1 2009.

We can see that REXI's Q1 operating profit was about $1 million in each of the past two years. For the previous three years, the annual operating profit was $11.6 million in 2006, $9.8 million in 2007, and $8.9 million in 2008. We expect that the combination of a difficult environment, growth in the distressed real estate business, and cost cutting will result in roughly $8 million of operating profit in this segment in FY 2009.

We then adjust this for the profit REXI earns from rental property since we include the value of this property in our calculation of intrinsic value and we don't want to double count. This was $525,000 in Q1 2009 or roughly $2 million annualized, so our adjusted annual estimate of real estate operating profit is $6 million.

Table 9.4   Real Estate Operations Income Statement (000s)

	Three Months Ended	
	12/31/08	**12/31/07**
Revenues:		
Management fees:		
Asset management fees	$ 995	$ 649
Resource Residential property management fees	$ 984	$ 232
REIT management fees from RCC	$1,085	$1,776
	$3,064	$2,657
Fee income from sponsorship of partnerships and TIC property interests	$1,511	$1,299
Master lease revenues	$ 982	$ 877
Rental property income and FIN 46-R revenues	$1,292	$1,109
Interest, including accreted loan discount	$ 240	$ 419
Equity in losses of unconsolidated entities	–$ 199	–$ 60
Net gains on sale of TIC property interests	$ 0	$ 171
Total Revenues	**$6,890**	**$6,472**
Costs and expenses:		
General and administrative	$2,959	$2,947
Resource Residential expenses	$ 992	$ 783
Master lease expenses	$1,200	$ 946
Rental property and FIN 46-R expenses	$ 767	$ 790
Total Expenses	**$5,918**	**$5,466**
Real Estate Operating Profit	**$ 972**	**$1,006**
Minus net profit from rental property and FIN 46-R	$ 525	$ 319
Adjusted Real Estate Operating Profit	**$ 447**	**$ 687**

SOURCE: REXI 10-Q, Q1 2009.

It's hard to know what kind of multiple to put on these earnings, so we use a wide range of 5 to 10 times the $6 million of pretax operating profit, resulting in a $30 million to $60 million valuation estimate.

Commercial Finance

REXI's most valuable operation is its 85 percent stake in LEAF Financial (LEAF's management owns 15 percent), a small equipment leasing business. LEAF forms alliances with equipment vendors and investors and puts together investment pools (limited partnerships) that LEAF manages that do four-year-average-life leases on small-ticket items, with very wide diversification in terms of both the assets and the customers. LEAF generates three fee streams: (1) income spread until leases are sold down; (2) origination fees (175 to 200 basis points); and management fees (more than 100 basis points).

LEAF has grown both organically as well as by purchasing pools of leases from others. As of December 31, 2008, LEAF managed approximately 105,000 leases and loans that had an average original finance value of $23,000 with an average term of 52 months. Table 9.5 shows the assets under management in each area.

We think of LEAF as a manufacturing plant: it manufactures leases for companies that want to lease equipment and need financing for that. LEAF also manufactures the capital with which to do that through both equity and debt partnerships, raising equity dollars and then levering them. The problem today is that, with capital markets frozen, it's

Table 9.5   Commercial Finance Assets under Management

	As of Dec. 31	
Assets under Management (millions)	**2008**	**2007**
LEAF	$ 155	$ 492
LCFF	$ 0	$ 131
Merit Capital Advance	$ 9	$ 23
Managed for own account	$ 164	$ 646
Lease Equity Appreciation Fund I, L.P.	$ 96	$ 102
Lease Equity Appreciation Fund II, L.P.	$ 267	$ 343
LEAF Equipment Leasing Income Fund III, L.P.	$ 692	$ 502
Fund 4	$ 15	$ 0
LCFF	$ 184	$ 0
RCC	$ 104	$ 95
Other	$ 41	$ 11
Managed for others	$ 1,399	$ 1,053
Total	**$1,563**	**$1,699**

Source: REXI 10-Q, Q1 2009.

difficult for LEAF to raise both the equity and the debt it needs, as this paragraph in the Q1 2009 earnings release notes:

> LEAF began a public offering of up to $200.0 million of limited partnership interests in August 2008 for LEAF Equipment Finance Fund 4, L.P. ("Fund 4"), an equipment leasing partnership, and for LEAF Commercial Finance Fund ("LCFF"), a $25.0 million offering in the form of 8.25% promissory notes. Through February 3, 2009, LEAF had raised $52.0 million for Fund 4 and LCFF.

In other words, in six months LEAF had raised only $52 million of the $225 million it hoped to raise, so LEAF is shrinking dramatically, as shown in Table 9.6, the financial statement for REXI's commercial finance operations for Q1 2009.

We can see that REXI's commercial finance revenues fell 45 percent, which led to a 57 percent drop in operating profit. Annualized, the Q1 profit is $16.4 million, but we expect that once the capital markets thaw, operating profit will be in the $25 million to $30 million range.

Let's use $25 million and apply a 5 to 10 times earnings range to come up with a valuation of $125 million to $250 million REXI's 85 percent stake is therefore worth $106 million to $212 million. LEAF is a tremendous asset, and we believe that its value will eventually be realized through its sale or a spin-off.

Balance Sheet

There are many assets on REXI's balance sheet, but before we turn to them, let's analyze the liabilities, namely the $608.7 million of debt. There are many different kinds of debt—some are deadly and can lead to bankruptcy, and some are very favorable. Nearly all of REXI's debt is the best kind: nonrecourse. This means that, if there's a default, the debt holders can't come after REXI, but only the assets that secure the debt. It's like a mortgage on your home: If you default, the bank can foreclose and take the home, but that's it—it can't come after any other assets (whether this is a good thing is open to debate—in Canada, this is not the case, and that country didn't have a housing bubble, perhaps because Canadian homeowners are more cautious when they know that if they default on their mortgages, the bank can come after *all* of their assets).

Table 9.6   Commercial Finance Operations Income Statement

	Three Months Ended	
	12/31/08	12/31/07
Revenues:		
LEAF	$ 6,934	$14,259
Merit	$ 923	$ 2,168
Acquisition fees	$ 1,355	$ 5,704
Fund management fees	$ 5,602	$ 3,997
Other	$ 570	$ 1,837
Total Revenues	**$15,384**	**$27,965**
Costs and expenses:		
Wage and benefit costs:		
LEAF	$ 3,203	$ 4,949
Merit	$ 386	$ 592
	$ 3,589	$ 5,541
Other costs and expenses:		
LEAF	$ 3,588	$ 3,041
Merit	$ 272	$ 799
	$ 3,860	$ 3,840
Total Expenses	**$ 7,449**	**$ 9,381**
Commercial Finance Operating Profit	**$ 7,935**	**$18,584**

SOURCE: REXI 10-Q, Q1 2009.

NOTE: As with the FFM segment disclosure, the commercial finance income statement doesn't show approximately $3.8 million of interest expense, so operating profit was roughly $4.1 million, not $7.9 million.

REXI explained its debt situation in its Q1 2009 earnings release:

As of December 31, 2008, the Company reduced its total consolidated borrowings outstanding to $608.7 million from $1.05 billion at December 31, 2007, a decrease of $441.8 million (42%). At December 31, 2008, borrowings include $213.5 million of borrowings consolidated under FIN 46-R as to which there is no recourse to the Company, $327.7 million of non-recourse revolving credit facilities and promissory notes at LEAF and $67.5 million of other debt, which includes $13.7 million of mortgage debt secured by properties owned by the Company's subsidiaries.

So, REXI has only $53.8 million ($67.5 minus $13.7) of debt that is recourse to the company and it has $16.1 million in cash, so that's only $37.7 million of net recourse debt.

Now let's turn to REXI's assets. Table 9.7 shows the asset side of REXI's balance sheet as of December 31, 2008.

Table 9.8 shows our range of estimated values of REXI's assets, less its recourse debt. Let's go through it line by line:

- Investment securities available for sale of $16.9 million on the 12/31/08 balance sheet are comprised of three assets: REXI owns two million shares of Resource Capital Corporation (ticker: RSO) that were worth $7.7 million on December 31, 2008; the value was $4.2 million as of March 6, 2009. It also owns 118,400 shares of The Bancorp, Inc. (ticker: TBBK) that were worth $444,000 on December 31, 2008; the value was $317,000 as of March 6, 2009. Finally, REXI's stakes in CDOs that it sponsored and manages were valued at $8.7 million on December 31, 2008. At the very least, we

Table 9.7   Resource America Balance Sheet: Assets

Assets	12/31/08	9/30/08
Cash	$ 16,082	$ 14,910
Restricted cash	$ 21,421	$ 23,689
Receivables	$ 2,638	$ 2,014
Receivables from managed entities and related parties	$ 36,769	$ 35,674
Loans sold, not settled, at fair value	$ 0	$ 662
Loans held for investment, net	$223,326	$219,664
Investments in commercial finance—held for investment, net	$239,583	$182,315
Investments in commercial finance—held for sale, at fair value	$103,023	$110,773
Investments in real estate, net	$ 36,961	$ 37,972
Investment securities available for sale, at fair value	$ 16,895	$ 22,746
Investments in unconsolidated entities	$ 17,313	$ 18,523
Property and equipment, net	$ 15,950	$ 16,886
Deferred tax assets	$ 53,956	$ 44,467
Goodwill	$ 7,969	$ 7,969
Intangible assets, net	$ 4,173	$ 4,329
Other assets	$ 11,989	$ 15,764
Total Assets	**$808,048**	**$758,357**

SOURCE: REXI 10-Q, Q1 2009.

Table 9.8   Estimated Value of Resource America's Assets Less Recourse Debt

	Low	High
Investment securities available for sale, at fair value	$ 0	$ 13
Investment in Apidos VI	$ 0	$ 16
Investments in unconsolidated entities	$ 0	$ 17
Investments in real estate, net	$ 23	$ 33
Cash and receivables from managed entities and related parties	$ 16	$ 53
Subtotal Investments	**$39**	**$132**
Debt revolver	−$54	−$ 54
Total Net Investments	**−$15**	**$ 78**

SOURCE: REXI 10-Q, Q1 2009, T2 Partners estimates.

haircut the $16.9 million by the decline in value of the two stocks, so this is now $13.2 million. If we want to be really conservative, we'll value all of it at zero.

- REXI's investment in Apidos VI, which is embedded in "Loans held for investment, net," was valued at $16 million as of December 31, 2008. At the high end, we valued this at $16 million, and at the low end, nothing.

- Investments in unconsolidated entities are investments REXI has made in the commercial finance, real estate, and financial fund management investment vehicles it has sponsored and manages. At the high end, these could be worth the $17.3 million they're carried for on the balance sheet, and at the low end, zero.

- We think REXI's investments in real estate of $23.3 million net ($37.0 from the balance sheet minus "$13.7 million of mortgage debt secured by properties owned by the Company's subsidiaries" from the Q1 2009 press release) are carried at very conservative values and could easily be worth $10 million more, so at the low end we value them at $23 million and at $33 million at the high end.

- Cash is $16.1 million, and receivables from managed entities and related parties are another $36.8 million. At the high end, this item is worth $52.9 million (for example, if the business were sold, the bulk of the receivables would be drawn down and converted to cash); at the low end, some analysts choose not to count the receivables as part of REXI's intrinsic value, so we would add only the $16.1 million of cash.

Valuation

In Table 9.9 we add up all of the pieces using both our low and high estimates, then subtract the debt to come up with the estimated intrinsic value of REXI's equity. Then we divide by the number of shares to arrive at our per-share estimate of intrinsic value of $8.66 and $22.04 using our low and high estimates, respectively. In other words, using our most conservative estimates, the stock is worth nearly triple its current price and, in an upside scenario, could be worth 7x more—and even at that price it would be lower than where it was less than two years ago.

Conclusion

Stocks like REXI are being punished to an unbelievable degree in this market—and we've sure felt the pain. But we're convinced that REXI's intrinsic value is multiples of today's share price and that we will be well rewarded for our patience and conviction.

Table 9.9   Estimates of Resource America's Intrinsic Value

(Millions except per share)	Low	Comment	High	Comment
Financial fund management	$ 40	Fee runoff	$ 60	6× '09 pretax
Real estate	$ 30	4× '09 pretax	$ 60	10× '09 pretax
Commercial finance	$ 106	4× '09 pretax	$ 212	10× '09 pretax
Assets	$ 39		$ 132	
Subtotal	$ 215		$ 464	
Debt	–$ 54		–$ 54	
Estimated intrinsic value of the equity	**$ 161**		**$ 410**	
Diluted shares outstanding	18.6		18.6	
Estimated intrinsic value per share	**$ 8.66**		**$ 22.04**	
Current share price (3/10/09)	$ 3.19		$ 3.19	
Multiple of today's share price	**2.7**		**6.9**	

SOURCE: T2 Partners estimates.

Chapter 10

Opportunities in Pools
of Distressed Mortgages

Case Study: Long Beach Mortgage Loan Trust 2006-8

W e are equity investors, but in mid–December 2008 we made our first debt investment when we bought a piece of a 2006 bubble-era subprime pool of mortgages suffering from catastrophic defaults. Were we crazy? You decide. . . .

The securitized pool of mortgages (called a residential mortgage-backed security or RMBS) is called the Long Beach Mortgage Loan Trust 2006-8, and it's a fairly typical pool of subprime mortgages from near the peak of the bubble in 2006. It contained 6,447 mortgages, valued at $1.38 billion (later increased to 6,647 loans totaling $1.42 billion), and was structured at inception as shown in Table 10.1. Over 80 percent of the pool was rated AAA, and nearly all was rated investment grade (98 percent by S&P and 96 percent by Moody's).

Table 10.1   Structure of Long Beach Mortgage Loan Trust 2006-8

Class	Expected Rating (S&P/Moody's)	Principal Balance ($)	Credit Enhancement
I-A	AAA/Aaa	$ 366,091,000	18.60%
II-A1	AAA/Aaa	$ 322,788,000	18.60%
II-A2	AAA/Aaa	$ 124,929,000	18.60%
II-A3	AAA/Aaa	$ 236,928,000	18.60%
II-A4	AAA/Aaa	$ 73,178,000	18.60%
M-1	[AA+]/Aa1	$ 43,493,000	15.45%
M-2	[AA+]/Aa2	$ 39,351,000	12.60%
M-3	[AA]/Aa3	$ 24,853,000	10.80%
M-4	[AA]/A1	$ 22,092,000	9.20%
M-5	[AA–]/A2	$ 21,401,000	7.65%
M-6	[A+]/A3	$ 19,330,000	6.25%
M-7	[A]/Baa1	$ 13,807,000	5.25%
M-8	[A–]/Baa2	$ 11,046,000	4.45%
M-9	[BBB+]/Baa3	$ 10,355,000	3.70%
M-10	[BBB]/Ba1	$ 8,975,000	3.05%
M-11	[BBB–]/Ba2	$ 13,807,000	2.05%
C	Unrated	$ 28,303,000	
Total		$1,380,727,000	

SOURCE: Long Beach Mortgage Loan Trust 2006-8 Prospectus Supplement, September 15, 2006.

Table 10.2 shows that the loans in the pool are high-interest-rate (8.46 percent) loans to deep subprime borrowers (639 average FICO score) who are really stretching to make payments (39.4 percent average debt-to-income ratio—and you can be sure many were lying about their incomes). Almost 83 percent are adjustable-rate mortgages, more than half of which reset within two years. More than half are in California and Florida, and almost 48 percent are stated-income/limited-documentation/no-doc loans.

Performance of Long Beach Mortgage Loan Trust 2006–8

The layering of risk factors is astonishing—borrowers with very poor credit histories, high-interest adjustable-rate mortgages, lots of liar's loans, a concentration in bubble markets—so it's not surprising that this

Table 10.2   Information about the Mortgages in the Long Beach Mortgage Loan Trust 2006-8

Trust Statistics

Total scheduled principal balance	$1,380,727,000
Average scheduled principal balance	$214,166
Number of mortgage loans	6,447
Weighted average gross coupon	8.46%
Weighted average FICO score	639
Weighted average combined original LTV	89.87%
Weighted average debt-to-income ratio	39.41%
Weighted average months to roll	33 months
Product Type:	
Adjustable-rate mortgage	82.59%
Fixed-rate mortgage	17.41%
Not interest–only	92.46%
Interest–only	7.54%
Documentation Level:	
Full documentation	52.33%
Limited documentation	5.80%
Stated income	41.87%
Purpose:	
Cash–out refi	41.33%
Purchase	51.74%
Rate/term refi	6.93%
Top Five Locations:	
California	39.55%
Florida	11.84%
Texas	4.60%
Maryland	4.51%
Washington	4.37%

Source: Long Beach Mortgage Loan Trust 2006-8 Prospectus Supplement, September 15, 2006.

RMBS is a complete train wreck. Figure 10.1 shows the status of the loans in the pool after only 30 months, through January 2009.

Starting from the top, we can see the funds that have been paid back to the pool: $253 million from the 18 percent of mortgages that refinanced and $114 million in recoveries, a 40 percent recovery rate on the $296 million of mortgages (original face value) that went through the entire process from default to foreclosure, real estate owned (REO), and, finally, sale.

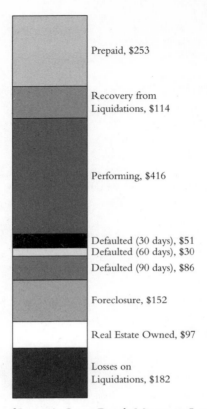

Figure 10.1   Status of Loans in Long Beach Mortgage Loan Trust 2006-8, January 2009
Source: Amherst Securities. Amounts are in millions of dollars.

Next, $416 million (30 percent of the original balance) of mortgages are still performing, $51 million have missed one payment, $30 million have missed two payments, $86 million have missed three payments, $152 million are in foreclosure, and $97 million are REO. Finally, the realized losses in the pool are $182 million, based on average severity of 61.5 percent on the $296 million of liquidated houses. Table 10.3 has further details on the pool.

Figure 10.2 shows the cumulative default rate since the inception of this RMBS. It's truly mind-boggling to think that more than 60 percent of the mortgages have defaulted in little over two years—and there's no sign of a slowdown, though the Obama administration's new

Table 10.3 Data on the Long Beach Mortgage Loan Trust 2006-8, January 2009

Date	Loss ($M)	Severity	CDX	sTr	cTr	SMM	vPr
1/1/09	$ 0.0	0.0%	62.4%	4.5%	42.5%	0.1%	1.2%
12/1/08	$12.2	73.4%	61.4%	6.6%	55.9%	0.5%	5.8%
11/1/08	$12.7	74.5%	59.7%	5.8%	51.2%	0.8%	9.2%
10/1/08	$18.9	58.5%	58.2%	6.9%	57.6%	0.8%	9.2%
9/1/08	$16.2	61.6%	56.2%	5.2%	47.3%	1.2%	13.5%
8/1/08	$14.7	58.6%	54.6%	5.4%	48.6%	0.9%	10.3%
7/1/08	$13.1	59.5%	52.8%	4.9%	45.3%	0.6%	7.0%
6/1/08	$13.0	54.9%	51.1%	4.7%	43.9%	0.7%	8.1%
5/1/08	$11.7	57.2%	49.4%	4.7%	43.9%	1.1%	12.4%
4/1/08	$10.7	64.2%	47.5%	5.2%	47.3%	0.7%	8.1%
3/1/08	$ 7.7	61.4%	45.4%	4.4%	41.7%	0.7%	8.1%
2/1/08	$ 4.7	64.2%	43.4%	4.8%	44.6%	0.6%	7.0%
1/1/08	$ 6.7	58.4%	41.2%	5.8%	51.2%	0.9%	10.3%
12/1/07	$ 6.6	66.2%	38.4%	5.2%	47.3%	0.7%	8.1%
11/1/07	$ 5.4	62.5%	35.7%	4.9%	45.3%	0.9%	10.3%
10/1/07	$ 4.4	49.9%	32.9%	5.4%	48.6%	0.6%	7.0%
9/1/07	$ 2.2	54.7%	29.7%	4.1%	39.5%	1.0%	11.4%
8/1/07	$ 5.9	69.8%	27.1%	4.2%	40.2%	1.0%	11.4%
7/1/07	$ 0.5	40.4%	24.3%	3.4%	34.0%	1.4%	15.6%
6/1/07	$ 6.0	106.7%	22.0%	3.3%	33.1%	1.3%	14.5%
5/1/07	$ 0.2	34.8%	19.5%	3.4%	34.0%	1.2%	13.5%
4/1/07	$ 0.2	66.7%	17.0%	3.6%	35.6%	1.2%	13.5%
3/1/07	$ 0.0	0.0%	14.1%	3.3%	33.1%	1.5%	16.6%
2/1/07	$ 0.0	0.0%	11.3%	3.7%	36.4%	1.2%	13.5%
1/1/07	$ 0.0	0.0%	8.0%	3.7%	36.4%	1.6%	17.6%
12/1/06	$ 0.0	0.0%	4.7%	3.4%	34.0%	1.5%	16.6%
11/1/06	$ 0.0	0.0%	1.4%	1.4%	15.6%	1.1%	12.4%
10/1/06	$ 0.0	0.0%	0.0%	0.0%	0.0%	0.5%	5.8%
9/1/06	$ 0.0	0.0%	0.0%	0.0%	0.0%	0.0%	0.0%

SOURCE: Amherst Securities.

Here are the definitions of the terms:

Loss: Realized loss for the entire pool during the month.

Severity: The percentage of the face value of the mortgage that was lost upon liquidation e.g., if $20 million in mortgages (face value) liquidates during the month with 60 percent severity, the loss is $12 million and $8 million is remitted back to the RMBS).

CDX: Cumulative default rate since the inception of the pool.

sTr: The percentage of performing mortgages at the beginning of the month that defaulted during the month (default here means missing a third payment or 90 days, so this captures the mortgages that began the month having already missed two payments and then missed the third payment during the month).

cTr: The annual default rate of a pool if the monthly default rate stays constant.

SMM: The percentage of mortgages that prepaid during the month.

vPr: The annual prepayment rate of the pool if the monthly prepayment rate stays constant (i.e., annualize that month's SMM).

Table 10.4:   Homes Sold, Recovery and Losses Realized

Month	Loss (mm)	Severity	Face Value Liquidated (mm)	Recovery to Pool
10/2008	$18.9	58.5%	$32.3	$13.4
11/2008	$12.7	74.5%	$17.0	$ 4.3
12/2008	$12.2	73.4%	$16.6	$ 4.4

SOURCE: Amherst Securities, T2 Partners calculations.

Homeowner Affordability and Stability Plan (HASP) may make a substantial impact.

Let's focus on the last three months of 2008 (excluding January 2009, for which the data is incomplete). Table 10.4 takes the loss and severity from Table 10.3 and calculates the total amount of face value of mortgages liquidated during the month and the cash recovered for the pool. For example, in October 2008 the face value of mortgages liquidated was $18.9 million in losses, divided by the severity, 58.5 percent or 0.585, which equals $32.3 million. The recovery to the pool is the difference between the amount liquidated and the loss, or $32.3 minus $18.9, which equals $13.4 million.

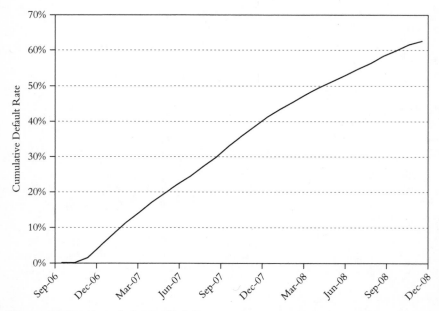

Figure 10.2   Cumulative Default Rate
SOURCE: Amherst Securities.

We can see that the number of houses that were sold (liquidated) fell by nearly half in November and December 2008, plus the severity spiked so the cash recovered for the pool dropped by two-thirds. This is very bad news for the senior tranches of the pool, which had been getting paid down rapidly. All three of these factors are a sharp departure from their trends, as shown in Figure 10.3.

The jump in severity can't be due to home prices declining so much in one month. These are mortgages with an average face value of $214,166 (per Table 10.2), so the 58.5 percent severity in October 2008 means that there's a $125,287 loss and a recovery of $88,879. But the loss captured by the severity number includes the costs of foreclosure, eviction, selling the home, and so forth, and let's say those costs total $25,000. That means the average house was sold for roughly $114,000, $100,000 below the cost of the mortgage.

If we apply November's 74.5 percent severity to this example, it would mean a $159,554 loss and a recovery of only $54,612. Assuming the same $25,000 in costs, that would mean the average house was sold for about $80,000, 30 percent less than the previous month. Home prices may be falling fast, but they're not falling *that* fast!

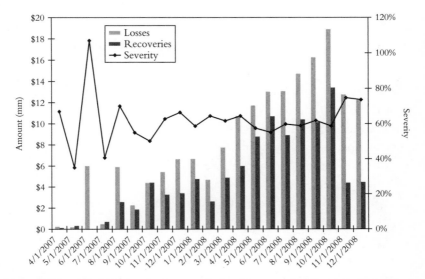

Figure 10.3   Monthly Losses, Recoveries, and Severity for the Long Beach Mortgage Loan Trust 2006-8
Source: Amherst Securities.

So if the jump in severity can't be explained by declining home prices, what might have caused it? One possibility is that the servicer started dumping houses at fire-sale prices, during the slowest months of the year no less, to recoup the money it had advanced to the pool. (When a homeowner stops paying, the servicer is obligated to continue paying the RMBS pools as if the homeowner were still paying, and then gets reimbursed when the homeowner catches up or, far more likely, when the home is eventually sold. But in the meantime, having to advance payments can cause cash flow problems for servicers. To alleviate this problem, servicers might hold a fire sale because, since they're getting paid back first, they don't really care how much the houses sell for.)

Another possibility is that, upon the election of Barack Obama, the servicer of the pool stopped selling nicer houses or those with better-off homeowners in the hope that the new administration would implement a government-subsidized plan that would help keep people in their homes and/or give servicers incentives to do so.

In fact, this is precisely what has happened in the form of HASP, which is great for servicers not only because of the direct incentives to them, but also because it will help keep people in their homes, meaning that a servicer can continue collecting fees for servicing the mortgages.

More broadly, HASP is a windfall for servicers and is likely to help millions of homeowners, which is why we support it, but it is probably very bad for virtually all tranches of RMBS pools, as Amherst Securities pointed out in a research note on March 9, 2009:

> This Housing Affordability and Stability Plan contains an inherent conflict of interest between servicers and investors. The plan, in combination with the servicer safe harbor, leaves the current first lien holders with no protection. It is the equivalent of having the fox guard the hen house, with the fox in possession of the only set of keys.
>
> And it potentially corrupts the integrity of the securitization market. In any structured security, the prioritization of claims is integral to valuation. Once the precedent is set to violate this hierarchy, by making the first lien holders incur losses without touching the second lien cash flows, the integrity is breached.[1]

Thus, the effects of HASP must be carefully considered when evaluating an RMBS tranche.

That said, the sharp decline in house liquidations, the increase in severity, and the sharply lower recovery in November and December 2008 are likely to be anomalies, though the monthly recoveries to the Long Beach Mortgage Loan Trust 2006-8 may be permanently impaired to some degree. To see the impact, we need to examine the structure and current status of this pool in greater detail.

How Payments Flow to the Tranches

Table 10.5 shows the status of the remaining tranches in the RMBS. Note that tranches M-5 through M-11 and the equity tranche have already been wiped out and there's almost nothing left of the M-4 tranche.

This table shows that tranche IA has been paid down from $366 million to $223 million and the IIA1 tranche has been paid down from $323 million to only $52 million—and no other tranches have been paid anything. A total of $413 million has gone to the top two tranches in this pool: $253 million from prepays plus $114 million of recovery from liquidations plus $46 million in interest payments made by performing loans.

Figure 10.4 shows why two tranches are being paid off simultaneously. When this RMBS was created, it was split into four pieces labeled 3, 4, 5, and 6. The recoveries from pieces 3 and 4 pay down tranche IA, while the recoveries from pieces 5 and 6 pay down tranche IIA1 first;

Table 10.5   Current Balances of Surviving Tranches

	Original (mm)	Current (mm)
IA	$366.1	$222.8
IIA1	$322.8	$ 51.8
IIA2	$124.9	$124.9
IIA3	$236.9	$236.9
IIA4	$ 73.2	$ 73.2
M1	$ 43.5	$ 43.5
M2	$ 39.4	$ 39.4
M3	$ 24.9	$ 24.9
M4	$ 22.1	$ 14.2
M5 and below	wiped out	

SOURCE: Amherst Securities.

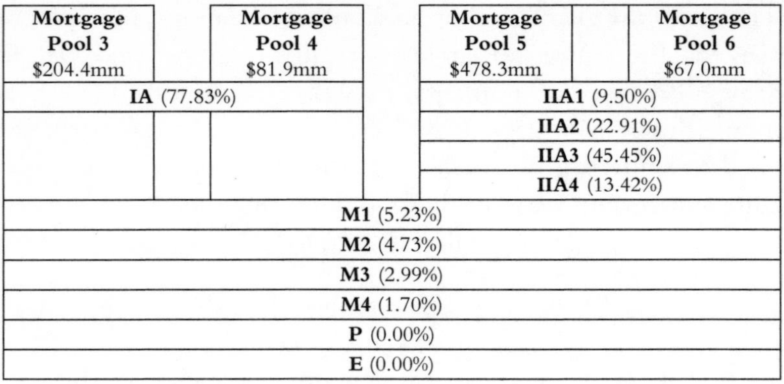

Mortgage Pool 3 $204.4mm	Mortgage Pool 4 $81.9mm	Mortgage Pool 5 $478.3mm	Mortgage Pool 6 $67.0mm
IA (77.83%)		IIA1 (9.50%)	
		IIA2 (22.91%)	
		IIA3 (45.45%)	
		IIA4 (13.42%)	
M1 (5.23%)			
M2 (4.73%)			
M3 (2.99%)			
M4 (1.70%)			
P (0.00%)			
E (0.00%)			

Figure 10.4   Structure of Long Beach Mortgage Loan Trust 2006-8
Source: Amherst Securities.

then, when it's paid off in full, the recoveries from pieces 5 and 6 pay down tranche IIA2, and so forth. Note that losses from the entire pool impact the mezzanine tranches.

And here's one more twist to consider: Once all of the mezzanine tranches are wiped out, the payments from pieces 5 and 6 go *pari passu* to the remaining IIA tranches. For example, at the point that the M1 tranche is wiped out, let's say that half ($62 million) of the IIA2 tranche remains, plus all of the IIA3 ($237 million) and IIA4 ($73 million). In this case, the IIA2 tranche would go from receiving 100 percent of the cash coming in from pieces 5 and 6 to receiving only 16.7 percent: $62 \div (62 + 237 + 73)$.

What We Bought and Its Prospects

We care a lot about this because we bought $3.8 million of the IIA2 tranche at 34 cents on the dollar. This tranche has a face value of $125 million, and we bought it at a value of $42.5 million, so we own 8.9 percent of it ($3.8 \div 42.5$).

Now there's a horse race going on between cash coming into the pool that is paying down the tranche above ours and losses wiping out the tranches beneath us. Specifically, there's $51.8 million remaining to be paid off in the tranche above us (IIA1), and there's $121.8 million in the M1 through M4 tranches. Our hope is that the $51.8 million gets paid off more quickly than $121.8 in losses hit the pool so that we can have many months of collecting 100 percent of the cash coming in from pieces 5 and 6.

Based on the October 2008 numbers, we were in good shape, because while there were $18.9 million in losses, there were also $13.4 million in recoveries, most of which went to pieces 5 and 6 to pay down the tranche above ours. However, if the November and December trends of $12.5 million in losses and $4.4 million of recoveries continue, we will not do so well.

Even when the mezzanine tranches are wiped out, however, all is not lost for our tranche, because it has $310 million of protection beneath it in the IIA3 and IIA4 tranches, and only losses from pieces 5 and 6, not the entire pool, would be eroding the two tranches subordinate to ours. Once the IIA1 tranche above ours is paid off, the IIA2 tranche would start receiving 28.7 percent of the cash coming into pieces 5 and 6 (assuming no erosion of the IIA4 tranche): $125 \div (125 + 237 + 73)$.

Conclusion

We think there's a reasonable chance that the low recoveries in November and December 2008 were anomalies, driven by temporary actions by servicers. HASP will help keep some of the borrowers in this pool in their homes, but probably not very many, considering how low their FICO scores were and how far underwater nearly all of them are (the weighted average combined loan-to-value ratio at origination was 90 percent, the loans were written at the peak of the bubble, and more than half the houses are in California and Florida, where housing prices have collapsed more than 50 percent in many areas).

There are many variables to consider, but if we assume 6 percent monthly defaults, 3 percent annual prepayments, 70 percent severity on all mortgages that have already defaulted but have not yet been liquidated, and 75 percent severity for any currently performing mortgages that default, then we will earn approximately a 31 percent annualized cash return on this investment—less than what we had originally hoped for, but satisfactory nevertheless.

Chapter 11

An Introduction to Shorting

Before we dive into our analyses of two stocks we are short, allow us to give you some background and a warning: **For most people, we think shorting stocks is a very bad idea.**

Shorting a stock means betting that it will decline. To do so, you (or your broker) borrow a stock and immediately sell it. You keep the cash proceeds, but must eventually return the stock you borrowed to the lender. Your hope is that the stock will decline such that you can buy the stock back in the market at a lower price, return the shares to the lender, and pocket the profits.

For example, let's say you short 1,000 shares of a stock trading at $10. You receive $10,000. Then the stock falls to $6 and you decide to cover your short, so you buy the 1,000 shares back for $6,000 and keep a $4,000 profit. Note that since no stock can fall below zero, your profit is limited to the amount that you shorted.

The year 2008 was a marvelous time for shorting. It was like shooting fish in a barrel, as 95 percent of stocks declined, many by 90 percent or more. With the apparent ease of shorting and so much uncertainty about the market's future, perhaps you've considered shorting stocks to make money (or at least mitigate your losses) if the market continues to decline.

While it's an appealing idea, ultimately we believe it's a flawed one for most investors, especially today when stocks are so beaten down that a big rally is possible. Sure there are always a few stocks that make good shorts, but generally the best time to short is when markets are hitting highs and investors are confident and complacent, not a time like now when there's blood in the streets and expectations are low, when even a sliver of good news could send stocks soaring.

We believe there's no more easy money to be made on the short side, which is one of the reasons we have covered many of our shorts and have only two short case studies in this book (one of which, Wells Fargo, we now own, in fact). Some of our shorts, such as MBIA, we think are terminal—meaning that the stock will eventually go to zero—but most are not. In such cases, we are short the stock because of one or more company-specific or industry-specific issues, but if these issues are resolved or the stock price falls enough to fully reflect them, then we cover the position and move on. Sometimes, as in the cases of Wells Fargo or Fairfax Financial, we even end up buying a stock that we were once short.

Just as we warned in Chapter 6 about the mistake of falling in love with your stocks on the long side, it's equally important not to fall in love with your stocks on the short side. Any stock is a good long at a certain price and a good short at another price, so it's important to be disciplined about rationally assessing intrinsic value and selling or covering positions when they hit your price targets.

Isn't Shorting Evil?

Some people view short selling as something akin to flag burning. It's un-American to hope that a company stumbles and its stock plunges, right?

Some people even blame shorts for bringing down entire companies like Bear Stearns and Lehman Brothers. This is 99 percent nonsense (though we are certainly aware of occasional case in which short sellers behave badly, just as there are cases in which stocks are fraudulently pumped up). It's one reason we support reinstating the uptick rule, which means that a stock can be shorted only at a price higher than the previous trade. This prevents a wave of short selling from driving a stock price down. We question whether this happens very often—in our opinion, it's almost always waves of longs dumping their stock when they finally figure out a company is in trouble that drive the stock down; at that point, many short sellers are covering by buying the stock—but reinstating the uptick rule would remove all doubt.

Just as a healthy legal system needs both defense attorneys and prosecutors, healthy financial markets need people who will look at companies in a skeptical light, given that accountants, Wall Street analysts, and companies have such strong incentives to spin positive stories. Short sellers—and the handful of courageous journalists who cover them—are a valuable resource to regulators (hopefully going forward, anyway) as well as to savvy investors, even those who invest only on the long side. By reading and understanding the shorts' arguments, we have avoided or sold stocks that have subsequently declined significantly.

Famed short seller Jim Chanos of Kynikos Associates, when we interviewed him in *Value Investor Insight* in July 2005, commented on this:

> Short selling is now a lot more acceptable than it was, but it's still difficult. People question our motives and say things like "What's your vested interest? Aren't you saying that just because you expect the stock to go down?" Well, yeah ... don't people who are long say positive things because they think a stock's going to go up? We're held to a double standard sometimes, but I'm used to that.
>
> But the institutional client base understands short selling and why it's valuable. There's also been a significant amount of academic literature out in recent years about the need for it in efficient markets, which the SEC also talks about. Finally, in the last five years, in the face of all the brokerage firm and mutual fund scandals, the short sellers were among the few guys considered to be wearing white hats.[1]

Arguments against Short Selling

Shorting looked easy in 2008, but in reality it's a brutally tough business. In many ways, it appears to involve nothing more than applying the same analyses one uses when determining whether to buy a stock: On the long side, investors generally seek companies with good management, strong growth, high margins and returns on capital, little or no debt, clean balance sheets, and sustainable competitive advantages—all at a low price. Conversely, short sellers look for weak or dishonest management; low or negative growth, margins, and returns on capital; high and increasing debt, accounts receivable, and inventory; and weak competitive advantages—all at a ridiculously high price.

But shorting is not simply the opposite of long investing. It's much harder and more dangerous for a number of reasons:

- Your upside is capped and your downside is unlimited—precisely the opposite of long positions. When shorting stocks, you could be right 80 percent of the time, but the losses from the 20 percent of the time that you're wrong could exceed the accumulated profits. Worse yet, a once-a-century storm like the bursting of the Internet bubble might wipe you out entirely. If there's even a 1 percent annual risk of such an event, that tiny risk translates into a 39.5 percent chance of the freak event occurring over 50 years.

- To prevent such an occurrence, most short sellers use stop loss limits, meaning they will start covering the short if it runs against them a certain amount. This means short sellers have to be right not only about a stock, but also about the timing. If a stock rises significantly, many short sellers will lock in losses, even if they may later be proven correct.

- In order to short a stock, you first must borrow it from your broker, who has the power to call in the stock you've borrowed at any time—or, worse yet, buy stock to cover for you. Brokers are most likely to do these things if the stock is rising quickly, and they're probably doing it to other short sellers as well at the same time, so all of this buying pressure can cause a stock to rise even further, triggering even more covering. This vicious circle is called a "short squeeze," and it isn't pretty—we can show you our scars.

- Shorting has gotten much more competitive. There are now a few thousand hedge funds (and who knows how many individual investors) looking for the same handful of good shorts, in contrast to a few dozen a couple of decades ago. This results in crowded shorts, increasing the odds of a short squeeze.

- A short squeeze can also be created if the float—the number of shares that trade freely—is suddenly reduced. Such a case occurred in October 2008 when Porsche, which owned 35 percent of Volkswagen, unexpectedly disclosed that it had raised its stake in Volkswagen to 74.1 percent through the use of derivatives. The German state of Lower Saxony, where Volkswagen is based, owned 20 percent, so that left a float of only about 5 percent of VW shares on the market. Three popular hedge fund trades had been (1) to short VW based on weakening car demand, (2) to go long Porsche and short out its ownership of VW to "create" only Porsche, or (3) to go long VW preferred stock and short the common stock, betting on the relative underperformance of the common. In any case, for whatever reason, nearly 13 percent of all VW common shares were short, so moments after Porsche announced its higher stake, the mother of all short squeezes ensued and the stock quintupled from $200 to over $1,000, momentarily making VW the most valuable company in the world. This was extraordinarily painful for many shorts.
- Short sellers used to earn interest on the cash they held while they were short a stock, but this has all but disappeared due to low interest rates—and brokers even charge "negative rebates" on hard-to-borrow stocks, meaning that short sellers have to pay 5 percent, 10 percent, 15 percent, or more in annual interest to borrow the stock.
- The long-term upward trend of the market works against you (yes, believe it or not, markets used to go up most of the time).
- Gains are taxed at the highest, short-term rate.
- It generally requires many more investment decisions, thereby increasing the chances of making a serious mistake.
- It's a short-term, high-stress, trading-oriented style of investing that requires constant oversight.
- Mistakes hurt your portfolio more as they compound. If you make a mistake with a long position, it becomes a smaller percentage of your portfolio as it drops. A mistaken short, however, grows larger as it appreciates.

It's no wonder famed short seller Joe Feshbach wrote in early 2006 in a column for *Value Investor Insight*, "The landscape is littered with the carcasses of short-only funds that never made money, while long-term winners are about as numerous as those in the airline industry."[2]

So Why Do We Short?

In light of all of this, why do we short? The answer is easy today because shorting has been so profitable for the past year-and-a-half or so it has literally kept us in business, given the poor performance of our long portfolio.

But it wasn't an easy answer in early 2006, as we had done nothing but lose money shorting stocks for three consecutive years. In the January 2006 issue of *Value Investor Insight*, we published the following column:[3]

Bear Necessities

Given how our bearish bets have performed in the past couple of years, we've asked ourselves why we bother betting on the downside at all. Here's why.

Given the long-term upward trend in equity prices and frequent bouts of excessive investor optimism—"Markets can remain irrational longer than you can remain solvent," John Maynard Keynes once warned—one might ask why make bearish bets at all. This question is particularly relevant to us given the money we've lost in this area over the past couple of years.

After carefully studying our experience, we're not swearing off negative bets for two main reasons: First, we still think we can make money on them. In addition, they remain a great tool for hedging against risk. That said, some refinements in our strategy are in order as we learn from our mistakes.

Be Specific

Two years ago we became convinced that the technology sector in general—and semiconductor stocks in particular—had become significantly overvalued. Following its nearly 80% decline from March 10, 2000 through October 9, 2002, the

Nasdaq had rallied dramatically, rising 80% from its 2002 low through the end of 2003. We were amazed to see the froth returning to the very stocks that had obliterated investors only a couple of years earlier and believed that, across the technology sector, the fundamentals did not remotely support the stock prices.

Rather than shorting or buying puts on individual tech stocks, we felt the best way to profit from the perceived overvaluation was to buy puts on two baskets of stocks: the Nasdaq-100 Trust [QQQQ] and Semiconductor HOLDRS [SMH]. While we might not understand many of the companies that make up these baskets well enough to make a bearish investment, we believed, in aggregate, that these indices were sure to decline materially.

Initially, our investment worked well as the Nasdaq-100 and SMH were down more than 12% and 30%, respectively, over the first seven-and-a-half months we held them. Alas, we weren't clever enough to take our profits and instead held as both indices rallied through the end of 2005. Of course, the passage of time was also eroding the value of the puts. We sold these positions at a loss late last year and don't plan to reinitiate them.

We made two mistakes here: First, we strayed outside our circle of competence—always a bad idea—and tried to compensate by buying a basket of stocks. Second, for us, a basket is a poor way to express an investment opinion, bullish or bearish. Our advantage as investors is detailed, bottom-up stock research, and we give up much of that advantage when we invest in a basket. Assuming we sufficiently understand at least certain companies within a sector, we will almost certainly be better off buying or shorting the most undervalued or overvalued stocks in the sector rather than investing in a basket. . . .

While we've abandoned making bearish bets on baskets as a way to make money, we still use puts on such indices as the S&P 500 and Russell 2000 for hedging because: (1) it reduces risk, defined as the permanent loss of capital; (2) in the event of a major correction, it will provide us with substantial cash to invest at bargain prices, thereby enhancing returns; and (3) it allows us to remain invested in certain stocks we otherwise might sell prematurely, which should also enhance returns.

Hedging 80-Cent Dollars

The last point warrants further discussion. Like many value investors, we tend to sell our winners much too early. Because we're so conservative, our estimates of intrinsic value are usually low and, even if they aren't, the market often tends to push our winners far above intrinsic value—at least for a time. There are few things more annoying than buying a stock at $10, selling it from $15 to $20 and then watching it go to $50.

Here's an example of how we've hedged one of our favorite positions to avoid selling too soon—and why we don't regret losing money on the hedging so far: We think McDonald's [MCD, $35.78] is easily worth $40 per share, based on a 16x multiple of the $2.50 per share of free cash flow we think the company can earn in the not-too-distant future. When the stock hit $32 in late 2004—having risen steadily from a low of around $12 in March 2003, when we last purchased it—it was, in our opinion, the proverbial 80-cent dollar.

In the past we might have sold and locked in our gains, but this would have triggered big taxes and, more importantly, denied us the healthy long-term compounding we expect from this stock over many years to come. Instead we bought long-dated puts on the S&P 500, which we felt were very attractively priced, with a notional value proportional to our holdings in McDonald's. In this way, we could hedge our McDonald's position against the possibility of a substantial market decline, yet still benefit from the upside of an undervalued stock that we believed was highly likely to outperform the S&P 500 over time.

So what has happened? The S&P 500 has risen, volatility has fallen and time has elapsed, all of which have caused the S&P

500 put position to decline. Multiply this across a number of positions and it's easy to see how this strategy lost us a lot of money.

Is hedging 80-cent dollars—when the cost of hedging is at or near all-time lows—the wrong strategy? We don't believe so. Buying insurance always looks wrong in hindsight when the event you insured against doesn't happen. But the fact that our home didn't burn down last year doesn't mean we're upset that we lost 100% of our "investment" in our home insurance policy—and it doesn't keep us from renewing our policy.

Capital preservation is far more important to us than keeping up with the S&P 500 over short time periods. We do believe, however, that we erred somewhat in how we sized our "insurance" policies—in essence, we took a good idea and overdid it. All of our index put positions tended to move together, so we effectively had more insurance than we needed. This served us well during the down months of 2005, but cost us for the year as a whole. In addition, our buying of at-the-money puts was, in hindsight, a mistake. We're not trying to hedge against modest 5–10% declines, but against a much larger correction, so we've recently been buying 10% out-of-the-money puts. Finally, our macro concerns lessened our confidence in our long stock positions more than they should have. We're still hedging our 80-cent dollars, but at what we now think are more appropriate levels.

Our January 2006 column also contained a table with a list of seven stocks we were short at that time. Table 11.1 reproduces the table, with two columns added: the stock price as of March 6, 2009, and the percentage change since we published our column.

More than three years later, we are still short Farmer Mac (the first stock we ever shorted), MBIA, Planar, and Research in Motion, and are now long Fairfax Financial. We actually did better on these stocks than the table indicates, because we added aggressively to our MBIA short and covered our Fairfax short for a nice gain, changed our minds about the company and its management, bought it more than a year later, and profited on the rebound.

Table 11.1   Stocks We Were Short in January 2006

Company	Ticker	Price 1/30/06	Price 3/6/09	% Change
Fairfax Financial	FFH	$151.10	$227.38	50%
Farmer Mac	AGM	$ 28.50	$ 2.48	−91%
MBIA	MBI	$ 62.68	$ 2.53	−96%
OmniVision	OVTI	$ 25.22	$ 6.65	−74%
Palm	PALM	$ 36.47	$ 6.15	−83%
Planar Systems	PLNR	$ 13.25	$ 0.50	−96%
Research in Motion	RIMM	$ 22.27	$ 36.34	63%
Average:				−47%

Originally published in *Value Investor Insight*, 1/28/06.

Good Places to Short

We hope we've dissuaded you from shorting, but if we haven't, we'd like to share some advice that Jim Chanos gave when we interviewed him in 2005 about the categories for his best short ideas:[4]

What are the broad categories your ideas tend to fall into?

JC: The first and most lucrative are the booms that go bust. We've had our most success with debt-financed asset bubbles—as opposed to just plain asset bubbles—where there are ticking time bombs in terms of debt needing to be repaid, and where there are people ahead of the shareholders in the bankruptcy or workout process. The "debt-financed" distinction is important. It kept us from shorting the Internet in the 90s—that was a valuation bubble more than anything else.

A classic example here was the commercial real estate bubble in the late 1980s. More recently was the bursting of the telecom bubble. We made a lot of money on that—much more than on Enron, for which we get so much credit. We looked at a company like Lucent and discovered to our amazement that they were essentially financing their whole business through venture-capital investing in start-ups. They'd invest in a start-up, which would then take the equity money it got from Lucent to use it as a down payment for Lucent equipment. So Lucent would book a 10-year revenue commitment, backed by a very non-credit-worthy set of receivables, when no net new money had changed hands.

Speaking of potential asset bubbles, what's your take on the residential housing market today?

JC: We've watched with amazement as this has played out, but we're not short the homebuilders because they're getting their money out. By and large, it's the consumer who is leveraged and is going to be the patsy. When prices adjust, the effects are going to be very broad, but not as specific to companies as we'd like to see as short sellers. Other than a pause in homebuilders' activity levels, we don't see most of them being in financial distress. . . .

What's the second broad category in which you've found good ideas?

JC: Technological obsolescence. Economists talk quite rightly about the benefits of "creative destruction," where new technologies and innovations advance mankind and grow GDPs. But such changes also render whole industries obsolete. Disruptive technologies have two sides and always have. You saw it in the 1980s as personal computers wiped out the word-processor and minicomputer markets.

What's playing out now is the transformation from an analog to a digital world. While that's created great fortunes like Google's, it's also wiping out whole businesses. Traditional music retailing was one of the first to start going. Then came the ongoing problems in video rental. My value-investor friends buying Blockbuster are completely wrong. Studios selling DVDs directly through outlets like Wal-Mart is killing video rental, before we even talk about the rise of video-on-demand or piracy. . . .

Many of your past big winners have involved account-ing irregularities. Is that still a fruitful area for you?

JC: No question. This can run the gamut from simple over-statement of earnings, often a gray area, to outright fraud. We're trying to find cases where the economic reality is significantly divorced from the accounting presentation of the business. It's not GE managing earnings—everybody does that. We want to see something way beyond that, where management is going out of its way to mislead.

It could be the hiding of losses in offshore subsidiaries like Enron. It could be abusing mark-to-market accounting like Baldwin-United and many others. It could be Boston Chicken, a big winner for us in the 1990s, lending money to franchisees to cover losses and not reserving for the receivables.

The biggest abuse in accounting today, often legally, is in acquisition accounting. This is still wide open to manage-ment estimates for things like writing down assets, writing up liabilities and setting reserves. Often the target company, right before a purchase, is instructed to withhold sales and front-end expenses. Tyco was a master of that. Suddenly, right after the acquisition, things would look wildly accretive, but it was very misleading. When you get on that treadmill, you have to do bigger and bigger acquisitions to keep the game going.

Another general area in which there's a real propensity for abuse is any case where companies are making long-term assumptions about the value of assets and have the ability to book them immediately into profits. We scrutinize that very carefully. . . .

Are there specific metrics you look for that signal prob-lems with the numbers?

JC: Managements have gotten so good at playing Wall Street that I've actually become more skeptical of the metrics they want you to focus on. For example, when people would question the earnings at Tyco, former management would say "There can't be anything wrong with earnings, just look at our cash flow."

It turns out that just about every cash-flow lever possible was being gamed at Tyco. Capital spending never seemed to grow, until you looked at the footnotes on future contingencies and saw they were calling everything operating leases that never showed up in the capital spending.

Any other broad categories where you find good ideas?

JC: The last big one would be consumer fads. This is when investors—typically retail investors—use recent experience to extrapolate *ad infinitum* into the future what is clearly a one-time growth ramp of a product. People are consistently way too optimistic and underestimate just how competitive the U.S. economy is in these types of things: Cabbage Patch Kids in the 1980s, NordicTrack in the early 1990s and, more recently, Salton with the George Foreman grills.

We're short Palm right now, based on the Treo Smartphone. It's a nifty product, but that's all they have. They lose money on their PDAs. And you have Samsung, Nokia, Sony Ericsson and everybody looking to have their own product like the Treo. The biggest problem is that Palm doesn't control the Treo software—it's just a box. Boxes with chips in them tend to be very good shorts if that's all they are. . . .

Before we turn to our analysis of MBIA and Wells Fargo, we'll again repeat that, especially in this environment, **for most people, we think shorting stocks is a very bad idea.**

Chapter 12

A Case of
Questionable Reserves

Case Study: MBIA Inc

We've been short MBIA's stock for the better part of the past six years, very publicly for most of this period, warning anyone who would listen about the many dangers we saw. For the first four years, we looked quite foolish as the stock roughly doubled to above $70, but since then it has collapsed to around $5 as of late March 2009.

We believe the stock is terminal—meaning we think it will be worthless—so we have added to our short position as the stock has declined, and on occasion bounces, and have little interest in covering our position even at today's depressed levels. **However, we do not recommend shorting MBIA stock at this price.** There is a scenario—not a likely one, but a possibility—that the company could be successful in walling off its toxic liabilities, in which case the stock could rise manyfold, crushing shorts. This is an extremely complex situation and must be followed carefully. The reason we're using it as a case study is *not* because it's our favorite short idea at this time and price, but because we believe our analysis of it will teach our readers much about the risks of both highly leveraged financial companies and bubble-era mortgage-backed structured finance products.

History

MBIA insures bonds. Specifically, its core business since its inception in 1973 has been insuring domestic municipal bonds (in fact, the company used to be known as Municipal Bond Insurance Association). Few municipalities are AAA rated, as MBIA was until 2008, so to lower interest costs and make it easier to sell their debt offerings, municipalities paid MBIA to insure their bonds, thereby making them AAA rated. This was a stable, profitable, steadily growing, minimal-loss business that MBIA used to dominate, achieving a 42.4 percent market share in 1997.

Because of its apparent profitability, however, the business of insuring muni bonds became much more competitive over time and MBIA's market share fell steadily. Despite this dramatic loss of share in its core business, however, until 2007 MBIA continued to grow its earnings, book value, and premiums at its historic low-teens to mid-teens rate.

How was this possible? Simply because MBIA aggressively began insuring a wide range of bonds backed by subprime loans on new and used autos, aircraft leases and equipment trusts, credit card receivables, investor-owned utilities, health care equipment financing, student loans, emerging market CDOs, credit default swaps, and, most ominously, structured finance products based on U.S. mortgages like residential mortgage-backed securities (RMBSs) and collateralized debt obligations (CDOs). In 1990, MBIA hadn't guaranteed a single structured finance product, but by the end of 2008 it had over $200 billion of exposure, equal to 25.8 percent of its total insured portfolio.

Any time a company materially changes its business, there is a significant chance of something going wrong because of execution risk, unfamiliarity with the new lines of business, and so forth. The potential downside should any of these risks materialize is, of course, magnified dramatically in the case of a highly leveraged financial institution like MBIA. As MBIA has discovered, there are vast differences between municipal bonds and structured finance products. The domestic public finance business has been around for a long time, so it can be modeled with a reasonable degree of accuracy, and MBIA successfully participated in the market for decades. In marked contrast, the structured finance products Wall Street was peddling during the housing bubble were relatively recent creations with risks that were unknown to MBIA (and, as we now know, to the rating agencies who misrated them, the banks that sold them, the regulators that failed to regulate them, and the institutional investors that bought them).

MBIA is a classic story of a company stretching to continue its long-accustomed growth by getting into areas it had no business being in—and the company and its shareholders have paid a terrible price. As the housing bubble burst and the credit crunch hit with full force, MBIA suffered blow after blow, including multiple rating downgrades and losses that crushed book value per share from $53.43 at the end of 2006 to $4.78 only two years later.

MBIA's Business Model

MBIA's business model is to collect a small amount of money up front (insurance premiums) in exchange for a promise to pay potentially large but unlikely-to-occur losses in the future—in most cases, decades into the future. The best analogy for this business model is picking up pennies in front of a steamroller—it's nicely profitable until something goes wrong, and then . . . *splat!*

This is a very different type of business model from, for instance, an auto insurer like GEICO, which collects premiums up front to insure a car for a certain period (generally six to twelve months), so it knows almost exactly what its losses will be within a short period of time. In contrast, nobody—not MBIA, its investors, its regulators, or anyone else—can estimate with any degree of precision whatsoever what its losses might be decades from now on an insurance policy sold today. Given that losses (claims) are an insurance company's primary expense (this is especially true at MBIA, which, at its peak, had only about 500 employees), this presents an accounting conundrum: What does an insurance company report for earnings when it doesn't know what its costs will be?

The answer for all companies, not just insurers, is that they must estimate what their losses will be and recognize them at the same time they recognize the associated premium revenue. But for a handful of companies like MBIA, where there is a very long time between collecting the money and paying out claims, and where the amount of the ultimate claims is so uncertain, management has *enormous* leeway to estimate losses. The enormity of this leeway is matched only by the incentives to estimate minimal losses, thereby inflating profits, capital levels, and, of course, the share price. Imagine the incentives for a CEO to write risky new lines of business and set aside inadequate reserves; in the short run, profits would soar and it's very likely that long before anyone realized the onerous consequences of these reckless and irresponsible actions, the CEO would have long since cashed in his stock options and retired.

This is pretty much what happened to MBIA. It turns out that the company was massively underreserved, and the combination of actual payouts and credit impairments against expected future payouts has crushed book value by more than 90 percent. In an ironic twist, the longtime CEO, who had indeed earned a bundle and retired before the stock collapsed from losses on business written under his watch, is now back as CEO, trying to save the company (and his reputation).

We highlight these risk factors because we think they apply not only to MBIA, but also to many other companies, so investors need to be very cautious when investing in companies with business models like MBIA's.

Good Bank/Bad Bank

Before we share our analysis of MBIA's likely losses, we need to explain a recent restructuring of the company undertaken by management, which, if it stands, could change our analysis dramatically. MBIA has effectively been in a runoff mode for quite some time, having written "minimal new business in 2008," according to its Q4 2008 earnings release. In an attempt to get back into business, MBIA announced on February 18, 2009, that it was creating a separate public finance bond insurance company called National Public Finance Guarantee Corporation or simply National, which caused the stock to pop 30 percent for a day before it continued its tumble. Figure 12.1 shows MBIA's new structure.

MBIA Inc. is the public holding company, so when investors buy MBIA's stock, this is the entity they own a stake in. Its primary asset and source of revenues is MBIA Insurance Corporation (MBIA Corp.), its regulated insurance subsidiary. This is the entity that writes the insurance—at least it used to when it had an AAA rating—and then it upstreams (dividends) its profits to MBIA Inc.

To capitalize National, MBIA Inc. took $2.1 billion in cash from MBIA Corp. and transferred it to the new entity. In addition, according to MBIA's Q4 2008 investor presentation, "MBIA Corp. reinsured $554 billion net par of domestic public finance business to National" and noted that "$2.89 billion of net UPR [unearned premium reserves], less ceding commission, and loss reserves transferred to National."

In other words, MBIA Inc. took $554 billion of par insured of MBIA Corp.'s good business, *plus* $2.1 billion in cash *plus* another $2.89 billion in cash reflecting prepaid premiums by muni policyholders, leaving MBIA Corp. with virtually all of the riskiest assets, yet 41 percent fewer claims-paying resources ($8.8 billion vs. $15.0 billion), as shown in Table 12.1.

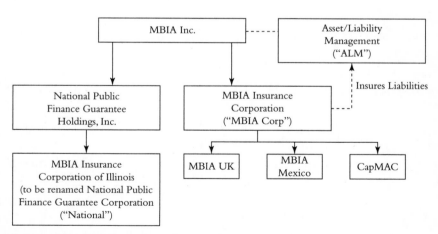

Figure 12.1   MBIA Inc. Partial Organizational Chart
SOURCE: MBIA Q4 2008 investor presentation, March 3, 2009, p. 35.

Table 12.1 Summary of MBIA Corp.'s Claims-Paying Resources as of December 31, 2008

(in millions)	Actual	Pro Forma	
	MBIA Corp.	**MBIA Corp.**	**National**
Capital and surplus	$ 3,503	$3,087	$ 416
Contingency reserve	$ 2,596	$1,238	$1,357
Capital Base	**$ 6,098**	**$4,325**	**$1,773**
Unearned premium reserve	$ 4,170	$ 691	$3,479
Present value of installment premiums	$ 2,386	$2,088	$ 298
Premium resources	$ 6,556	$2,779	$3,777
Loss and LAE* reserves	$ 1,871	$1,692	$ 179
Soft capital credit facilities	$ 450	—†	—
Total Claims-Paying Resources	**$14,975**	**$8,796**	**$5,729**

SOURCE: MBIA Q4 2008 investor presentation, March 3, 2009, p. 41.
*Loss adjustment expense.
†Does not include $450 million soft capital facility covering net insured losses on U.S. public finance policies that remain with MBIA Corp.

Figures 12.2 and 12.3 break down the insured portfolios of National and the remainder of MBIA Corp., highlighting the fact that MBIA gave the former all of its good businesses, while leaving the latter with the toxic sludge.

What MBIA is trying to do (while vehemently denying it[1]) is analogous to a good bank/bad bank model, which companies often try to undertake when saddled with big losses in one area. The idea is to split into two and wall off the good businesses from the liabilities of the bad business. While many companies contemplate such a plan, it rarely happens (notable exceptions being First National Bank of Houston and Mellon Bank of Pittsburgh in 1988).

MBIA cleverly tiptoed around the issue of whether MBIA Corp.'s policyholders can come after National's profits and assets if the former's losses exceed its claims-paying assets. Here's what CEO Jay Brown wrote in his February 18, 2009 letter to shareholders:

> Our U.S. public finance policyholders need to know that our municipal business will operate as a separate entity and will not subsidize our structured business—this split formalizes our commitment. Our structured finance policyholders should also feel

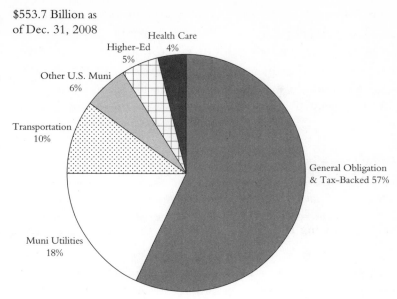

Figure 12.2 Breakdown of Insured Portfolio of National
Source: MBIA Q4 2008 investor presentation, March 3, 2009, p. 41.

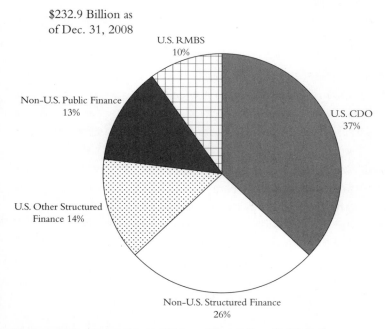

Figure 12.3 Breakdown of Insured Portfolio of MBIA Corp.
Source: MBIA Q4 2008 investor presentation, March 3, 2009, p. 41.

very comfortable that their policies remain in an entity with ample claims-paying resources to meet any expected claims, even under our stress loss scenarios. It is also important to note that, in the process of securing our transformation, we hired outside advisors while our regulator did its own background work, and both came to the same conclusion: that we would continue to have the resources to pay all expected claims as they come due.[2]

Brown tried his best to leave the impression that National is walled off from MBIA Corp.'s possible losses, but he didn't explicitly say this—and if he could have, he surely would have.

If MBIA is successful in walling off National, doing it would be wonderful for the executives and shareholders of the holding company, as they would essentially walk away from the consequences of their disastrous miscalculations in the structured finance area and get a do-over, starting a clean, well-capitalized new bond insurer in an environment that is very favorable now because many competitors have gone out of business.

The problem is that, in our opinion, this plan is a breach of what MBIA Inc. promised the policyholders and debt holders of MBIA Corp. and could be overturned by a court (though MBIA's regulator approved it[3]). MBIA's business relies on trust: It pockets up-front payments in exchange for long-term promises to policyholders who are buying the insurance only because they believe it's backed by all of the assets of the company. Now that unexpected losses have hit, is it right for management to take $5 billion out of MBIA Corp. and leave the policyholders who remain without this money? What about the buyers of the surplus notes, $1 billion of debt that MBIA Corp. sold to investors in January 2008? That $5 billion of cash isn't there to support them, either. (Even if MBIA gets away with this plan, it certainly raises the question of who would buy insurance from National, which is run by the same people who behaved in this fashion toward their previous policyholders.)

If MBIA Corp. does not end up having sufficient resources to pay claims due to the losses from the billions of dollars of structured finance guarantees on its books—which we and the market, based on where the stock has been trading, think is very likely—we suspect many policyholders will sue based on laws against "fraudulent transfer" (also known as "fraudulent conveyance"), which *Black's Law Dictionary* defines as:

A transfer of property for little or no consideration, made for the purpose of hindering or delaying a creditor by putting the property beyond the creditor's reach; a transaction by which the owner of real or personal property seeks to place the property beyond the reach of creditors.[4]

Indeed, on March 11, 2009, two hedge funds that owned securities guaranteed by MBIA, which had dropped dramatically in value after MBIA announced its good bank/bad bank plan, filed a class action lawsuit calling MBIA's actions a "looting" and accusing MBIA of:

> . . . a massive fraudulent conveyance transaction engaged in by the MBIA Defendants in breach of their covenant of good faith and fair dealing with their financial guaranty policyholders. . . . In this transaction, . . . the MBIA Defendants stripped over $5.4 billion of assets from MBIA Insurance, in a calculated and cynical effort to enrich structurally junior economic stakeholders of the parent company, MBIA Inc., including its senior executives and shareholders, while leaving some $241 billion of policyholders stranded in a denuded insurer that will be unable to meet its obligations as they come due.[5]

The plaintiffs also pointed out that MBIA could have restructured the company by putting National beneath MBIA Corp. (rather than beneath a holding company), such that its profits would flow first to MBIA Corp. and then, if MBIA Corp. were sufficiently capitalized, through to MBIA Inc. The only scenario by which management would be worse off under this alternative structure is if MBIA Corp.'s reserves turn out to be insufficient. Thus, management's actions speak volumes, as the plaintiffs note:

> The motivation for this choice could not be clearer—MBIA Inc. seeks to benefit its shareholders, bondholders, and senior executives by diverting value that would otherwise be needed to pay the policyholders stranded at MBIA Insurance. This choice of structure belies all pretense by MBIA Inc. that MBIA Insurance is solvent. . . . Plainly, MBIA Inc. was not prepared to run the risk of such an insolvency—preferring to shift it instead solely to the policyholders left behind at MBIA Insurance.

A final interesting point: Even if MBIA's plan succeeds, it might not save the holding company, because its debt has cross-default provisions with MBIA Corp. such that if the latter is taken over by regulators or deemed insolvent, the holding company debt defaults.

All of this is moot, of course, if we're wrong about how large the losses will be in MBIA's portfolio, so let's take a look at this issue.

Areas of Losses

We focus our analysis on the structured finance products that MBIA guaranteed, but before we turn to this we want to highlight that National may face real losses over time. Historically, the muni bond business has been almost a zero loss business, but as Warren Buffett pointed out in his 2008 annual letter to Berkshire Hathaway shareholders, that might change drastically in the future:

> Local governments are going to face *far* tougher fiscal problems in the future than they have to date. The pension liabilities I talked about in last year's report will be a huge contributor to these woes. Many cities and states were surely horrified when they inspected the status of their funding at year-end 2008. The gap between assets and a realistic actuarial valuation of present liabilities is simply staggering. . . .
>
> . . . Insuring tax-exempts, therefore, has the look today of a dangerous business—one with similarities, in fact, to the insuring of natural catastrophes. In both cases, a string of loss-free years can be followed by a devastating experience that more than wipes out all earlier profits. We will try, therefore, to proceed carefully in this business, eschewing many classes of bonds that other monolines [bond insurers] regularly embrace.[6]

That said, our investment thesis on MBIA doesn't depend on a dime of losses in the muni business, so let's turn our attention to the structured finance business, in particular to MBIA's exposures to RMBSs and CDOs, which we break down in Table 12.2.

We can see that MBIA has $124.9 billion of exposure to CDOs of various types and $31.8 billion of exposure to five different types of RMBSs—a total of $156.7 billion of exposure to highly risky assets,

Table 12.2 MBIA's Exposure to CDOs and RMBSs

	Exposure (Bn)	Impairments Taken (Bn)
CDO Exposure:		
CDOs of high-grade U.S. ABSs	$ 14.5	$0.6
CDOs of mezzanine U.S. ABSs	$ 2.7	$0.1
CDO-squareds	$ 8.3	$0.5
Other multisector CDOs	$ 2.2	$0.0
Inv. grade and structured corp. credit	$ 39.4	$0.0
High yield corporate	$ 12.7	$0.0
CMBS and commercial real estate	$ 44.9	$0.0
Emerging market	$ 0.2	$0.0
Total CDO	**$124.9**	**$1.2**
RMBS Exposure:		
Prime first lien	$ 8.2	
Alt-A first lien	$ 3.4	
Subprime first lien	$ 4.0	
HELOC	$ 7.5	
Closed-end second lien	$ 8.7	
Total RMBS	**$ 31.8**	**$2.1**
Grand Total	**$156.7**	**$3.3**

SOURCE: MBIA 2008 10-K and Q4 2008 investor presentation.

against which it has taken a mere $3.3 billion of impairments. Before we proceed with our analysis, which shows that MBIA's losses will likely be exponentially higher than what the company is admitting to, allow us to explain the structure of a CDO.

Structure of a CDO

In Chapter 10, we analyzed one RMBS in great depth. RMBSs were a money machine for Wall Street, as we explained in Chapter 2, but there was a problem: It was easy to sell the AAA-rated tranches to the institutional investors of the world and to sell the lower-rated, high-yielding tranches to hedge funds and other yield-seeking investors (also known as "yield whores" because they'd sell their mothers for an extra 50 basis points of yield), but the BBB and A tranches were harder to sell because they didn't have a high-enough interest rate to attract the yield-seeking investors, yet had a low-enough rating that institutional investors weren't interested, either.

The solution: a CDO, which is structured just like an RMBS, but instead of owning actual loans, *it owns tranches of other asset-backed securities* like RMBSs. As Table 12.2 shows, there are many different types of CDOs, just as there are many different types of asset-backed securities, because Wall Street securitizes many different types of debt: not just mortgages, but also credit card debt, student loans, auto loans, corporate debt, commercial real estate, and so forth. Our analysis of MBIA will focus on CDOs that are comprised of tranches from RMBSs.

Figure 12.4 shows what a typical mezzanine CDO looks like, comprised nearly entirely of BBB-rated tranches (a CDO comprised mostly of A-rated tranches is known as a high-grade CDO—that name will go down in the oxymoron hall of fame).

Note that the CDO is comprised of low-rated tranches, yet the rating agencies were willing to give as much as 95 percent of a typical CDO an AAA rating (we're not making this up). Voilà! Nearly all of a collection of low-rated, barely investment-grade tranches from RMBS pools were turned into an AAA-rated product that could easily be sold.

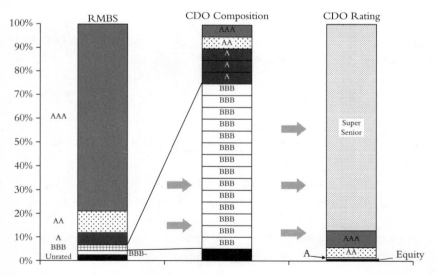

Figure 12.4   Structure of a Typical RMBS and CDO
SOURCE: T2 Partners.

Thanks to the magic of Wall Street alchemy and the foolishness and/or corruption of the rating agencies, turds were turned into gold.

CDOs are second-derivative products, which makes them highly leveraged and unstable. Because the tranches that comprise a CDO are usually very thin—each are a mere 1 to 3 percentage points of the underlying RMBS—they are likely to suffer either 0 percent losses or 100 percent losses. And if the RMBSs whose tranches comprise the CDO are correlated, as is the case with bubble-era U.S. mortgage pools, then the CDO is likely to have only one of two outcomes: Either the underlying RMBSs perform well enough such that the BBB and A tranches are protected, in which case the CDO will likely suffer almost no losses, or the RMBSs deteriorate to a point where the BBB and A tranches are wiped out, in which case the CDO is as well.

MBIA's RMBS Exposure

Let's turn our attention first to MBIA's RMBS exposure. As noted earlier, MBIA had $31.8 billion of exposure to RMBSs at the end of 2008, broken down by sector and vintage in Figure 12.5.

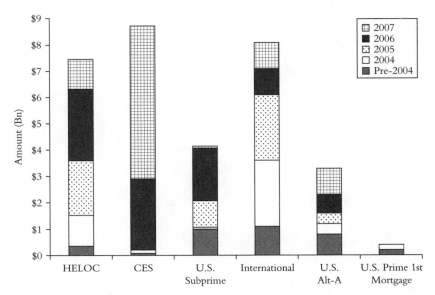

Figure 12.5 MBIA RMBS Exposure, Sector, and Vintage Composition
SOURCE: MBIA Q4 2008 investor presentation, March 3, 2009, p. 25.

Figure 12.5 provides a number of key pieces of information. First, note the adverse selection of which MBIA was a victim. The Wall Street firms knew that their U.S. prime first mortgage pools would likely perform well, so they didn't bother paying MBIA to guarantee them—hence, the tiny bar on the right of Figure 12.5. Instead, they paid MBIA to guarantee only their riskiest pools of home equity lines of credit (HELOCs), closed-end second liens (CESs), subprime, international, and Alt-A loans.

Also, note that more than half of MBIA's RMBS exposure consists of HELOCs and closed-end second mortgages, which cause particularly onerous losses because upon default the lender has no collateral to seize (like a house), so severities can exceed 100 percent. MBIA agrees with our 100 percent severity assumption, noting in its 2008 10-K (page 55) that "we assumed that all defaulted [HELOC and CES] loans will result in a total loss of principal." As we highlighted in Chapter 4, HELOCs and CESs are now defaulting at catastrophic rates, especially the 2005–2007 vintages, as was shown in Figure 4.28.

Unfortunately for MBIA, the significant majority of the HELOC and CES pools it has guaranteed are filled with mortgages from precisely the wrong mortgage companies (in descending order, Countrywide, ResCap, and IndyMac) that were written at precisely the wrong time (2005 to 2007), as shown in Table 12.3.

In particular, consider that two-thirds of MBIA's CES exposure ($5.8 billion) is of 2007 vintage, and then recall Figure 4.29, which showed an Ambac-guaranteed 2007-vintage CES pool that is likely to lose well over 80 percent of its value. In its Q4 2008 investor presentation,

Table 12.3   Vintage of HELOC and CES RMBSs Guaranteed by MBIA

Year	HELOC % of Total	CES % of Total
2007	15.2%	66.7%
2006	36.7%	30.9%
2005	27.7%	0.0%
2004 and prior	20.4%	2.4%

SOURCE: MBIA 10-K 2008, p. 85.

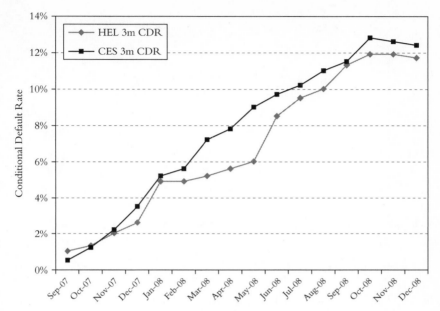

Figure 12.6   Conditional Default Rate for HELOCs and CESs
SOURCE: MBIA Q4 2008 investor presentation, March 3, 2009, p. 25.

MBIA presented Figure 12.6, which shows that HELOCs and CESs (it's not clear if this data is for what MBIA has guaranteed or for all HELOCs and CESs) are seeing steep increases in defaults: as of December 2008, both had conditional default rates (CDRs) of 12 to 13 percent, meaning that roughly 1 percent of the loans are defaulting every month—less than the Ambac-guaranteed pool shown in Figure 4.29, but catastrophic nevertheless.

MBIA has already paid out well over $1 billion in claims on its HELOC and CES exposure, as shown in Figure 12.7.

As noted earlier, MBIA has taken only $2.1 billion of impairments against its RMBS exposure, or 6.6 percent of the $31.8 billion total. While MBIA hasn't revealed enough information about its exposures in this area for us to know for sure, our knowledge of how virtually all bubble-era RMBS pools are performing leads us to conclude that MBIA's actual losses will be many multiples of the *de minimis* impairments it has taken to date.

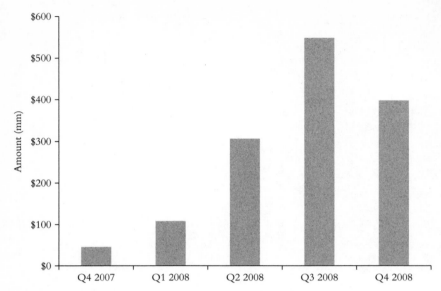

Figure 12.7   HELOC and CES Claims Paid by MBIA, by Quarter
SOURCE: MBIA 10-Qs, 10-Ks, and conference calls, Q4 2007 to Q4 2008.

Table 12.4   MBIA's CDO Exposure and Impairments Taken

	Exposure (Bn)	Impairments Taken (Bn)
CDOs of high-grade U.S. ABSs	$14.5	$0.6
CDOs of mezzanine U.S. ABSs	$ 2.7	$0.1
CDO-squareds	$ 8.3	$0.5
Total	**$25.5**	**$1.2**

SOURCE: MBIA 2008 10-K.

MBIA's CDO Exposure

As noted earlier, MBIA has $124.9 billion of exposure to CDOs and has taken $1.2 billion of impairments, all against its $25.5 billion on multisector CDO exposure, broken down as shown in Table 12.4.

Let's focus on these three categories of multisector CDOs. Table 12.5 shows the exact securities that MBIA had guaranteed as of the end of 2007 (MBIA has not disclosed this information since then, but the numbers haven't changed much).

Table 12.5 Details of MBIA's Multisector CDO Exposure

Year	Deal Type/Name	Net Par Insured (MM)
CDOs of High–Grade U.S. ABSs Containing RMBS Collateral		
2004	TBD—no expected losses	$ 656
2004	TBD—no expected losses	$ 653
2005	TBD—no expected losses	$ 600
2006	Broderick 2 CDO	$ 1,118
2006	ART CDO 2006-1	$ 828
2006	Wadsworth CDO	$ 601
2006	Harp I CDO	$ 723
2007	Jupiter V	$ 1,190
2007	Broderick 3	$ 1,203
2007	Newbury Street	$ 1,684
2007	Highbridge ABS CDO I	$ 1,177
2007	Faxtor HG 2007-1	$ 950
2007	**Longshore 2007–III**	**$ 896**
2007	Bernoulli II	$ 563
2007	Silver Marlin I	$ 469
2007	Forge ABS High Grade CDO	$ 450
2007	West Trade III	$ 1,015
2007	Tazina II	$ 563
2007	Robeco High Grade I	$ 413
2007	Biltmore 2007-1	$ 375
Subtotal		**$16,127**
CDOs of Mezzanine U.S. ABSs Containing RMBS Collateral		
2004	TBD—no expected losses	$ 198
2004	TBD—no expected losses	$ 179
2004	TBD—no expected losses	$ 218
2007	Sagittarius I	$ 473
Subtotal		**$ 1,068**
CDOs of Multisector High-Grade Collateral		
2004	TBD—no expected losses	$ 1,350
2005	TBD—no expected losses	$ 1,430
2006	Logan II	$ 1,115
2006	Menton III	$ 1,077
2007	Logan III	$ 990
2007	Menton IV—no expected losses	$ 2,175
Subtotal		**$ 8,137**
Total		**$25,332**

SOURCE: MBIA Form 424B5, filed February 7, 2008; Pershing Square's Open Source Model, January 30, 2008.

And as you can see in Table 12.6, more than two-thirds of these CDOs are 2006 and 2007 vintage.

An Analysis of One CDO

To show how significant MBIA's impairments are, let's drill into one CDO highlighted in Table 12.5, Longshore 2007-III. This is a $1.3 billion 2007 vintage high-grade CDO (meaning that most of the tranches that comprise Longshore were originally rated A+, A, or A–), broken into seven tranches as shown in Table 12.7.

We can see that Longshore had three AAA-rated tranches, comprising 94.2 percent of the CDO, and that the super-senior A1 tranche,

Table 12.6   Vintage of CDOs Guaranteed by MBIA

Year	High-Grade ABS % of Total	Mezzanine % of Total	CDO-Squared % of Total	Total Weighted by Dollars
2007	62.2%	0.0%	39.1%	48.1%
2006	22.9%	0.0%	21.4%	20.0%
2005	4.5%	13.4%	17.1%	9.5%
2004 and prior	10.4%	86.6%	22.4%	22.4%

Source: MBIA 2008 10-K.

Table 12.7   Longshore CDO Funding 2007-III

Class	Original Balance (MM)	Current Balance (MM)	Percent	Original Rating	Current Rating	Credit Enhancement
A1	$1,131	$1,100	86.5%	AAA	Ca	13.5%
A2	$ 50	$ 50	3.9%	AAA	C	9.6%
A3	$ 44	$ 44	3.4%	AAA	C	6.2%
B	$ 38	$ 38	3.0%	AA	C	3.2%
C	$ 18	$ 20	1.6%	A	C	1.7%
D	$ 10	$ 11	0.9%	BBB	C	0.8%
Equity	$ 10	$ 10	0.8%	Not rated	Not rated	0.0%
Total	**$1,300**	**$1,272**				

Source: Amherst Securities, T2 Partners estimates.

Table 12.8 Information about the Tranches That Make Up Longshore

	Percent	Current Balance (MM)	Weighted Thickness	Weighted Credit Enhancement
RMBS	51%	$ 651	3.1%	7.7%
CMBS	25%	$ 322	6.6%	11.4%
CDO	23%	$ 299	14.2%	N/A
	100%	$1,272	6.6%	

SOURCE: Amherst Securities, T2 Partners estimates.

which MBIA guaranteed, was $1.13 billion and comprised 87.0 percent of the pool, meaning there was 13 percent credit enhancement or $169 million of protection beneath it in the pool. MBIA reinsured 20.9 percent of its $1.13 billion exposure, so its net exposure shown in Table 12.5 is $896 million.

Longshore is comprised of well over 100 tranches from RMBSs, commercial mortgage-backed securities (CMBSs), and other CDOs, in some cases directly and in other cases synthetically via credit-default swaps. As we can see in Table 12.8, more than half of the Longshore CDO is backed by tranches from RMBS pools (more than half of which are subprime). The balance of Longshore is roughly equally split between tranches of CMBS pools and other CDOs (i.e., 23 percent of Longshore is a CDO-squared).

We can see that the average RMBS tranche is only 3.1 percentage points thick and has only 7.7 percent credit enhancement, meaning that if the average RMBS pool that underlies more than 50 percent of Longshore suffers losses of more than 10.8 percent, then the tranches will be wiped out—and so will most of Longshore.

Amherst Securities provided us with data on the 90 RMBS tranches and the pools they are part of that make up the majority of Longshore. The great majority of these RMBSs are performing similarly, so we took the first one on the list, called the ABFC (Asset Backed Funding Corporation) 2006-OPT2 Trust, and drilled down into it. It is a $1.1 billion typical 2006 bubble-era subprime pool, structured very similarly to the one we analyzed in Chapter 10, as shown in Table 12.9.

Longshore has exposure to $10 million of the M-5 tranche of this pool, so Longshore will begin to take losses when this pool suffers

Table 12.9　Structure of the ABFC 2006–OPT2 Trust

Class	Initial Rating (S&P/Moody's)	Principal Balance	Credit Enhancement	
A-2	AAA/Aaa	$ 232,459,000	21.20%	78.80% of the pool was rated AAA
A-2	AAA/Aaa	$ 232,465,000	21.20%	
A-3A	AAA/Aaa	$ 205,493,000	21.20%	
A-3B	AAA/Aaa	$ 52,911,000	21.20%	
A-3C	AAA/Aaa	$ 96,963,000	21.20%	
A-3D	AAA/Aaa	$ 45,929,000	21.20%	
M-1	AA+/Aa1	$ 49,466,000	16.70%	
M-2	AA/Aa2	$ 30,622,000	13.91%	96.55% of the pool was rated investment grade by S&P and Moody's
M-3	AA- /Aa3	$ 21,593,000	11.95%	
M-4	A+/A1	$ 19,237,000	10.20%	
M-5	A/A2	$ 19,237,000	8.45%	
M-6	A- /A3	$ 18,687,000	6.75%	
M-7	BBB+/Baa1	$ 17,039,000	5.20%	
M-8	BBB/Baa2	$ 10,443,000	4.25%	
M-9	BBB- /Baa3	$ 8,794,000	3.45%	
B	BB+/Ba1	$ 10,993,000	2.45%	
CE	Not Rated	$ 26,933,882		
Total		**$1,099,264,882**		

SOURCE: Prospectus October 5, 2006.

losses of $93 million and will lose the entire $10 million when the pool suffers $112 million in losses.

The ABFC 2006–OPT2 Trust was filled with 5,052 of the worst loans imaginable: They have high interest rates (average of 8.67 percent) and were issued to deep subprime borrowers (607 average FICO score) who are really stretching to make payments (43 percent average debt-to-income ratio). Eighty-five percent are adjustable-rate mortgages, nearly 90 percent of which reset within two years of origination. Nearly 40 percent are in California and Florida, and 42 percent are stated-income/limited- or no-documentation loans (i.e., liar's loans).

Similar to the RMBS analyzed in Chapter 10, this pool is a complete train wreck. As shown in Table 12.8, after only 29 months (through January 2009) 31 percent of the loans had prepaid (but the prepayment rate had shrunk to almost nil), 34 percent had defaulted, and, of the 35 percent of the loans that were still performing, 6 to 8 percent were defaulting *every month*, with 65 percent severity in recent months.

So what are the prospects for the M-5 tranche held by Longshore? As of January 2009, the tranche was 3 percent thick and was senior to

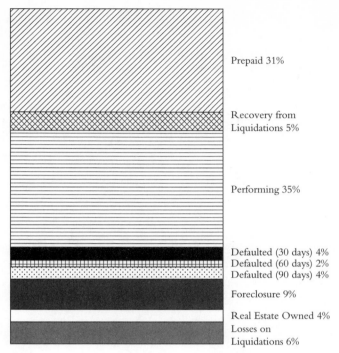

Figure 12.8   Status of the Original Loans in the ABFC 2006-OPT2 Trust, January 2008
SOURCE: Amherst Securities.

9.4 percent of the Trust, meaning there was only $59.5 million sub-ordinate to this tranche. In only 29 months, the Trust has already lost $67.3 million and has $251.8 million in defaults—in total, an expected accumulated loss of $134.2 million (assuming a 53.3 percent loss on the defaulted loans). The $134.2 million loss is $74.7 million more than the $59.5 million subordinate to the M-5 tranche—and there are 330 months to go. Thus, we believe that it is nearly certain that 100 percent of this tranche will be wiped out. Amherst Securities is pricing a tranche like this as the present value of its remaining interest payments only (i.e., at most, 1 cent on the dollar).

We asked Amherst Securities to analyze the other RMBS, CMBS, and CDO tranches held by Longshore, and the firm estimates a 1 percent recovery on the RMBS and CDO tranches and a 10 percent recovery for the CMBS tranches, which results in an implied price for Longshore of 3.3 cents on the dollar, as shown in Table 12.10.

Table 12.10   Amherst Securities Estimated Fair Value for the Tranches That
Make Up Longshore

	Percent	Current Balance (MM)	Fair Market Value (MM)	Implied Price for Longshore CDO
RMBS	51%	$ 651	$ 7	1
CMBS	25%	$ 322	$32	10
CDO	23%	$ 299	$ 3	1
	100%	$1,272	$42	3.3 cents

SOURCE: Amherst Securities, T2 Partners estimates.

Thus, MBIA's losses on Longshore are likely to be nearly 100
percent, equal to roughly $850 million to $1.1 billion, depending on
whether you think MBIA's reinsurance is good (in which case its exposure to Longshore would be "only" $896 million) or not (we don't,
and think MBIA's real exposure is close to the gross amount of $1.13
billion).

We have looked at the other high-grade multisector CDOs like
Longshore to which MBIA is exposed, 85.1 percent of which are 2006
and 2007 vintage, and we believe that Longshore is representative of the
group. Yet MBIA has taken impairments for less than 5 percent of its
multisector CDOs—and not a penny for its $97.2 billion of exposure to
other CDOs.

In summary, our analysis leads us to believe that MBIA's underreserving for its CDO exposure is even more extreme than for its RMBS
exposure and that it will probably take losses in excess of $10 billion
just on its $25.5 billion of multisector CDO exposure alone.

Conclusion

In our entire careers, we have never seen a company as underreserved
as MBIA—without even considering the likely losses it will have in
its nonstructured finance portfolio and guaranteed investment contract
business. We think MBIA's losses will significantly exceed the company's reserves, and will far exceed the $944 million of equity at MBIA
Inc., the holding company, and the claims-paying resources of the

insurance subsidiary, MBIA Corp., even if one includes the money that was transferred to National.

Our analysis suggests that the real losses to come will become clear over the course of 2009, and that when this happens MBIA's regulator will take over the company, remove the senior management, and put it into runoff. In addition, the creation of National will be seen for what we believe it is—a fraudulent transfer—and will be undone. Holders of the stock, holding company debt, and surplus notes will be wiped out entirely, and policyholders will get only a fraction of the amount they are owed (the exact amount will depend on the magnitude of the losses relative to MBIA's claims-paying resources).

Despite all of this, however, we will repeat our earlier warning: **We do not recommend shorting MBIA stock at $5.** There is a scenario—not a likely one, but a possibility—that the company could be successful in walling off its toxic liabilities, in which case the stock could rise manyfold, crushing shorts.

Chapter 13

An Ill-Fated Acquisition?

Case Study: Wells Fargo

G iven that we covered our remaining short position in Wells Fargo at around $10 during the first week of March 2009—and are now long the stock—you might wonder why we're writing about it here. There are two answers: first, because when we decided to write this book in early January 2009, it was one of our favorite short ideas because the stock was around $30—it's truly stunning how quickly the stock fell in only two months. Second, because it's an interesting case study of how a company can be a great short at one time and price, but one that should be covered, or even be a long position, at another time and price.

As the credit crunch deepened over the course of 2008, we profitably shorted a number of banks like Washington Mutual and Wachovia that we believed had not reserved adequately for likely losses. Wells Fargo was not on our list because we thought it had a great franchise and that its reserves might be sufficient. However, when it became clear that Wells Fargo would be acquiring Wachovia, we shorted it at around $30.

Our investment thesis rested on two pillars: First, having been short Wachovia, we thought Wells Fargo was buying some big losses, especially in Wachovia's option ARM and home equity portfolios. Second, we thought Wells Fargo's stock price reflected an unrealistically rosy scenario in light of what was happening in the overall mortgage and credit markets. When we first shorted it, the stock was trading at roughly 3 times and 12 times our estimates for book value and earnings, respectively, at the time, so we thought there was a lot of room for the stock to fall if our investment thesis was correct—and it was unlikely to run against us very much if we were wrong. This is precisely the type of "heads we win a lot, tails we don't lose very much" scenario that makes for a good investment, long or short.

The Bull Case for Wells Fargo

There is much to admire about Wells Fargo. By all accounts it has a great management team and a very strong franchise that will likely become even stronger with the acquisition of Wachovia, which gives it a coast-to-coast presence and propels it to the top, or near the top, of U.S. banks. The combined company is number one in bank branches (6,610), small business lending, middle market commercial lending, agriculture lending, commercial real estate lending and brokerage, and bank-owned insurance brokerage (number five worldwide). It's also number two in banking deposits in the United States (11.2 percent, a hair behind Bank of America, which has 11.3 percent), mortgage originations and servicing, retail brokerage, and debit cards.

Wells Fargo's pre-Wachovia business was highly profitable, earning $19.6 billion pretax in 2008 before provisions for loan losses (which were enormous—net income was only $2.9 billion; peak net income was $8.4 billion in 2006). Figure 13.1 shows the dramatic growth over the six years between 2003 and 2008.

Wells Fargo's robust earnings were primarily driven by the company's net interest margin, which in 2008 vastly exceeded the margins of its three largest competitors, as shown in Figure 13.2.

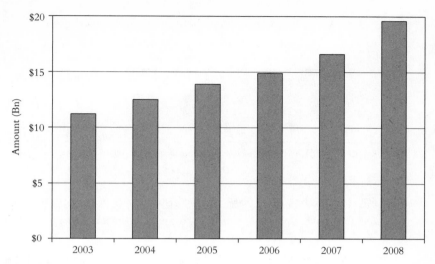

Figure 13.1 Wells Fargo Pretax, Preprovision Earnings, 2003–2008
SOURCE: Wells Fargo Q4 2008 financial results presentation, January 28, 2009, p. 10.

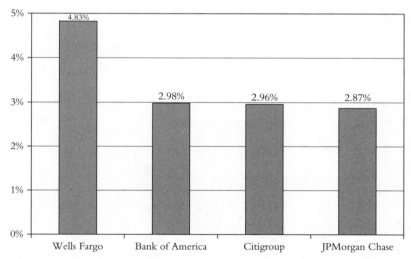

Figure 13.2 Net Interest Margin of the Four Largest U.S. Banks, 2008
SOURCE: Wells Fargo Q4 2008 financial results presentation, January 28, 2009, p. 15.

Wells Fargo not only had higher margins, but was also growing its revenues and pretax, preprovision earnings faster than its peers, as shown in Table 13.1.

Table 13.1   Growth in Pretax, Preprovision Earnings and Revenue

	Pretax, Preprovision Earnings Growth		Revenue Growth
	2008	**5 Years**	**2008**
Wells Fargo	17.4%	11.3%	6.1%
JPMorgan, Citigroup, BofA	−60.5%	−60.4%	−16.7%
Top 9 peers	−47.9%	−41.7%	−2.1%

SOURCE: Wells Fargo Q4 2008 financial results presentation, January 28, 2009.

Turning to Wachovia, Figure 13.3 shows its pretax, preprovision earnings for the past six years, which are approximately 60 percent of Wells Fargo's.

The combined earnings power of the two companies is enormous. We estimate that with interest spreads at record levels currently, the pretax, preprovision income of the original Wells Fargo will rise slightly to between $20 billion and $22 billion in 2009, plus we add $10 billion to $12 billion from Wachovia, so that's $30 billion to $34 billion. On top of this, Wells Fargo estimates $5 billion in cost savings and synergies, so let's assume savings of $4 billion to $6 billion, for a grand total of

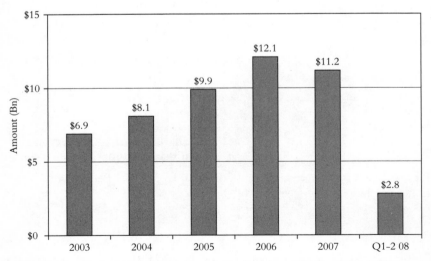

Figure 13.3   Wachovia Pretax, Preprovision Earnings, 2003 to Mid-2008
SOURCE: Wachovia 10-K 2007 and 10-Q, Q3 2008.

$34 billion to $40 billion in normalized pretax, preprovision earnings (it may take a little while to realize the cost savings). This is consistent with what Warren Buffett estimated when he was interviewed by CNBC on March 9, 2009: "I would expect $40 billion a year preprovision income."

Buffett added: "And under normal conditions, I would expect maybe $10–$12 billion a year of losses." That's 25 to 30 percent of $40 billion, so applying the same percentage to $34 billion, that's $8.5 billion to $10.2 billion in losses, leaving pretax income of between $23.8 billion and $25.5 billion. Now subtract 33 percent for taxes and divide by 4.2 billion shares, and the result is earnings per share (EPS) of between $3.78 and $4.05. The same calculations at $40 billion of pretax, preprovision income, minus $10–$12 billion of losses, result in EPS of $4.44 to $4.76. Any way you cut it, that's a lot of earnings for a stock that closed on March 12, 2009, at $13.95.

The first quarter of 2009 is off to a good start according to CFO Howard Atkins, who made some bullish comments in a press release on March 6, 2009: "Our strong operating results for the first two months of 2009 have been driven by continued growth in lending, deposits and mortgage volumes. Mortgage originations for the first two months alone were $59 billion, exceeding in two months the exceptionally strong fourth quarter of 2008, and mortgage applications were $107 billion."[1]

Regarding its balance sheet, in the same press release Wells Fargo announced that it was cutting its dividend by 85 percent, which will save the company $5 billion annually—a very smart move. In another smart move, Wells Fargo was aggressive in booking impairments and taking write-downs in Wachovia's portfolio, as shown in Table 13.2.

Table 13.2   Credit Impairments and Write-Downs Taken by Wells Fargo on Wachovia

Portfolio	Credit Impaired Loan Balance (Bn)	Credit Write-Down (Bn)
Pick-a-Pay mortgages (option ARMs)	$ 59.8	$ 24.3
Other consumer loans	$ 5.1	$ 2.8
Commercial real estate	$ 20.5	$ 7.7
Other commercial loans	$ 5.9	$ 1.5
Other	$ 2.6	$ 0.9
Total	**$93.9**	**$37.2**

Source: Wells Fargo Q4 2008 financial results presentation, January 28, 2009.

In the March 6 press release, Atkins summarized why Wells Fargo believes that its capital position is strong:[2]

> Our capital position, adjusted for risk, is near the top of our peer group. At December 31, 2008, stockholders' equity was $99 billion with Tier 1 Capital at 7.84 percent—30 percent above the 6 percent regulatory minimum for well-capitalized banks. Our tangible common equity was $36 billion, 2.86 percent of tangible assets and 3.32 percent of regulatory risk-weighted assets. These ratios are after significantly reducing the risk in the Wachovia loan and securities portfolios, about half of the combined balance sheet of the new Wells Fargo. By immediately writing down loans and securities at Wachovia through purchase accounting adjustments at close, we have already significantly reduced the risk of loss to tangible common equity. Since these losses have already been recognized, our future earnings will be higher and therefore tangible common equity can now grow faster. Adjusted for the fact that we already accounted for these future losses, our tangible common equity as a percent of regulatory risk-weighted assets would have been 5.2 percent at December 31, 2008.

Buffett certainly thinks Wells Fargo is attractive, but worries about what the government might do. Here's what he said during the March 9 CNBC interview:

Warren Buffett: . . . Our stocks we plan to hold a very long time. . . . Overall I like to buy them with the idea of owning forever. And the quotes don't make much difference.

Now, if I looked at the performance of Wells Fargo . . . in a couple years—and management doesn't have anything to do with what I'm saying here—I would expect $40 billion a year preprovision income. And under normal conditions I would expect maybe $10 to $12 billion a year of losses. I mean, you lose money in banking; you just try not to lose too much.

So, you know, you get to very interesting figures. I mean, the spreads are enormous on what they're doing. They're getting the money at bargain rates. So if there were no quote on Wells Fargo and I just owned it like I own my farm, I would look at the way the business is developing, and I would say, you know, "These are a couple of tough years for losses in the banking business, but you expect a couple tough years every now and then," and that the earning power is . . . going to be greater by far than it's ever been when you get all through with it.

The only worry in that is the government will force you to sell shares at some terribly low price. And I hope they're wise enough not to do that. That's what's spooking the banking market to a big extent.

Becky Quick, CNBC: You worry about that, too.

Warren Buffett: Yeah, sure.

Becky Quick: That's why you'd like some clarity out of Washington on what they're planning to do. . . .

Warren Buffett: I think clarity is a good thing for the whole country. . . . Any issue to do with people's money, clarity's important. People want to be clear about their money. But I would say that . . . Wells Fargo, their prospects three years out are better than ever.

To summarize, Buffett loves the stock, it's trading at 3 to 4 times normalized earnings, and the company has taken large write-downs for Wachovia, so why isn't every investor buying it? The answer lies in the balance sheet, in particular a minimal amount of equity, which may yet put Wells Fargo in the same dire position as Citigroup.

Wells Fargo's Balance Sheet

Table 13.3 shows Wells Fargo's balance sheet, which includes Wachovia, as it appears in the 2008 10-K. You might think it would be easy to determine Wells Fargo's stockholders' equity, the single most important element of the balance sheet—just read the second-to-last line at the bottom of the balance sheet, right? But it's not so easy. (For more discussion of equity, see the appendix at the end of this chapter.)

What we, as investors, care about is Wells Fargo's ability to weather the current storm, so we want to focus on tangible common equity—the word *tangible* meaning that it excludes goodwill and other intangibles, and the word *common* meaning it includes only common stock, not preferred stock. Intangibles are excluded because, as noted earlier, things like

Table 13.3   Wells Fargo's Balance Sheet

(in millions)	December 31	
	2008	**2007**
Assets:		
Cash and due from banks	$ 23,763	$ 14,757
Federal funds sold, securities purchased under resale agreements, and other short-term investments	$ 49,433	$ 2,754
Trading assets	$ 54,884	$ 7,727
Securities available for sale	$ 151,569	$ 72,951
Mortgages held for sale (includes $18,754 and $24,998 carried at fair value)	$ 20,088	$ 26,815
Loans held for sale (includes $398 carried at fair value at December 31, 2008)	$ 6,228	$ 948
Loans	$ 864,830	$ 382,195
Allowance for loan losses	$ 21,013	$ 5,307
Net loans	$ 843,817	$ 376,888
Mortgage servicing rights:		
Measured at fair value (residential MSRs)	$ 14,714	$ 16,763
Amortized	$ 1,446	$ 466
Premises and equipment, net	$ 11,269	$ 5,122
Goodwill	$ 22,627	$ 13,106
Other assets	$ 109,801	$ 37,145
Total Assets	**$1,309,639**	**$ 575,442**
Liabilities:		
Noninterest-bearing deposits	$ 150,837	$ 84,348
Interest-bearing deposits	630,565	260,112
Total deposits	781,402	344,460
Short-term borrowings	108,074	53,255
Accrued expenses and other liabilities	53,921	30,706
Long-term debt	267,158	99,393
Total Liabilities	**1,210,555**	**527,814**
Stockholders' Equity:		
Preferred stock	31,332	450
Common stock $1.67 par value, authorized 6 billion shares; issued 4.4 billion shares and 3.5 billion shares	7,273	5,788
Additional paid-in capital	36,026	8,212
Retained earnings	36,543	38,970
Cumulative other comprehensive income (loss)	−6,869	725
Treasury stock 135,290,540 shares and 175,659,842 shares	−4,666	−6,035
Unearned ESOP shares	−555	−482
Total Stockholders' Equity	**99,084**	**47,628**
Total Liabilities and Stockholders' Equity	**$1,309,639**	**$575,442**

SOURCE: Wells Fargo 2008 10-K.

brands don't help cover losses. As for preferred stock, it's a hybrid security that has characteristics of both debt and equity since it typically pays a dividend, but often can also be converted into common stock. It's valuable capital in that it can absorb losses and help avert a company's possible bankruptcy, but it's senior to the common stock, meaning the common stockholders usually takes all losses until they're wiped out before the preferred stockholders start to take losses. Therefore, shareholders of Wells Fargo's stock should be most concerned with the amount of tangible common equity.

So we start with stated equity of $99,084 (all numbers hereafter in millions) and then subtract $31,332 of preferred stock and $22,627 of goodwill, for a total of $45,125 ($45.1 billion). But wait, there's more.

Due to some odd twist in generally accepted accounting principles (GAAP), mortgage servicing rights (MSRs) appear on the balance sheet. Wells Fargo is in the business of servicing mortgages, and the value of this business, based on Wells Fargo's estimate of future profits, appears as an asset. This makes no sense, as this is clearly intangible asset—in fact, the Financial Accounting Standards Board (FASB) defines *all* servicing rights as intangible assets. So, $45,125 minus $14,714 of "Measured at fair value (residential MSRs)" and $1,446 of amortized MSRs results in tangible common equity of $28,965 ($29.0 billion).

We're not done yet, however. Wells Fargo has "Other assets" of $109,801, and when one reads the footnotes in the 10-K, one sees that the company has buried some intangible assets in this line rather than breaking them out separately. Table 13.4 appears in note 7 of Wells Fargo's 2008 10-K.

The two lines in italics, "Core deposit intangibles" and "Customer relationship and other intangibles," totaling $15,515 ($15.5 billion) also need to be subtracted in the calculation of tangible common equity, so $28,965 − $15,515 = $13,450 ($13.5 billion). (Incidentally, note the huge rise to $44.2 billion of "Other," up from $12.1 billion the previous year. A sum this large should be broken down and described in detail, but it's not. Such a big increase almost certainly has to do with the Wachovia acquisition, and part of it could be intangibles as well.)

Phew! All done, right? Nope. One more step. Once a year, accounting rules (specifically FAS 107, "Disclosures about Fair Value of Financial Instruments") require companies to report "fair value

Table 13.4   Wells Fargo's Other Assets

(in millions)	December 31 2008	2007
Total nonmarketable equity investments	$ 16,782	$ 6,930
Operating lease assets	$ 2,251	$ 2,218
Accounts receivable	$ 22,493	$ 10,913
Interest receivable	$ 5,746	$ 2,977
Core deposit intangibles	*$ 11,999*	*$ 435*
Customer relationship and other intangibles	*$ 3,516*	*$ 319*
Foreclosed assets:		
GNMA loans	$ 667	$ 535
Other	$ 1,526	$ 649
Due from customers on acceptances	$ 615	$ 62
Other	$ 44,206	$ 12,107
Total Other Assets	**$109,801**	**$37,145**

Source: Wells Fargo's 2008 10-K, note 7, p. 110.

estimates . . . for financial instruments . . . for which carrying amounts approximate fair value, and excluding financial instruments recorded at fair value on a recurring basis."[3] In the case of Wells Fargo, FAS 107 requires the company to value the loans on its balance sheet (as well as certain other assets) at market value, rather than simply carrying them at par, which it normally does unless a write-down is taken. Companies are often slow to take write-downs, so FAS 107 can provide insight into this. Table 13.5 shows a table that appears in note 17 of Wells Fargo's 2008 10-K.

We can see that in 2007, there was virtually no difference between the carrying amount and estimated fair value for either financial assets or liabilities, but it was quite a different story in 2008. In particular, Wells Fargo discloses that the $843.8 billion of loans held on its balance sheet have a fair (i.e., market) value of only $829.6 billion, $14.2 billion less. (Note that fair value is determined by the company, which obviously has strong incentives to estimate as high a number as possible.)

Calculating the differences across all FAS 107 financial assets and liabilities results in a net difference in 2008 of fair value being $13,583 million lower than what Wells Fargo reports on its balance sheet—quite a difference from 2007, when it was $1,459 million higher.

Table 13.5   FAS 107: Disclosures about Fair Value of Financial Instruments

(in millions)	December 31, 2008		December 31, 2007	
	Carrying Amount	Estimated Fair Value	Carrying Amount	Estimated Fair Value
Financial Assets:				
Mortgages held for sale	$ 1,334	$ 1,333	$ 1,817	$ 1,817
Loans held for sale	$ 5,830	$ 5,876	$ 948	$ 955
Loans, net	$ 843,817	$ 829,603	$ 376,888	$ 377,219
Nonmarketable equity investments (cost method)	$ 11,104	$ 11,220	$ 5,855	$ 6,076
Total	**$ 862,085**	**$ 848,032**	**$385,508**	**$386,067**
Difference		**−$ 14,053**		$ 559
Financial Liabilities:				
Deposits	$ 781,402	$ 781,964	$ 344,460	$ 344,484
Long-term debt	$ 267,055	$ 266,023	$ 99,373	$ 98,449
Total	**$1,048,457**	**$1,047,987**	**$443,833**	**$442,933**
Difference		−$ 470		−$ 900
Net Difference		**−$ 13,583**		$ 1,459

SOURCE: Wells Fargo's 2008 10-K, note 17, p. 143.

So this is the final adjustment we make to Wells Fargo's equity: $13,450 minus the FAS 107 adjustment of $13,583 results in the company having adjusted tangible common equity of *negative* $133 million!

Reasonable people would argue whether this means that Wells Fargo is insolvent, but there's no question that the company has virtually no cushion on its current balance sheet to withstand future losses beyond its $21.7 billion provision for credit losses.

Losses

Wells Fargo, to its credit, did not become involved to any meaningful degree in toxic securitized products, as did so many of its peers, so the analysis of possible losses focuses on the loans Wells Fargo holds on its balance sheet. Table 13.6 shows the breakdown of Wells Fargo's

Table 13.6 Wells Fargo Loan Portfolio with Estimated Losses

	Wells Fargo 12/31/08 (Bn)	Estimated Range of Cumulative Losses (%)	Estimated Range of Cumulative Losses (Bn)
Commercial and Commercial Real Estate:			
Commercial	$202		
Other real estate mortgage	$103		
Real estate construction	$ 35		
Lease financing	$ 16		
Total Commercial and Commercial Real Estate	**$356**	**5–10%**	**$ 18–$36**
Consumer:			
Real estate 1–4 family first mortgage— option ARMs*	$ 95	6–40%	$ 6–$39
Real estate 1–4 family first mortgage	$153	5–10%	$ 8–$15
Real estate 1–4 family junior lien mortgage	$110	10–15%	$ 11–$17
Credit card	$ 24	7–12%	$ 2–$3
Other revolving credit and installment	$ 93	7–12%	$ 7–$11
Total Consumer	**$475**		
Foreign	$ 34	3–10%	$ 1–$3
Total Loans	**$865**		**$52–$124**

SOURCE: Wells Fargo Q4 2008 earnings release, January 28, 2009, p. 25; T2 estimates.
*NOTE: We break out option ARMs separately from "Real estate 1–4 family first mortgage," using the table on page 38 of the earnings release. Also, the $6 billion to $39 billion of estimated option ARM losses are in addition to the $24.3 billion write-down taken to date.

$864.8 billions of loans (including Wachovia's book) as of year-end 2008, with our range of loss estimates for each category, discussed further later.

While it's virtually impossible to estimate losses on such a large and complex loan book, based on the data and trends analyzed in the first half of this book, we are able to make some estimates, especially in the consumer loan area.

Option ARMs

Let's start with option ARMs. Table 13.7 appears on page 38 of Wells Fargo's Q4 2008 earnings release, reflecting Wachovia's "Pick-a-Pay" portfolio (its name for option ARMs; to its credit, Wells Fargo never wrote a single one of these toxic loans).

What this table is showing us is that Wells Fargo, when it acquired Wachovia, went through its $119.6 billion option ARM portfolio, separated the best $57.7 billion worth into a non-credit-impaired portfolio, and put the remaining $61.9 billion of risky/defaulted loans into a credit-impaired portfolio (labeled "SOP 03-3 loans"). Then, it wrote down the credit-impaired loans by $24.3 billion, leaving $37.6 billion. Thus, Wells Fargo's total option ARM portfolio as of year-end 2008 was $57.7 billion plus $37.6 billion = $95.3 billion. Of these loans, 56 percent are in California and 10 percent are in Florida.

The $57.7 billion of non-credit-impaired loans are performing extremely well so far, with only 0.10 percent having missed even one payment and a loan-to-value of 80 percent based on November 2008 home prices. This sounds impressive until one considers that by definition

Table 13.7   Wells Fargo's Pick-a-Pay (Option ARM) Loan Portfolio

December 31, 2008

	Non-SOP 03-3 Loans		SOP 03-3 Loans			
(in millions)	Outstanding Balance	Current LTV Ratio	Balance Prior to Nonaccretable Discount	Current LTV Ratio	Carrying Amount	Ratio of Carrying Amount to Current Value
California	$28,107	86%	$42,650	133%	$25,472	85%
Florida	$ 6,099	89%	$ 5,992	119%	$ 3,439	76%
New Jersey	$ 3,545	74%	$ 1,809	94%	$ 1,246	60%
Texas	$ 2,231	61%	$ 562	72%	$ 385	49%
Arizona	$ 1,449	95%	$ 1,552	133%	$ 895	85%
Other states	$16,269	75%	$ 9,381	92%	$ 6,178	61%
Total	**$57,700**		**$61,946**		**$37,615**	

Source: Wells Fargo Q4 2008 earnings release, January 28, 2009, p. 38.

this portfolio should be performing exceptionally well—because Wells Fargo cherry-picked only performing loans to be part of it!

As we showed in Chapter 4, option ARMs are defaulting at catastrophic rates, but that's driven almost entirely by the loans that have hit their resets—before then, roughly 80 percent of the borrowers are paying only the ultralow teaser rate, so very few will default no matter what the LTV is. Wells Fargo doesn't disclose what percentage of its non-credit-impaired loans have hit their reset (our bet: almost none), nor what percentage are negatively amortizing (our bet: the vast majority).

Wells Fargo tried to put lipstick on this pig during its Q4 earnings call when it said: "We do believe that Wachovia's option ARM portfolio, or Pick-a-Pay, is the highest-quality option ARM portfolio in the industry." To us, that's like claiming to be the best downhill skier in Somalia.

And while it might appear that Wells Fargo was very conservative in writing down Wachovia's option ARMs by $24.3 billion, or 20.3 percent, we think more losses are in store. In Chapter 4, we estimated that of all option ARMs ever written (Wachovia had roughly one-sixth of them), 70 percent would default with 60 percent severity, resulting in 42 percent losses. If we give Wells Fargo the benefit of the doubt and assume that 50 percent of the original $119.6 billion will default with 50 percent severity, that's a 25 percent loss or $29.9 billion, $5.6 billion more than the write-down Wells Fargo has taken to date. But we wouldn't be surprised to see 70 percent default with 70 percent severity, a 49 percent loss or $58.6 billion loss—$34.3 billion more than the write-down taken to date.

Home Equity Portfolio

Our second-biggest area of concern is Wells Fargo's home equity portfolio, which grew by approximately $55 billion (more than 50 percent) with the acquisition of Wachovia. Here's some data on the portfolio, as disclosed on page 37 of the Q4 2008 earnings release and during the January 28, 2009 conference call:

- The combined portfolio as of year-end 2008 was $129.5 billion;
- Wells Fargo categorized $10.3 billion (8 percent) as the "liquidating portfolio," similar to the option ARM credit-impaired portfolio;
- Seventy-six percent of the liquidating portfolio and 40 percent of the core portfolio (43 percent overall) have a combined loan-to-value above 90 percent, a worrisome level given how rapidly home prices

are falling, especially in Wells Fargo's two biggest home equity loan markets, California and Florida;

- Fully 27.5 percent of the loans are in California and 9.5 percent are in Florida, a total of 37 percent, a *very* worrisome level;
- Only 15 percent of the loans are first lien; the remaining 85 percent are second lien, meaning that upon default, severity will likely approach 100 percent; and
- Only 2.48 percent of the loans were two or more payments past due as of year-end 2008, and the annualized loss rate is 2.87 percent, both good numbers (assisted by Wachovia's 1.62 percent and 1.84 percent figures, respectively), but the delinquency trend is rising.

In Chapter 4, we estimate that home equity loan losses across the entire $1.1 trillion outstanding will ultimately be 15 to 25 percent. Again, if we give Wells Fargo the benefit of the doubt and assume its losses will be 10 to 15 percent and apply this only to the $110 billion of second lien home equity loans, that's $11 billion to $17 billion in losses.

First Lien Mortgages

Wells Fargo has $153 billion of first lien mortgages (excluding option ARMs) of which $18.7 billion are home equity loans. Of the $153 billion, 21 percent are in California and 11 percent are in Florida, for a total of 32 percent. It's difficult to estimate the possible losses here because Wells Fargo doesn't break out delinquencies for this segment, nor do we know how many are jumbo loans, but we'd guess they comprise the majority of the California and Florida loans, given how high home prices got in those states (also, if they weren't jumbo loans, Wells Fargo would probably have sold them to the government-sponsored enterprises [GSEs], Fannie and Freddie).

In Chapter 4 we estimated that all prime loans will show 5 to 10 percent losses and jumbo loans will have 7 to 12 percent losses, so let's use the low end for Wells Fargo, 5 to 10 percent. Applied to a $153 billion portfolio, that's $8 billion to $15 billion in losses.

Other Consumer Loans

Based on our knowledge of the credit card industry, we estimate that Wells Fargo's credit card, other revolving credit, and installment loan portfolio will incur losses in the 7 to 12 percent range, equal to $9 billion to $14 billion.

Commercial and Commercial Real Estate

It's difficult to estimate what the losses might be for Wells Fargo's $356 billion of commercial and commercial real estate loans, which account for 41 percent of the company's total loan book. The only area for which the company provides meaningful disclosure is in commercial real estate and construction, where the original Wells Fargo had $68 billion in outstanding loans with a 0.55 percent annualized charge-off rate in Q4 2008, more than double the previous quarter's 0.27 percent and 8 times the 0.07 percent in Q4 2007. Wachovia's $70 billion portfolio was showing much greater stress, with a 5.92 percent annualized charge-off rate in Q4 2008, more than double the previous quarter's 2.64 percent and 5 times the 1.09 percent in Q4 2007.

Commercial real estate, to which Wells Fargo has $103 billion of exposure, is going to be an enormous train wreck, but actually losses and charge-offs to date remain quite low, primarily because the loans typically don't reset for at least five years, so the bad loans written during the peak bubble years of 2005 to 2007 haven't reset and therefore banks can hold them at or near par.

Real estate construction loans, to which Wells Fargo has $35 billion of exposure, will likely be an even bigger train wreck.

In total, we estimate that Wells Fargo will have 5 to 10 percent losses across its commercial and commercial real estate loan book, which translates into another $18 billion to $36 billion in losses.

Conclusion

In total, as noted in Table 13.6, we estimate that Wells Fargo will incur $52 billion to $124 billion of losses on its $865 billion loan book, or 6 to 14 percent. Even the low end is more than double Wells Fargo's $21.7 billion provision for credit losses, so in light of the company having little or no real equity, does this mean we think Wells Fargo is likely to meet the same fate as Citigroup? Not necessarily. Allow us to explain.

Wells Fargo is currently in a race for its life. Its losses are digging a hole every quarter, which will continue for the foreseeable future, so Wells Fargo's challenge is to earn profits fast enough to fill the hole before it engulfs the company. We think it's likely to do so, which is why we now own the stock. It's going to be a close call, however, which is why it's not a very big position—there's still a real possibility of a bad outcome.

Everything hinges on how quickly the losses come in and how much money Wells Fargo can earn. The $21.7 billion provision for credit losses provides a bit of a cushion, which Wells Fargo said during its January 28, 2009, conference call "covers 12 months of estimated losses for consumer loans and at least 24 months for commercial loans." We think that's optimistic, but it still underscores the good news for the company that its loans will take time to default. Unlike toxic securitized finance products like RMBSs and CDOs, which have to be marked down very quickly, actual loans take time to season, and companies have some leeway as to when they take charge-offs and recognize losses. For example, Wells Fargo is aggressive working with many at-risk homeowners and businesses to modify loans and reduce the chances of default. In a race against time, it's critically important that Wells Fargo have these tools at its disposal.

Another plus is that Wells Fargo's management finally seems to have awakened to how perilous the situation really is, which led it to slash the dividend and even more aggressively cut costs.

As we showed at the beginning of this chapter, Wells Fargo is generating pretax, preprovision earnings of approximately $30 billion to $34 billion annually ($7.5 billion to $8.5 billion per quarter) even before $5 billion in cost cuts and synergies kick in, which will likely boost this to $10 billion per quarter.

When combined with the $21.7 billion provision for credit losses, are these profits enough for Wells Fargo to keep ahead of the $52 billion to $124 billion of losses to come? We think it's likely, but it depends on the level of profits and losses and, equally important, their timing. If big losses materialize quickly but profits are weaker than we expect, Wells Fargo will be in big trouble.

Figure 13.4 shows Wells Fargo's net loan charge-offs and its provision for credit losses for each of the past five quarters. The good news is that the loan charge-offs in every quarter are lower than the credit losses being taken, meaning the company is building its total provision for credit losses, especially in the fourth quarter of 2008 when it took a huge charge to boost its reserves upon acquiring Wachovia.

Figure 13.5 shows the same data for Wachovia over the same period (excluding Q4 2008 due to the acquisition).

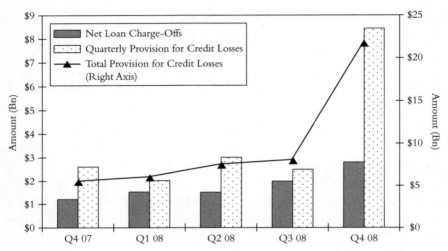

Figure 13.4   Wells Fargo (pre-Wachovia) Quarterly Net Loan Charge-Offs and Provision for Credit Losses, and Total Provision for Credit Losses
SOURCE: Wells Fargo Q4 2008 earnings release, January 28, 2009, p. 27.

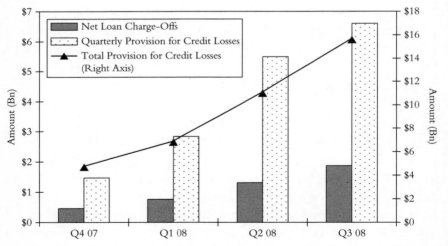

Figure 13.5   Wachovia Quarterly Net Loan Charge-Offs and Provision for Credit Losses, and Total Provision for Credit Losses
SOURCE: Wachovia 10-Q, Q3 2008, p. 33.

Note how Wachovia massively increased its provision for credit losses in its last two quarters of existence, far above the increase in loan charge-offs. This was a desperate—and ultimately unsuccessful—attempt to catch up from prior periods of underreserving and stave off distress. By Q3 2008, it had built its total provision for credit losses to $15.6 billion, but investors judged this inadequate and crushed the stock, forcing Wachovia into the arms of Wells Fargo. (It turns out that investors were right, given that Wells Fargo took $37.2 billion in write-downs upon acquiring Wachovia, as shown earlier in Table 13.2.)

Now we have the information to estimate what the combined company's quarterly loan charge-offs and provision for credit losses might be. We can see that Wachovia's loan charge-offs were rising rapidly before it was acquired. Assuming that these trends in Wachovia's loan book continue, quarterly loan charge-offs might be $3 billion in Q1 2009, rising to $4 billion by the end of 2009 and then stabilizing, so to keep ahead of this, let's assume that Wells Fargo will want to take a $4 billion provision for credit losses in Q1 2009 and then increase this to $5 billion by the end of 2009.

Coincidentally, Wells Fargo's loan losses prior to the acquisition were running at a similar pace, so let's assume its charge-offs and credit losses rise similarly as well. This would imply that the combined company's quarterly provision for credit losses would be $8 billion in early 2009, rising to $10 billion by the end of the year.

As high as this is, it is almost precisely matched by the $8 billion to $10 billion of quarterly pretax, preprovision profits we expect Wells Fargo to earn, so its current $21.7 billion cushion would see little impairment and the company would probably make it through the storm. As noted earlier, however, if some combination of weaker profits and higher losses occurs, Wells Fargo might end up a ward of the government, like Citigroup.

In summary, we think if Wells Fargo makes it through the storm without significant dilution of its shareholders, perhaps a 70 percent likelihood in our estimation, it will earn $4 to $5 per share, which would translate into a $40 to $60 stock. That kind of upside offsets the very real downside risk and makes the risk-reward equation highly favorable when the stock is priced in the $10 to $15 range, which is why we now own it.

Appendix: Background on Equity

The single most important figure on a balance sheet is equity. Mathematically, assets are equal to liabilities plus equity ($A = L + E$)—that's why it's called a balance sheet: assets must balance liabilities plus equity. Another way to think about equity is that it's the amount by which assets exceed liabilities ($E = A - L$). Thus, equity is a measure of financial strength: A company with $100 billion in equity (like Berkshire Hathaway) is financially stronger than a company like Resource America, which has $141 million in equity, because Berkshire has a $100 billion asset cushion above all of its liabilities to withstand such shocks to the business as a loss of assets (writing down inventory, for example) or an unexpected jump in liabilities (e.g., insurance claims from a big hurricane).

From a shareholder's perspective, equity is both good and bad. It's good because it provides a company with protection against unexpected calamities such as the economic environment we're currently experiencing. Companies of all sorts, not just financial institutions, that have lots of equity will weather this storm and may even profit from it by being able to take market share from or acquire weaker competitors.

But equity also represents shareholders' capital that's tied up in the business—that's why its full name is "stockholders' equity" (it's also known as "book value"). But as an investor, I don't want my capital tied up in a business—I'd prefer that the business use as little capital as possible because that increases the return on equity and lets me keep more of my capital so that I can invest it elsewhere.

Pretty much every business requires a certain amount of equity to operate, but above a minimum level, boards and management teams have a great deal of latitude as to how to capitalize a business, which raises tough questions with no clear answers. For example, if a company is profitable over time and accumulates a lot of cash, should it hold on to the cash in case a recession hits or a juicy acquisition target comes along? Or should the company return the capital to shareholders in the form of dividends or share repurchases, thereby reducing its equity? Shareholders generally love dividends and share repurchases, but consider how many companies returned billions in cash to shareholders only a year or two ago and are now desperately in need of capital amid the current crisis.

The reason this is important is that the U.S. (and world) financial system is on its knees because most companies don't have enough equity to withstand the losses that are occurring. Even using generous definitions of equity, Wall Street firms were levered 25 to 1 and even up to 35 to 1, meaning their assets were 25 to 35 times as large as their equity—and banks weren't far behind. For example, in its March 6, 2009, press release, Wells Fargo noted that its Tier 1 capital (the most generous equitylike measure) was at 7.84 percent. While that was "30 percent above the 6 percent regulatory minimum for well-capitalized banks," according to CFO Atkins, it's still 12.8 times leverage. And if you use tangible equity rather than Tier 1 capital, the leverage jumps to 35:1! (Of course, Wells Fargo's leverage is infinite if you use our calculations that show its equity is negative.) Wells Fargo, like most financial institutions, is highly leveraged and has little margin for error.

Goodwill and Intangible Assets

It's not just the dollar amount of equity that matters—it's often more important exactly what are the assets and liabilities that determine the equity. In some cases, a company's assets aren't worth what they're carried on the books for or the company has hidden liabilities, both of which would make actual equity lower than reported.

The most important adjustment that often needs to be made to equity is to subtract intangible assets, the largest of which is usually goodwill, which is created when a company acquires another for more than its asset value. For example, imagine a company paid cash to acquire Coca-Cola for its current market capitalization of $95 billion. Coke has $16 billion of tangible book value, so the acquirer would see its cash balance go down by $95 billion and it would take Coke's assets and liabilities onto its own balance sheet. Because Coke's tangible assets exceed its liabilities by $16 billion, this would offset the decline in cash, resulting in a $79 billion decline on the assets side of the acquirer's balance sheet.

This presents an accounting quandary, however. Remember, $A = L + E$. Assets just went down by $79 billion net, so the equation is no longer in balance. Should the acquirer be required to write down its equity by $79 billion as a reflection of the fact that it grossly overpaid for Coke? Think about it: Why would someone buy Coke for more than its tangible assets? The obvious answer is that Coke's value is not embedded in its cash, receivables, inventory, trucks, computers, buildings, and all other assets that appear on its balance sheet. Rather, by far its most valuable asset is its brand, which has been built, cultivated, and nurtured by the company since its inception in 1892. It's the brand that, more than anything, allowed the company to earn nearly $6 billion in profits in 2007 and 2008, which in turn justifies the $95 billion market cap (as of March 12, 2009).

So the acquiring company is paying $79 billion above the tangible asset value for Coke's intangible assets. To resolve the accounting quandary and balance the balance sheet, therefore, the acquiring company would add $79 billion to its balance sheet on a line under assets called "Goodwill."

There are other types of intangible assets, which usually appear on a separate line under assets on the balance sheet called "Intangible assets" or "Other intangible assets." For example, imagine a pharmaceutical company that buys a patent from another company for $1 billion, giving it the right to produce a lucrative drug. In this case, the acquirer's cash would go down by $1 billion and intangible assets would go up by $1 billion.

When calculating a company's financial strength, many analysts exclude goodwill and other intangibles primarily because if a company runs into trouble, its intangible assets are likely to be worth little or nothing, whereas its tangible assets like cash, receivables, inventory, and even sometimes property, plant, and equipment can be monetized to, say, pay off debt.

Conclusion

W e hope this book has given you a better understanding of the housing crisis and how the tools of value investing can help you take advantage of it—or at least avoid the pitfalls. We'd like to leave you with some suggestions if you'd like to learn more— and if you want to be a successful investor, you must *constantly* be learning.

Our first suggestion would be to check out our website at www.more mortgagemeltdown.com, which has an up-to-date version of these recommendations. We've also posted our latest thoughts on the companies we analyze in this book, on the mortgage and housing market, and on the credit crisis. Finally, there will be updated (and color!) versions of many of the figures in this book, as well as lots of material (speeches, letters, articles, meeting notes, etc.) about Buffett and Munger.

On a daily basis, we absorb the *Wall Street Journal* and the business section of the *New York Times*. We also read *Fortune, Forbes, BusinessWeek*, and *Barron's* and are subscribers to *Grant's Interest Rate Observer*, the *Value Line Investment Survey*, and Fred Hickey's *The High Tech Strategist* newsletters. We also enjoy reading the regular missives by Bill Gross of PIMCO (www.pimco.com), Jeremy Grantham of GMO (www.gmo.com) and Howard Marks of Oaktree (www.oaktreecapital.com/memo.aspx).

Even if we weren't the co-founders, we also highly recommend that you attend the Value Investing Congress twice a year and subscribe to *Value Investor Insight*, which every month publishes in-depth interviews with top value-oriented investors, and *SuperInvestor Insight*, which tracks the quarterly buying and selling activities of two dozen of the world's greatest investors. Many of these investors speak at the Value Investing Congress, which takes place in New York City in the fall and Pasadena, California in the first week of May.

Book Recommendations

For an up close and personal view of the total depravity that took place on the ground during the mortgage bubble, we recommend *Confessions of a Subprime Lender: An Insider's Tale of Greed, Fraud, and Ignorance* by Richard Bitner and *Chain of Blame: How Wall Street Caused the Mortgage and Credit Crisis* by Paul Muolo and Mathew Padilla. To better understand what happened on Wall Street and the rise of increasingly complex derivatives, we recommend *FIASCO: The Inside Story of a Wall Street Trader* by Frank Partnoy and *A Demon of Our Own Design: Markets, Hedge Funds, and the Perils of Financial Innovation* by Richard Bookstaber. Finally, there are lots of good statistics in *The Two Trillion Dollar Meltdown: Easy Money, High Rollers, and the Great Credit Crash* by Charles Morris and *Financial Shock: A 360° Look at the Subprime Mortgage Implosion, and How to Avoid the Next Financial Crisis* by Mark Zandi.

Turning to investing, start with Ben Graham's *The Intelligent Investor: The Definitive Book on Value Investing*. Graham was Warren Buffett's teacher at Columbia Business School and lifetime mentor. We agree with Buffett that this is the best book ever on investing. If you want something more in-depth, try Graham and Dodd's classic, *Security Analysis*, though at 766 pages it's not for the faint of heart.

Then read all of Warren Buffett's Berkshire Hathaway annual letters, dating back to 1977, which are available for free at www.berkshirehathaway.com. A better way to read these letters is via *The Essays of Warren Buffett: Lessons for Corporate America* by Lawrence Cunningham. This book organizes Buffett's annual letters to shareholders by topic—a far more efficient (albeit slightly more expensive) way to read them.

Turning from Buffett to Munger, we highly recommend *Poor Charlie's Almanack: The Wit and Wisdom of Charles T. Munger*, edited by Wesco board member Peter Kaufman—and not just because we wrote Chapter 3, "Mungerisms: Charlie Unscripted, Highlights from Recent Berkshire Hathaway and Wesco Financial Annual Meetings," which captured the highlights of what Munger had to say at the 1999 to 2004 Berkshire and Wesco meetings. At 548 pages with thick, glossy paper and lots of pictures, it's coffee-table quality. And the content is great; most important, it has transcripts of Munger's 11 major speeches/writings over the past 20 years, plus the story of his life. Munger may be less well known than Buffett, but he is an investment genius in his own right and is one of the most interesting thinkers we've ever encountered.

If you liked the investing case studies in this book, you'll enjoy *You Can Be a Stock Market Genius: Uncover the Secret Hiding Places of Stock Market Profits* by Joel Greenblatt. If you've heard of Greenblatt, it's probably because of his best seller, *The Little Book That Beats the Market*, which is, by far, the best investing book for beginners. While he wrote *You Can Be a Stock Market Genius* more than a decade ago, its lessons and case studies, focused on special situations like spin-offs, restructurings, and rights offerings, are timeless. Incidentally, Greenblatt is the founder of the ValueInvestorsClub.com web site, which we highly recommend.

Another great case study book is *Fooling Some of the People All of the Time: A Long Short Story* by Greenlight Capital's David Einhorn. The entire book is a fascinating case study of one company, Allied Capital, and Einhorn's dogged, courageous quest to uncover the truth about this company, which, precisely as he predicted, has completely collapsed. (We were already short Allied's stock when we read his book, but as soon as we finished it, we immediately shorted a lot more—and remain short the stock as of early March 2009 despite its price around $1 because we think it's terminal.)

If you can get a copy of *Margin of Safety: Risk-Averse Value Investing Strategies for the Thoughtful Investor* by Baupost's Seth Klarman without paying $1,000 or more (the going price—no joke), it's a classic. In addition, Klarman's annual letters are truly brilliant, though they're not easy to get hold of.

Another classic from 1958 is *Common Stocks and Uncommon Profits* by Philip Fisher, who was one of the pioneers of modern investment theory and may be the most underrated investment thinker of all time. He focused on identifying growth stocks that can be held for the long run.

Finally, turning to behavioral finance, we'll repeat Buffett's quote from Chapter 6: "Investing is not a game where the guy with the 160 IQ beats the guy with the 130 IQ. . . . Once you have ordinary intelligence, what you need is the temperament to control the urges that get other people into trouble in investing."

Our favorite book in this area, though it's not about investing, is *Influence: The Psychology of Persuasion* by Robert Cialdini. Munger raves about this book, which explains the six psychological principles that drive our powerful impulse to comply with the pressures of others and shows how we can defend ourselves against manipulation (or put the principles to work for our own interest). While not aimed at investors, its lessons have critical implications for rational investing.

For advanced books on investor irrationality, we suggest *Your Money and Your Brain: How the New Science of Neuroeconomics Can Help Make You Rich* by Jason Zweig and *Behavioural Investing: A Practitioner's Guide to Applying Behavioural Finance* by James Montier. If you're looking for a quicker read on the basics, try *Why Smart People Make Big Money Mistakes and How to Correct Them: Lessons from the New Science of Behavioral Economics* by Gary Belsky and Thomas Gilovich.

Happy reading!

Notes

Chapter 1 What Happened during the Housing Bubble?

1. Frank McKenna, "Income Fraud Involving Stated and Full Document Loan Programs," www.nationalmortgagenews.com/fraud/stories/?id=40.

2. www.myfico.com/CreditEducation/CreditScores.aspx.

3. "Clawing Your Way Out of the Subprime and Alt-A Market," www.smartmoney.com/personal-finance/real-estate/clawing-your-way-out-of-the-subprime-and-alt-a-market-21068.

4. "The Giant Pool of Money," National Public Radio, *This American Life*, Program #355. Originally aired May 9, 2008. Produced by Chicago Public Radio and distributed by Public Radio International. This episode was a collaboration between *This American Life* and NPR News. Reported by Alex Blumberg and Adam Davidson. © 2008 Ira Glass, WBEZ Alliance, Inc. and the individual reporters.

5. George Packer, "The Ponzi State," *New Yorker*, February 9, 2009, www.newyorker.com/reporting/2009/02/09/090209fa_fact_packer.

6. "House of Cards: The Mortgage Mess," *60 Minutes*, January 27, 2008, www.cbsnews.com/stories/2008/01/25/60minutes/main3752515.shtml.

7. "House of Cards," CNBC, February 25, 2009, www.cnbc.com/id/28892719.

8. Niall Ferguson, *The Ascent of Money: A Financial History of the World* (New York: Penguin Press, 2008), 264–265.

9. "The Giant Pool of Money."

10. "How Could So Many of Us Have Been So Wrong?" *St. Louis (MO) Beacon*, January 28, 2009, http://stlmortgagecrisis.wordpress.com/2009/01/29/st-louis-beacon-how-could-so-many-of-us-have-been-so-wrong/.

11. James Hagerty, "In Maricopa, Ariz., a Paradise Found and Lost," *Wall Street Journal*, February 24, 2009, http://online.wsj.com/article/SB123543721679054667.html.

12. Michael Phillips, "Would You Pay $103,000 for This Arizona Fixer-Upper?" *Wall Street Journal*, January 3, 2009, http://online.wsj.com/article/SB123093614987850083.html.

13. Packer, "Ponzi State," original investigation of Sonny Kim was done by Michael Van Sickler. St. Petersburg Times, 11/28/08, www.tampabay.com/news/humaninterest/article919554.ece.

Chapter 2   What Caused the Bubble?

1. www.federalreserve.gov/boarddocs/testimony/2002/20021113/default.htm.

2. "The Giant Pool of Money."

3. Ibid.

4. Gretchen Morgenson, "After Losses, a Move to Reclaim Executives' Pay," *New York Times*, February 21, 2009, www.nytimes.com/2009/02/22/business/22pay.html.

5. Louise Story, "On Wall Street, Bonuses, Not Profits, Were Real," *New York Times*, December 18, 2008, www.nytimes.com/2008/12/18/business/18pay.html.

6. Joe Nocera, "The Heresy That Made Them Rich," *New York Times*, October 29, 2005, http://select.nytimes.com/2005/10/29/business/29nocera.html?pagewanted=all.

7. "The Giant Pool of Money."

8. Anthony Faiola, Ellen Nakashima, and Jill Drew, "What Went Wrong?" *Washington Post*, October 15, 2008, www.washingtonpost.com/wp-dyn/content/article/2008/10/14/AR2008101403343_pf.html.

9. Jo Becker, Sheryl Gay Stolberg, and Stephen Labaton, "White House Philosophy Stoked Mortgage Bonfire," *New York Times*, December 20, 2008, www.nytimes.com/2008/12/21/business/21admin.html.

10. Eliot Spitzer, "Predatory Lenders' Partner in Crime: How the Bush Administration Stopped the States from Stepping in to Help Consumers," *Washington Post*, February 14, 2008, www.washingtonpost.com/wp-dyn/content/article/2008/02/13/AR2008021302783.html.

11. Stephen Labaton, "S.E.C. Concedes Oversight Flaws Fueled Collapse," *New York Times*, September 26, 2008, www.nytimes.com/2008/09/27/business/27sec.html.

12. Alan Greenspan, "Understanding Household Debt Obligations," speech at Credit Union National Association 2004 Governmental Affairs Conference, www.federalreserve.gov/boarddocs/speeches/2004/20040223/.

13. Allen Fishbein and Patrick Woodall, "Exotic or Toxic? An Examination of the Non-Traditional Mortgage Market," Consumer Federation of America, May 2006, www.consumerfed.org/pdfs/Exotic_Toxic_Mortgage_Report0506.pdf.

Chapter 3   What Are the Consequences of the Bubble Bursting?

1. "Foreclosure Update: Over 8 Million Foreclosures Expected," Credit Suisse, December 4, 2008.

2. National Association of Realtors press release, February 25, 2009, www.realtor.org/files/research/oewljdsxcidwewdsadfs/pressrelease.htm.

3. Matt Carter, "Banks to Unleash Flood of REOs," *Inman News*, January 26, 2009, www.inman.com/news/2009/01/26/banks-unleash-flood-reos.

4. Report of February 27, 2009, cited in "REOs Dominate Many Markets," *Inman News*, February 23, 2009, www.inman.com/news/2009/02/23/reos-dominate-many-markets.

5. "Endless Housing Inventory—Shadow Inventory," Field Check Group report, January 30, 2009.

6. Yongheng Deng, John M. Quigley, and Robert Van Order, "Mortgage Default and Low Downpayment Loans: The Costs of Public Subsidy," National Bureau of Economic Research Working Paper No. 5184, July 1995, www.nber.org/papers/w5184.

7. Christopher L. Foote, Kristopher Gerardi, and Paul S. Willen, "Negative Equity and Foreclosure: Theory and Evidence," Federal Reserve Bank of Boston, June 5, 2008, www.bos.frb.org/economic/ppdp/2008/ppdp0803.pdf.

8. www.bea.gov/newsreleases/national/gdp/2009/gdp408p.htm.

Chapter 4   What Are the Problem Areas?

1. "Home Prices and Credit Losses: Projections and Policy Options," Goldman Sachs Global Economics Paper No. 177, January 13, 2009.

2. "Rebooting the Financial System," Goldman Sachs, January 23, 2009.

3. "Home Prices and Credit Losses."

4. "Rebooting the Financial System."

5. "Home Prices and Credit Losses."

6. Fitch report cited in *CNNMoney* article, "Pick-a-Payment Loans Turn Poisonous," September 3, 2008.

7. "Rebooting the Financial System."

8. Field Check Group research report, December 10, 2008.

9. Jody Shenn, "S&P to Adjust Subprime, Prime Methods, Downgrade Debt," *Bloomberg*, February 11, 2009, www.bloomberg.com/apps/news?pid=206010 09&sid=aRH2S0KvOEF8; Jody Shenn, "JPMorgan Analysts Double Jumbo-Mortgage Loss Forecast," *Bloomberg*, February 9, 2009, www.bloomberg.com/apps/news?pid=20601087&sid=aHd1M2bqYfUU; "Rebooting the Financial System," Goldman Sachs, January 23, 2009.

10. Field Check Group research report, December 10, 2008.

11. CNW Marketing Research, *New York Times*.

12. "2007 Review and 2008 Outlook: Home Equity ABS," Moody's Investors Service, February 7, 2008.

13. American Bankers Association Q3 2008 consumer credit delinquency bulletin.

14. "Rebooting the Financial System."

Chapter 5   What's Next?

1. National Association of Realtors, www.realtor.org/press_room/news_releases/2009/02/4th_quarter_metro_area_home_prices_down; MDA Dataquick.

2. www.ustreas.gov/press/releases/tg33.htm.

3. *Bridgewater Daily Observations*, February 19, 2009.

4. "Foreclosure Update: Over 8 Million Foreclosures Expected," Credit Suisse, December 4, 2008.

5. Monetary Policy Report submitted to the U.S. Congress on February 24, 2009, www.federalreserve.gov/monetarypolicy/mpr_20090224_part4.htm.

6. Ibid.

7. Ben Bernanake, Semiannual Monetary Policy Report to the Congress Before the Committee on Banking, Housing and Urban Affairs, U.S. Senate, Washington, D.C., February 24, 2009, www.federalreserve.gov/newsevents/testimony/bernanke20090224a.htm.

8. All data from Bank of America's earnings release on January 16, 2009, http://investor.bankofamerica.com/phoenix.zhtml?c=71595&p=irol-newsArticle&ID=1245457&highlight; note that these figures include Countrywide, but not Merrill Lynch.

Chapter 6   Advice for All Investors

1. U.S. Equity Strategy FLASH, JPMorgan, March 2, 2009, 4–5.

2. David Leonhardt, "Stocks Finally Start Looking Affordable," *New York Times*, March 2, 2009, http://economix.blogs.nytimes.com/2009/03/02/stocks-finally-start-looking-affordable.

3. Howard Marks, "The Long View," Oaktree Capital, 1/9/09, www.oaktreecapital.com/Memos/ThelongView.htm.

4. Howard Marks, "The Limits to Negativism," memo to Oaktree Clients, October 16, 2008.

5. Warren E. Buffett, "Buy American. I Am." *New York Times*, October 16, 2008.

6. Ibid.

7. 2008 Berkshire Hathaway annual report, www.berkshirehathaway.com/2008ar/2008ar.pdf.

8. Baupost Group, L.L.C., Third Quarter Letter to Partners, October 10, 2008.

9. Baupost Group, L.L.C., 2008 Annual Letter to Partners, January 27, 2009.

10. Robert Hagstrom, *The Warren Buffett Way* (New York: John Wiley & Sons, 1997), 99.

11. Buffett, "Buy American. I Am."

12. Baupost Group, 2008 Annual Letter to Partners.

13. Mark Twain, *Roughing It* (New York: Harper & Brothers, 1913), 276.

14. Jason Zweig, *Your Money and Your Brain* (New York: Simon & Schuster, 2007), 65.

15. *Value Investor Insight*, January 30, 2009, 20.

16. Baupost Group, 2008 Annual Letter to Partners.

17. Warren Buffett, Chairman's Letter, March 3, 1983, www.berkshirehathaway.com/letters/1982.html.

18. Jason Zweig, "Wall Street's Wisest Man," *Money*, June 2001, www.jasonzweig.com/uploads/6.01Ellis.pdf.

19. Benjamin Graham, *The Intelligent Investor*, 4th ed. (New York: HarperCollins, 2005), ix.

20. Ibid, p. 203.

21. Ibid, p. 204–5.

22. Ibid, p. 512.

23. *Forbes* article, August 6, 1979, 25.

24. James Montier, *Behavioural Investing* (Hoboken, NJ: John Wiley & Sons, 2007), 300.

25. Fairholme Capital Management conference call, November 25, 2008, p. 5/6, www.fairholmefunds.com/player/nov25.pdf.

26. *Value Investor Insight*, November 22, 2005, 3.

27. Andy Kilpatrick, *Of Permanent Value: The Story of Warren Buffett* (AKPE, 2008), 1586.

28. Zweig, *Your Money and Your Brain*, 5.

29. Ibid., 161.

30. Brad M. Barber and Terrance Odean, "Boys Will Be Boys: Gender, Overconfidence and Common Stock Investment," *Quarterly Journal of Economics* (February 2001), 264, http://faculty.haas.berkeley.edu/odean/papers/gender/BoysWillBeBoys.pdf.

31. Lin Peng and Wei Xiong, "Investor Attention, Overconfidence and Category Learning," *Journal of Financial Economics* 80, Issue 3 (June 2006), 563–602.

32. Robert J. Shiller, *Irrational Exuberance* (New York: Broadway Books, 2001), xii.

33. Michael Mauboussin, "Decision-Making for Investors: Theory, Practice, and Pitfalls," Mauboussin on Strategy, Legg Mason Funds Management, May 24, 2004, 16, www.capatcolumbia.com/MM LMCM reports/Decision-Making for Investors.pdf.

34. Montier, *Behavioural Investing*, 22–23.

35. *Value Investor Insight*, December 22, 2006, 9.

36. Robert B. Cialdini, *Influence: The Psychology of Persuasion* (Scott, Foresman & Co., 1993), 57.

37. Philip A. Fisher, *Common Stocks and Uncommon Profits*, 78.

38. *Value Investor Insight*, December 22, 2006, 9.

39. *Value Investor Insight*, March 23, 2005, 3.

Chapter 7   False Alarm on Derivatives

1. Warren Buffett interview with Charlie Rose, June 26, 2006, http://video.google.com/videoplay?docid=515260011274566220.

2. From Buffett's 1990 letter to Berkshire Hathaway shareholders (www.berkshirehathaway.com/letters/1990.html): "Most insurers are financially unable to tolerate such swings. And if they have the ability to do so, they often lack the desire. They may back away, for example, because they write gobs of primary property insurance that would deliver them dismal results at the very time they would be experiencing major losses on super-cat[astrophe] reinsurance. In addition, most corporate managements believe that their shareholders dislike volatility in results.

"We can take a different tack: Our business in primary property insurance is small and we believe that Berkshire shareholders, if properly informed, can handle unusual volatility in profits so long as the swings carry with them the prospect of superior long-term results. (Charlie and I always have preferred a lumpy 15% return to a smooth 12%.)"

3. 2008 Berkshire Hathaway annual report, www.berkshirehathaway.com/2008ar/2008ar.pdf.

4. Alice Schroeder and Gregory Lapin, "Berkshire Hathaway: The Ultimate Conglomerate Discount," PaineWebber, January 1999.

5. 2002 Berkshire Hathaway annual report, 13–15, www.berkshirehathaway .com/letters/2002pdf.pdf.

6. CNBC, March 9, 2009, www.cnbc.com/id/19206666.

7. Ibid.

Chapter 8   A Battered Blue Chip

1. Warren Buffett interview with CNBC, March 9, 2009, www.cnbc .com/id/29614072.

Chapter 10   Opportunities in Pools of Distressed Mortgages

1. First Lien RMBS Holders–Beware!, Amherst Mortgage BULLETIN, Amherst Securities, 3/9/09.

Chapter 11   An Introduction to Shorting

1. *Value Investor Insight*, July 29, 2005, 5.

2. *Value Investor Insight*, February 28, 2006, 20.

3. *Value Investor Insight*, January 31, 2006, 18–19.

4. *Value Investor Insight*, July 29, 2005, 3–5.

Chapter 12   A Case of Questionable Reserves

1. "This is not a good bank/bad bank split, although that is how I expect many observers will report on the change." CEO Jay Brown, letter to shareholders, February 18, 2009, http://investor.mbia.com/phoenix .zhtml?c=88095&p=irol-newsArticle&ID=1257489&highlight=.

2. CEO Jay Brown, letter to shareholders, February 18, 2009.

3. "MBIA Corp. and National received the required regulatory approvals from New York and Illinois prior to executing this restructuring." Press release, February 18, 2009, http://investor.mbia.com/phoenix.zhtml?c= 88095&p=irol-newsArticle&ID=1257488&highlight=.

4. Henry Campbell Black and Joseph R. Nolan, *Black's Law Dictionary: Definitions of the terms and phrases of American and English jurisprudence ancient and modern.*

5. Class action lawsuit filed March 11, 2009, in the United States District Court, Southern District of New York, by affiliates of Aurelius and Fir Tree funds.

6. 2008 Berkshire Hathaway annual report, www.berkshirehathaway.com/ 2008ar/2008ar.pdf.

Chapter 13   An Ill-Fated Acquisition?

1. Wells Fargo press release, March 6, 2009, www.wellsfargo.com/press/ 2009/20090306_Dividend.

2. Ibid.

3. Wells Fargo's 2008 10-K, note 17, p. 143.

Index